D1565152

The End of Exurbia

The End of Exurbia

*Who Are All Those People
and Why Do They Want
to Ruin Our Town?*

JOHN J. TARRANT

STEIN AND DAY/*Publishers*/ New York

First published in 1976
Copyright © 1976 by John J. Tarrant
All rights reserved
Designed by Ed Kaplin
Printed in the United States of America
Stein and Day/*Publishers*/Scarborough House,
Briarcliff Manor, N.Y. 10510

Library of Congress Cataloging in Publication Data

Tarrant, John J
The end of exurbia.

Bibliography: p. 230
1. Westport, Conn.—Social conditions.   2.   Suburbs
United States.   I.   Title.
HN80.W45T37   301.36′2   76-10343
ISBN 0-8128-1899-7

To Dot

ACKNOWLEDGMENTS

I haven't the space to give adequate thanks to all of those who helped.

Government officials, institution executives, professionals, and private citizens were generous in providing data and telling me of their hopes, fears, and feelings. I am particularly indebted to the Suburban Action Institute for information on the costs of exclusion; to Mary Maynard for access to unpublished material on suburban school integration; the Westport school administration for pertinent statistics; and—in heavy measure—to the Community Council of Westport-Weston for information on a wide range of exurban trends and problems.

I looted library resources, including those of the Westport Public Library, the Connecticut state library information network, the New York Public Library, and the Mercantile Library Association of New York.

Louise Ligato, Donice Mellett, and Deborah Dinsdale performed prodigies in helping to get the manuscript into readable shape.

Above all, I am grateful to all those who were willing to talk with me. Though the conclusions are entirely my own, the reservoir of experience and feeling was filled by them.

John J. Tarrant
Westport, Connecticut
July, 1976

Contents

Preface

The author answers a few questions. . . .

Q. What is Exurbia?

A. Exurbia is where—and, more important, *how*—we live when we think that at last we have achieved the Good Life.

Q. Can Exurbia be located geographically?

A. Roughly, but not precisely. It is not a matter of political divisions. For example, Pasadena has become a fair-sized city. But Pasadena manifests exurban viewpoints and copes with exurban problems. Westport, Connecticut, is considered by many (including most of those who live there) as an exurban community. But people who live in smaller towns and villages nearby—and who go to Westport only to shop—tend to think of it as "the city."

Q. Then where is Exurbia?

A. It is a place within commuting distance of a city: a community in which people live in nice houses, send their kids to good schools, live the Good Life, and hope they can continue to afford it.

Q. How can an exurbanite be identified?

A. He is successful. He has arrived at the place in which he hopes to live out a happy, untroubled existence.

Q. Is the exurbanite a suburbanite?

A. He lives in the suburbs—the more affluent suburbs. But the suburbanite who is still hoping and scrambling to move to a bigger house, with more ground around it, farther out—is not yet a full-fledged exurbanite. He is, however, well on the way. He has the attitudes and the sense of values.

Q. And what's happening to Exurbia?

A. It is dying.

Q. Is that important?

A. Exurbia has come to represent the American Dream of the Good Life. The massive impulse to reach it has had a profound effect on our society. When a dream of such compelling magnitude dies, it's important.

Q. Why should anybody care what happens to Exurbia?

A. Exurbanites care, for obvious reasons. Those who are clamoring to get into Exurbia care. And since I believe the concept of Exurbia represents something central to our culture, maybe we should all care a little.

Q. And that makes it important?

A. That and something more. As "busing" diminishes as an issue, suburban zoning will heat up. Zoning is the next battleground.

Q. Are you objective about what you say is happening?

A. I am ambivalent. I don't know that I can say I'm objective.

Q. Do you have statistics to back up everything you say?

A. I have statistics. Do they back up everything I say? No. I project and I extrapolate. I feel and imagine as well as compute. The book is oriented to the times and to people rather than to numbers.

Q. You talk about Westport a lot. Is Westport Exurbia?

A. Westport is, I think, representative of Exurbia. I talk about it because I live in it and I know it. To the extent possible, I have checked my facts, trends, and conclusions against what I have found happening in other Exurbias.

Q. You are trying to predict what is going to happen. Are you a "futurist"?

A. Anyone who tries to write about what is happening in any segment of society must be, to some extent, a futurist.

Q. You say a lot of grim things about Exurbia. If you don't like the place, why do you live in it?

A. I love the place, but I am convinced it is about to disappear, and I am melancholy about our lack of preparation for that event.

The End of Exurbia

1

The Journey to Exurbia

The 5:05 pulls out of Grand Central. The train carries twenty-five hundred commuters. Most of them will get off at Westport, sixty-five miles and an hour and ten minutes away.

The 5:05 emerges from the tunnel into the daylight at Ninety-eighth Street. It runs on elevated tracks along upper Park Avenue. Old tenements flank the tracks. Their windows are broken; the interiors appear burned out. Other buildings look to be in no better shape, but they are occupied. It's a warm evening. A girl sits on a fire escape. A man, stripped to the waist, leans out a window. An old, fat woman waters a small plant on a sill. All these people are black. They look blankly at the passing train. The commuters inside the train do not look back. They talk; they read their newspapers; they poise briefcases on their knees, open them, and riffle through papers. Some pull down the shades.

The train stops at One Hundred Twenty-fifth Street. A few people get on. They do not look like the rest of the passengers. The train is crowded; there is no place for them to sit. The 5:05 gets under way again. The last landmark it passes before crossing the river is a large blocklike structure, the headquarters of the New York City Welfare Department.

Just past the marshaling yards in Mott Haven, the Bronx, the train stops. The commuters scarcely notice. Then there is a sudden shattering of glass. A commuter ducks away from his starred window. Two small black boys stand on the opposite embankment. One makes an obscene gesture. They run away.

The train groans into motion and lumbers on, to arrive in Westport twenty minutes late. Some of the commuters are still muttering that something has to be done about these kids who throw stones at the train.

These are exurbanites, en route from where they work to where they sleep and play.

A. C. Spectorsky coined the term "exurbanite" to describe the individual who can't abide the city and who thinks of the suburbs as meaning dull conformity, and who thus moves farther out into the country.

Exurbia is the epitome of conspicuous consumption. As Thorstein Veblen saw it, a beautiful lawn was the means by which a householder could display his wealth to the world. It was the equivalent of the potlatch, the feast at which the Indian of the American Northwest destroys and gives away his possessions to show that he is a man of stature. The lawn, used for neither food growing nor forage, proclaims to all that the owner is a man so well off that he need not raise animals or cultivate the land.

But Exurbia is more than that. Exurbia is a system of affluent enclaves across the country, from Westport to Pasadena. The inhabitants of this wealthy archipelago—in Winnetka, in University Park, in Webster Groves, in Petaluma—constitute an elite within the American society. The exurban elite is powerful. Its members operate the levers that control how we are entertained, what we buy, and how we live.

An elite provides leadership, sets standards, embodies a way of life to be emulated and goals to be striven for. The economic role of the titled classes in Great Britain dwindled in the early years of the nineteenth century, but the function of this group as setter and maintainer of social norms continued for more than a hundred years.

The concept of Exurbia has been built on four cornerstones:

Exclusion: zoning that mandates large, single-family homes on spacious grounds.
Education: public school systems of recognized superiority that propel the children of Exurbia on to college.
Women: wives who have been willing to take on the bulk of the parental role and, in addition, do volunteer work on which much of the community's functioning depends.
"Distancing": isolation and insulation from problems, cities, neighbors, and, indeed, the other members of one's family.

All four cornerstones are crumbling.
Exurbia—the Good Life—has meant a lot to Americans. Between

1950 and 1970 the population of suburbia grew by thirty-five million people, up 10 percent. In *The Real America*, Ben Wattenberg likens the migration to the suburbs to the American Dream of the 1930s and 1940s: "What is it? 'The little white house with a picket fence around it,' of course. That's where June Allyson always wanted to move."

This American Dream comprises certain elements. One is the *house*—not a room, not an apartment, not a semidetached, but a house of one's own. Another is *land.* That picket fence surrounds some grass, flowers, a few trees. Once, the possession of a piece of land was a necessity of human existence. It's no longer a matter of life or death, but we still have the urge to own ground.

There are other things that go with the house in the suburbs. Nationwide, the median family income of suburbia is about $3,000 more than outside suburbia. The schools are better. People have better jobs, live more bountiful lives.

But these blessings do not come with suburbia. They are more effect than cause. People who are better educated and have better jobs move to the suburbs. Those who have the best jobs move to the supersuburban purlieus of Exurbia. What they get when they arrive there is the opportunity to do what Wattenberg says that human beings want deeply: "to associate with their 'own kind.' " Wattenberg adds some words in defense of the American Dream as exemplified by the impulse toward *suburban* living:

A society that provides its citizens with what they want is not one to be dismissed lightly, particularly if it is a democratic society dedicated to the idea of the pursuit of happiness via the mechanism of self-government and self-determination. What is so incredible about the whole development is that just when the process can be shown somewhat conclusively to be working pretty well, there arises a chorus of voices, heard in every corner of the land, proclaiming first failure, then guilt. Incredible!

No doubt about it, there are voices raised in opposition to the whole idea of suburbia. Books of fact and fiction denigrate the *suburbs* as characterless boxes containing conformist neurotics. Social critics denounce the denizens of Exurbia as a bunch of exclusive snobs. Life there is presented as being sterile and rootless, leading to the fragmentation of families, the alienation of children, and the erosion of moral standards.

It would appear, though, that most Americans have paid little attention to the attackers, and are in little need of the assurance of suburbia's supporters. All they know is that they want to live there. Suburbia—and its acme, Exurbia—stand for Journey's End: the reward for all those who engage in the "pursuit of happiness" that Jefferson bequeathed to us in the Declaration of Independence. Typically, in a survey of national attitudes commissioned by *The New York Times* and carried out by the Gallup organization in 1975, people again and again expressed their chief aspiration in terms of "a nice home in the suburbs."

Those who are trying to reach Exurbia—and those who have already gotten there—describe the reasons for the quest in similar terms. They want good schools, a better chance for the kids, a nice place to live, fresh air, nice neighbors, and more fun out of life.

However, the exurban elite is now an endangered species. Exurbia is threatened. Its members are beset with problems. And, unlike the cases of such other endangered species as the whooping crane, nobody gives a damn about the exurbanite except the exurbanite.

Exurbia's end is coming because of forces inside Exurbia and outside of it. Outsiders hate the exurbanite, but at the same time they envy him or her. They want their share of the Good Life, and they want it now. Their numbers are mounting, and the pressure they exert is growing. They are thrusting at the structure on which the elite archipelago rests.

But as those who amassed the initiation fees flocked to suburbia, the state of those who did not make it declined. The gulf continues to widen. In the city of Hartford, according to the 1970 census, median income is $9,108. Mean income per family member is $2,877. In the suburb of West Hartford, median income is $15,451, and mean income per family member is $5,861. In Hartford City, 12.6 percent of the families are at less than poverty level, with 8.3 percent earning less than 75 percent of poverty level. In West Hartford, the picture is measurably brighter: 2.2 percent below poverty level, and 1.6 percent at less than three-quarters of poverty level.

Suburbia is as much a state of mind as it is a geographic location. It is achievement, peace, surcease from besetting troubles. It is concrete proof that life is worthwhile.

But when the movement is of such massive proportions as has been in evidence in the past twenty years, there are bound to be problems. One very apparent one is the yawning gap between the haves and the have-nots; a gap that can be geographically demarcated as lying between the city and an adjoining town. When, as in the Hartford area, mean income per suburban family member is more than double that of the urban family member—and there are nearly six times as many poverty families in the city as outside it to the west—it becomes apparent that something has to give.

A social San Andreas Fault now exists between city and suburb. It groans and shifts, and it is only a matter of time before it gives way, with startling results. Since the citizens of the inner city of Hartford, though deprived of the means to achieve the Good Life, do possess the vote, politicians are very sensitive to the tremors they feel along the fault.

People no longer "know their place." We are seeing not just a heightening of aspiration, but a vast broadening of aspiration as well. Those with no educational advantages, without good jobs, burdened additionally by disadvantages of background and race, are not content with their lot. They have seen the beer commercial proclaiming that we only go around once in this life and we are entitled to all the gusto we can get. These people have taken this notion to heart. They want all they can get, and they feel they are entitled to get it. Those more fortunate seem to live in the suburbs, so that is where those less fortunate want to go as well.

But conditions are changing. The prime land in Exurbia is taken. Not that it is being used to what might be called capacity; the density of land use is still very low. But the exurbanite wants to keep it that way.

Those outside—"they"—do not give a damn about "changing the character of the community." They are no longer willing to accept the proposition that the inability to purchase a $50,000 house is sufficient reason for them to remain in the city. Others find Exurbia desirable—they want it, too.

These interacting pressures, aspirations, and disappointments do not bring out the best in either side. The outsiders are sometimes driven to ugly extremes in their characterizations of exurbanites. And those within the gates are developing a garrison mentality. They are digging in. As the pressures increase and the chances of maintaining exclusivity decline, they devote themselves to fighting change, no matter how gradual or well planned.

Within Exurbia there are problems, too. It is getting harder to afford that house and that piece of ground. Many of the strongest reasons for the exurbanite's choice of life-style have become suspect. Life is not as much fun as he or she thought it was going to be. The kids are not turning out as expected. There are stresses on the family ties.

However, though the exurbanites' life is turning sour, they are still not willing to share it with others. They continue to fight like hell to keep the others out. Disillusioning as existence among the good schools and the open spaces may be, it could always get worse; and it will get worse, they reason, if we let "them" in.

The denizens of Exurbia do not provide assistance or offer solutions for the mounting problems of the urban regions outside their enclaves. On the contrary, the exurbanites cry that all that is somebody else's problem, not theirs. They ask to be left alone.

The exurban way of life no longer shines like a beacon for the ambitious striver. The problems of Exurbia are becoming too well known. Exurban living is an embarrassment; more than that, it is a danger. As America faces the possibilities of becoming an energy-minus nation, a way of life as highly wasteful of energy as that of Exurbia comes in for increasing critical scrutiny.

The exurbanites mean well. They feel that they have worked hard and successfully, and that their success entitles them to live the way they wish. The way they wish to live happens to entail certain elements that have been only dimly perceived until now. One of these elements is *distance*. A home in Exurbia enables the owner to put distance between him and the plague-ridden city where he makes his money, between him and the cares and pressures of the real world, between him and his neighbors, even between him and his wife and children.

The open spaces of Exurbia, providing as they do the opportunity for *distancing*, tend also to weaken the gravitational pull of the planetary family. They foster indifference to problems and remoteness from reality. The exurbanite has enjoyed the illusion of "getting away from it all"—but now "it all" is about to engulf him.

To many, this is a calamity. In my view, it is not.

In this book I will attempt to examine the meaning of the exurban concept, the forces that are closing this frontier of society, and the consequences—good and bad—that will be felt by exurbanites and nonexurbanites alike.

2

A Stroll along the Beach

I'm sitting in the sun, on the beach in Westport. This beach is mine. I live in Westport.

That means something. It means I've arrived. You don't live in Westport without money. Median family income in the town (according to the 1970 census) is $21,435. I worked to get here. I came here because, when you achieve a certain measure of success, it's the thing to do. All around me are people who've also made it; who are *entitled* to enjoy Exurbia.

We should all be relaxed and happy, right? But we're not.

Let's take a turn around the beach.

Within a dozen yards of where we've been sitting is a monument; two old cannons embedded in concrete, pointing out toward the aquamarine water of Long Island Sound. There's a plaque. In 1779 British troops under Sir William Tryon landed here, marched north through what is now Westport to Danbury, burned Danbury, then retraced their steps to reembark at the beach. Near the beach there is a bronze statue of a Minuteman, kneeling, musket at the ready, as he gazes toward the Sound. He commemorates the valor of the embattled farmers of the area who fought nobly against overwhelming odds to resist Tryon's soldiers.

There are carpers who dispute the legendary bravery of Westport's Minuteman, saying that the locals were a cowardly rabble who fled at the first shot. The aura of the Minuteman, they maintain, is as phony as the cannons, which are not Revolutionary guns at all but, rather, ordnance of a much later date.

But never mind the Minuteman. There's another invasion going on, right now.

Notice that group of roughly twenty people at the water's edge. They are not doing anything extraordinary. Nevertheless, they constitute a center of surreptitious attention. Nobody is looking directly at them, but everyone is conscious of them. They're different. For one thing, most of them are black.

These are "poor people." They are part of a demonstration. A man named Ned Coll—who is himself by no means a "poor person"— is causing a big stir by bringing these poor people around as visual reminders of his drive to "open up" the beaches of exurban Connecticut.

It's not that we keep people out, exactly. Anyone can come to our beach. But not everyone can *park* at our beach. If you don't have a sticker—which is issued only if you own a house here or rent one— it's pretty expensive to get into the parking lot. Since very few of us ever think of going anywhere except in a car, we might have felt that this was enough. But Mr. Coll brings his people down on a bus.

Over in Greenwich they're worried about Coll and his poor people. They passed a law making it illegal to transport more than eight people to the beach in any one vehicle. Of course the reformers laugh at that one and say the courts will throw it out. The courts probably will, but Greenwich has bought a little time, and maybe they will think of something else.

Here in Westport we consider ourselves to be much more liberal than Greenwich. Indeed, we do not feel that we have any of the common prejudices at all. And this summer, at least, the "open-beach" people are going easy on us. Today's showing is just a token, nothing more. On the whole, they are leaving us alone. Many assume that this is because the invaders have nothing to complain about with respect to Westport's beach policies. Some of us, however, are vaguely aware that our liberal administration—through a "left-wing" town lawyer—has worked out a truce with the invaders. But no one thinks it can last forever. And there is a certain political campaign starting, with the challenger muttering that the town administration's "lax" policies are allowing "outsiders" (an ominous and evocative term in Exurbia) to clog up the parking lots to the serious inconvenience of bona fide residents. True, the parking authorities have pointed out that on the peak day, July 4, there were no more than forty-five out-of-town automobiles parked at the beach; but that doesn't matter. We feel the looming presence of the "outsiders" in our gut. It's not that we're racial bigots. It's simply that we have *earned* exclusive rights to our greenery, our beach, our beautiful shorelands and sheltered cove; and *these outsiders have not.* Here's how one Westport resident puts it: "When Ned Coll and his group pay my beach sticker costs, boat mooring costs, repairs to beaches costs, car taxes, boat taxes, various town taxes, then *and only then* will I welcome free-loaders such as they to my town, beach and/or property. Is it inconceivable that we have *worked* (does that word need translation?) all our lives for the privilege of privacy on the small bit of land we and the bank own?"

Well, let's take a walk along the waterline.

There's a good turnout today, a fair sampling of Westport. A lot of young people. But not as many as there used to be. In Exurbia, we're getting old. Most of us are approaching middle age, to phrase it mildly. But we look pretty good. The women are tanned and lean. Reaching the age of fifty is no reason not to wear a string bikini. You see very few really fat women in Westport. They take care of themselves with tennis, golf, bicycling—and they can afford nonfattening eating habits.

The men don't look quite as good, on the whole; there are bellies, jowls, thinning hair, and worry lines. Yet even when they are twenty-five pounds overweight and wear trunks that hang too far toward the knee and do not come up far enough toward the belly button, you can tell that these are Men of Consequence. On Monday morning, at the train station, with their sharply pressed suits and their briefcases, you will get a truer measure of their *puissance*.

But there are problems. Here is a Man of Consequence, lazing on his lounge chair, nicely tanned, relaxed, projecting kinetic energy. This is *somebody*, you think; probably a Mr. Big in the communications jungles of the city. And he is, an advertising powerhouse. Only he's on the beach in more ways than one. He gets his regular train every morning, rides in with his regular cronies, and exchanges the usual banter of in-ness; but he's been out of work for eight months.

Unemployment is running about 10 percent in Westport. This is executive-style unemployment, including high-priced managers who are out of jobs. And the official rate does not really reflect the whole picture—the number of men who are trying to hang on with severely reduced incomes, or who have, perforce, done "what they always wanted to do" and set up in business for themselves—with little real business being done.

Of course, the majority still have jobs. But a lot of the men are worried. Today they look relaxed and carefree, but looking relaxed and carefree is damn hard work when you are thinking that you might get the black spot next week.

Another group. The women chat easily, applying superfluous

suntan lotion with self-caressing languor. The men have been talking about debentures and the idiocies of Washington, but all fall quiet now. They are looking at some teenagers who are fooling around at the water's edge.

The boys are tall, hard-muscled, and handsome in a somewhat unformed way. Kids in Exurbia are big. Male exurbanites tend to be taller than the general population, height being a function of executive-suite preferment, but their sons tower over them. The girls are lush and fully displayed. They are engaging in aquatic foreplay, hugging, nuzzling, casual hands on the bottoms and breasts.

The middle-aged exurbanites on the beach try to keep their expressions within the bounds of tolerant amusement, but they keep slipping into something else: envy, disapproval, *loathing*.

In Exurbia we don't understand our children; and if truth is told, we often hate them. The local police spend a lot of time settling fights between fathers and sons, although these rarely get on the blotter.

Look out into the Sound. There's a nice breeze, and more sailboats than you can count. There are equally as many power boats; there's a forty-five-foot cruiser just clearing the spit on its way out from the boat basin. We have fourteen hundred boat owners in Westport. They're not happy. Their moorings are inconvenient; they want the town to build a big new marina. And everything that has to do with owning a boat is soaring in cost. Fun is getting very expensive.

Here on the beach is another group, a little louder, a little more convivial. They are pouring drinks from the thermos jug; two more large jugs lie ready in the hamper. And what they are pouring is not lemonade. These are black-belt martini drinkers. Later it will be cocktails at home, wine and brandy with dinner at Manero's or the Café de la Plage, drinks at the Player's Tavern between the acts at the Playhouse, and nightcaps at Mario's. And after that, a lot of things may happen.

Alcoholism is reaching what some people call epidemic proportions in our neck of Exurbia. There are twenty-four liquor stores in town (there are about the same number of psychiatrists), and they are thriving, counter to the economy. Seventy-five percent of the cases handled by the local police are alcohol-connected. We drink a lot, and drinking is making many of us uglier than it used to. Our kids drink, too. The high school guidance and medical departments are heavily involved in case loads of kids who are drunks. It's less common in junior high, but it is by no means a rarity.

And here are some exurbanites who are sixty and up. But these are not your pitiable senior citizens, whose big moments come when they cut a birthday cake at the Golden Age Club. They are getting old, but the power is still there. Their flesh is aging, but it is covered by tanned, smooth skin. Everything that money can do is being done to deter the inroads of time.

The "elderly," once a voiceless remnant of a busy and successful population, have become a force in our town, and a powerful one. Town bodies listen to them; politicians cater to them. They want cheap housing, cut prices, easy transportation, and lower taxes. And they are getting them. The reversal of the population pyramid is putting them ever more firmly in control. Who of us is willing to oppose them strongly? You can't knock the elderly, it's not the thing to do; and besides, many of us are not too far from being there ourselves.

There are more "singles" on the beach than last year, and a lot more than five years ago. Divorce has never been a stranger to Exurbia, but now marriages are breaking up at a more rapid rate than ever. Since we're older, the kids are more likely to be out of school and off on their own. And even if the kids are still around, we don't care as much about them as we used to. Exurbanites don't keep the marriage going for the sake of the kids anymore. And exurban women don't have to keep it going for the sake of the dollar as much as they used to. A lot of them are working—no longer at volunteer jobs, but for pay, which, added to the alimony (when you can get it), makes it possible to stay in town. And you need not starve for companionship or sex. Later we can visit some of the places where singles (official or otherwise) meet each other, for one-nighters or more enduring relationships. Not-married-but-living-together or living-apart-but-sleeping-together is getting to be a legitimate category for couples attending even the most nonswinging parties.

A lot of us have discovered the joys of a new life-style. There's George, for example. George used to be a buttoned-up financial executive with American Can. Then came the departure of the kids, the consciousness-lifting of the wife, the encounter groups, the resignation from the rat race, the commitment to pot, acid, and grouping. Now there's George, fifty if he's a day, with a scruffy white beard and a rope holding up his ragged jeans. And that girl with him, well, she's just his latest, can't be more than twenty-five. Amazing how he does it. We jeer at him, but many of us conceal behind the jeering a hefty measure of curiosity, and maybe more than a touch of bitter envy. George's wife? She's still his wife, we suppose; last anybody heard she was in San Francisco, or was it New Mexico?

We raise our eyes a little. Up on the rise overlooking the Sound, we can see the houses along Bluewater Hill Drive. They go for $100,000 minimum, and most for a lot more—although lately they don't go at all, there being few takers. There are no apartments, of course; we zone them out. But we're beginning to wonder how long that situation will last. Every year the lawsuits against it creep closer to success. Every year the legislature and the courts rumble more ominously about destroying our cherished local zoning.

You can't get away from it. Even looking at the *National Geographic* is no escape. In its July 1976 issue the *Geographic* asks five pundits about the future. What do they say? "The great illusion of the suburban experience was that man can experience nature by owning pieces of it. And that is fundamentally incorrect. . . . In the next twenty years at the longest, the suburbs, where the jobs are already moving, will be open to blue-collar blacks. . . I think it is perfectly clear that we are going to see the end of suburbia."

We wonder how long the Good Life can last. We wonder if the Good Life is really all that good. And we sometimes wonder what it means, and what we mean, and whether it is worthwhile to struggle any longer to keep it the way it has been.

X-Rays of an Aging Town

As far as Westport is concerned, a few statistics give some idea of what is happening. The numbers vary, but the same thing is happening to the other affluent suburbs in the United States.

In 1960, 347 babies were born to Westport parents. There were 169 deaths in the town.

In 1970, there were 142 births and 208 deaths.

In 1965, the number of students in Westport schools was 6,634. Ten years later, the total had changed little: The 1975 school population was 6,689.

The difference lies in the distribution. In 1965, more than 60 percent of these children were enrolled in the primary grades. By

1975, the proportion was reversed: More than 60 percent of the students were in junior high or high school.

In 1960, 201 building permits were granted in Westport, at an average value of $20,620.

In 1974, there were 44 building permits. The average value was $61,352.

In 1960, the bulk of the adult population lay in the thirty-to-forty-four age range. In 1975, the bulk lay between forty and fifty-nine.

The trends indicated by the foregoing figures are, if anything, accelerating. And what is happening in Westport is happening in other exurban enclaves.

Residents are getting older, and there is no significant influx of younger people. As an example, a sales data organization ranked the three hundred leading market areas in the U.S. in terms of how many households were headed by people under twenty-five. Fairfield County ranked 294th. (It ranked number one in households earning more than $50,000 per year.) Kids are moving up, through, and out of the school system, and there are fewer young children coming in. Housing has grown extremely expensive, and activity in housing is virtually stagnant.

These trends have considerable meaning for Exurbia, and for a society in which exurban living is still the goal.

Our examination of Exurbia and where it's going will take place within this framework.

3

Zoning: The Shaky Foundation

There is little public statuary in Exurbia. The town is its own monument. Occasionally you will come upon a piece of sculpture commemorating the veterans of wars dating back as far as the Revolution. Once in a while you'll see a statue of some bygone prominent citizen or community benefactor.

In no exurb will you find a statue of Edward M. Bassett. This is an injustice, for Edward M. Bassett is probably the most important figure in exurban history. He is the Father of American Zoning.

To the exurbanite, zoning is one of the great foundation stones of civilization. It is zoning that preserves the "character of the community." It is the means by which a property owner with, say, one acre of land, can influence what ten thousand other property owners can do with their ten thousand acres of land.

"Preserving the character of the community" is a positive term. But zoning is essentially negative. As a practical matter, Exurbia's zoning regulations are devoted to saying: "You *can't* do this." "We will not permit that." "The town will not admit those people."

One of the first things the prospective home-buyer hears from the real-estate agent is some such statement as "This neighborhood has two-acre residential zoning." They need not discuss the implications. Zoning is a pledge to the prospective householder that nobody is going to build a tire factory or a supermarket down the road from his gateway. They will not erect a drug-rehabilitation center anywhere nearby.

But the guarantee runs beyond these assurances. The existence of zoning says, in effect, that the new exurbanite will not have to worry about being subjected to any distasteful manifestations of heterogeneity. His neighbors will be people "just like him." They will be white. They will have money. They will not be uncomfortably

26

young. The householder need not worry about any of these things because he is protected by the most effective of exclusionary devices—money. People who cannot pay a minimum of $90,000 for a house on two acres will not be permitted to live near him. There will be no modest houses on small plots; and, of course, there will be no apartments, big or small, "garden" or "high-rise." Indeed, in full-fledged Exurbia, not only is the resident protected from such abominations in his immediate neighborhood, but he can be sure that they will exist nowhere in the entire town, though the town may comprise forty thousand residents and hundreds of square miles. In this fashion, the exurbanite is insulated from any world but the one of his preference.

Zoning, as it is presently practiced in the United States, started in 1913 in an office on Fifth Avenue in New York City. The man who was most responsible for starting it was Edward M. Bassett. Bassett was—it is fitting to note—a lawyer. He was born in Brooklyn in 1863, and died in 1948. Bassett attended Columbia Law School and spent many hours studying with his friend and fellow law student, Charles Evans Hughes.

Bassett practiced in Buffalo for a time, and then returned to Brooklyn shortly after the turn of the century, where he served on school boards and was elected to a term in the House of Representatives. In 1907, Hughes, then governor of New York, appointed Bassett to the Public Service Commission.

In 1908, Bassett visited Germany. In its way, this trip was to be as significant as Darwin's voyage on the *Beagle*. For in Germany, and particularly in Düsseldorf, Bassett saw what could be done with a city when the municipal fathers were able to exert strong authority in the control of building. The city planner Werner Hegemann had prepared a sweeping scheme for Düsseldorf, and Bassett looked with awe at Hegemann's models and illustrations.

Visitors to German and Swedish cities—Düsseldorf, Berlin, Stockholm—are frequently struck by the orderliness and uniformity of the buildings. They look down broad avenues, along which the structures stand in harmonious rows. There are parks and trees; no building dominates another; everywhere one can see the sky.

City planning rests on the principle of zoning. Zoning—the legislative method of controlling the use of land through the establishment of standards—began in Germany and Sweden around 1875. City officials set up regulations regarding the heights and concentrations of buildings. These regulations were extremely detailed, were based on extensive official power, and—especially in Germany—were quite rigid.

These are the first examples of formal municipal zoning. However, this is not the concept of zoning that has come to mean so much to the exurbanite. We might note two points about the regulations that came into use in Europe during the latter part of the nineteenth century. They were confined to cities, and they focused on the forms in which buildings could be built, not on the uses to which they could be put. Refinements were to come later.

Of course, not everyone was happy. The new idea of zoning came into direct conflict with the old concept of property rights. The civilized world has been built on the proposition that the individual can do as he likes with what belongs to him, as long as he does not do harm to the person or property of another. This basic concept applied emphatically to the use of land.

If zoning had been an altogether novel notion, it is reasonable to suppose that it would have died at birth. But while codification of property use was new, the concept of zoning was not. There seems to be something in our genes that leads us to "zone" ourselves. In a sense, we are all segregationists. Lewis Mumford (*The City in History*) observes that occupational and caste stratification shaped the ancient city. At the highest point was the ruler, who caught the full rays of the sun. Around him, in descending order, were the courtiers, priests, scribes, merchants, craftsmen, and house servants. The lowest order, the slaves, lived always in the shadows.

People who follow certain occupations tend to group themselves spontaneously: Harley Street, Madison Avenue, Haight-Ashbury, and so forth. The visitor to Venice notes how the dominant pattern of St. Mark's is repeated on a smaller scale throughout the city. Each parish has its square, fountain, church, school, and so forth. What we are looking at here is a system of functional zoning. Moreover, functional zoning has been reflected in municipal legislation for a long time. Jean Gottmann (*Megalopolis*) says: "Zoning legislation in the urbanized areas is an indispensable foundation for organizing the community and its land space from within, preventing anarchy through various *limitations on the use of the land.*" Gottmann traces the practice back to the ordinances of Colonial days that prevented powder mills from being built near dwellings in Boston.

So, there is ample historic evidence to show that human beings are amenable to the basic concept of zoning. This tendency made it easier for the pioneering city planners of Northern Europe to impose their regulations. And as a result of their efforts, the possibilities of zoning struck Edward M. Bassett as an epiphany; he was, he declared, "taken off my feet by the impressions given me by these new fields of work."

It would not be long before Bassett was to have his opportunity to realize the intoxicating possibilities of zoning.

Many New Yorkers (then as now) were unhappy about what was happening to the city. In particular, a lot of influential citizens were depressed about the sorry state of the thoroughfare that they considered to be the crowning glory of the metropolis—Fifth Avenue. Fifth Avenue had once offered a civilized prospect of stately homes and luxurious hotels. Now its lower stretches had become unsightly warrens of factories and loft buildings. Periodically these eyesores would disgorge milling throngs of workers, causing offense to the aesthetic senses of onlookers and distress to merchants of the higher class. Worse, the blight was creeping uptown; and there did not seem to be any power to stem it.

In 1907, the Fifth Avenue Association was formed. At this point the eminent New Yorkers who made up the body could do little more than lament the chaos they saw spreading around them. But they were influential people, and their deliberations led to the appointment, in 1913, of what was to be called the Heights of Buildings Commission. This official group numbered nineteen. The membership—all prominent people—comprised veterans of the Fifth Avenue Association, realtors, lawyers, and architects.

Edward M. Bassett was chosen to be chairman of the commission. The report that the commission issued is the genesis of American zoning. Bassett considered it to be the great accomplishment of his life. "I realized that I had found the kind of work that interested me and I foresaw that the whole subject was almost unexplored in this country and that it offered a vast field of progressive legislation."

Zoning offered more than a challenge. It offered something even more seductive—*power*. Seymour I. Toll (*Zoned American*) says: "Put in the most elemental terms, terms which are by no means oversimplified, Bassett became convinced that many great improvements in city building could come *without government's having to pay private citizens for the restraints imposed on their property.* [Emphasis added.] He spent something like the next fifteen years of his professional life persuading New York City and then cities and courts in the rest of the nation that zoning was just such an improvement."

The specific recommendations that emerged in the report were less important than the rationale on which they were based. The commission was established to concentrate on the problems indicated by its title—the heights of buildings. Furthermore, it was implicitly concerned with one geographic area—Fifth Avenue. At this time there were more than ninety-three thousand structures on Manhattan Island, and not many more than 1 percent of these exceeded ten stories. In the end there came regulations relating to height, setbacks, fire control and prevention, and structural details. These laws were not all that startling in their effects at the time.

The truly revolutionary element of the report was its justification of zoning regulations. The formula developed by the association contains most of the dominant themes that have sounded through zoning legislation and controversy to this day. The builder was a villain. "It is high time to put a stop to the operations of a certain type of builders, who, growing more and more bold as the years have passed by, have ruthlessly invaded neighborhood after neighborhood in New York and entered upon a riot of building out of all proportion to the character and needs of the district." (A quotation from commission member Robert Grier Cooke, printed in *The New York Times*.)

This statement introduces us not only to the "ruthless" builder but also to the sanctity of the "character" of the neighborhood. There was a distinction between the property rights of older occupants of the district and the rights of the new, "ruthless" individuals who, in their "conscienceless" fashion, were damaging the property values of others.

Another problem was that of the "appalling" people who were brought to certain neighborhoods by the machinations of the demon builders. "Nothing so blasting to the best class of business and property interests has ever been seen or known in any great retail district in any large city as this vast flood of workers which sweeps down the pavements at noontime every day and literally overwhelms and engulfs shops, shopkeepers, and the shopping public." Obviously, all members of the public were not equal. There was the "shopping public" who patronized the "best class" of store; and then there were the "appalling" hordes who used the pavement but who did not patronize the shops.

Anyone who has attended zoning-board hearings will recognize the themes: the villainous builder, the destruction of property rights, the interference with legitimate commerce—and, above all, the scarcely veiled elitism. From its earliest moments, the main thrust of American zoning has been to keep "them" out of "our" neighborhood.

The conclusion of the commission report was clear. But how was it to be put into effect? After all, the Constitution did not distinguish between the property rights of those whom the establishment approved and those who were beyond the pale. Distasteful as it might be, the "conscienceless" builder had rights, too; zoning as recommended by the commission would deprive this person of his freedom to use and develop his property as he wished.

Logically, the recourse of the municipality under existing law would have to be the right of "eminent domain"—the sovereign power of the state to appropriate private property to public use, whether the owner consents or not. But there were difficulties with eminent domain. Telling a landowner what he cannot do with his property is not the same as appropriating it for public use. And—even if eminent domain were to apply—it is implicit that the owner must be compensated for the land of which he is deprived. This would lead to endless complications. The commission decided that "practically, such a conclusion is out of the question. The expense and burden of condemnation proceedings and litigation in multitudinous cases would create a tax burden that would increase rather than compensate for the injury to property interests." Besides, the owner in such a case was not entitled to compensation, since the restraints placed upon him were to conserve reasonable individual and public rights inherent in "this class of property."

So, if condemnation through eminent domain was not practicable, what was the answer? Fortunately, there was a solution right at hand. The government does not have merely the right of eminent domain. It has *police powers*. Police power costs less than eminent domain. (Justice Holmes would describe it as the cheap way: Regulate rather than acquire.)

Municipalities began to zone enthusiastically. They passed laws saying what could—or could not—be built. Lawsuits abounded. Those who objected to zoning cited the part of the Fourteenth Amendment that prohibits the state from depriving persons of life, liberty, or property without "due process of law."

Was zoning "due process"? For more than ten years there was no

definitive ruling from the U.S. Supreme Court on whether or not
zoning was an undue use of the police power. The big judicial
moment for zoning came in 1926, in *Village of Euclid* v. *Ambler
Realty Co.*

Euclid was then a suburb of Cleveland. In 1911, the Ambler
Realty Company had begun to assemble parcels of farmland with an
eye toward eventual erection of factories. In 1922, the Village of
Euclid adopted a comprehensive zoning ordinance that would
prevent Ambler from doing what it wished with its land. Ambler
sued, saying that the regulations had cut the value of its land from
$10,000 to $2,500 an acre, thus depriving the company of property
without due process. The village's defense cited the health, safety,
and general welfare of the community.

In 1924, a U.S. district judge struck down Euclid's zoning
ordinance, holding it in violation of the Ohio constitution and the
Fourteenth Amendment. In 1926, the case went to the Supreme
Court.

The Supreme Court of that time, under Chief Justice William
Howard Taft, was a very conservative court. Oliver Wendell Holmes
and Louis D. Brandeis were considered liberals and social activists.
All the others ranged from conservative to reactionary. The court
had, for six years, been mowing down social legislation. Since 1920, it
had ruled more laws unconstitutional under the Fifth or the
Fourteenth Amendments than previous Supreme Courts had done in
the fifty-two years since the passage of the Fourteenth Amendment.

This was a court devoted to the paramount rights of private
property, and thoroughly opposed to "social-planning" measures
that would diminish the right of private property.

On each side, liberal and conservative, the justices had to
reconcile certain conflicting drives. The liberals, Holmes and Brandeis, had to consider the tradition of individual liberty as against the
social good as expressed by the need for municipal planning. Both
liberals voted to uphold zoning.

The seven conservatives were obliged to weigh the revered
concept of private property against the protection of certain
residential amenities. Justices McReynolds, Van Devanter, and
Butler voted against zoning; Taft, Stone, Sanford, and Sutherland
voted for it.

By a 6–3 decision the Supreme Court reversed the decision of the
lower court. It upheld the zoning ordinance of the Village of
Euclid—and gave sanction to the concept of zoning.

This decision is a landmark. And yet, to lawyers and even to the most zealous proponents of zoning, it is a curiously unsatisfactory decision.

One problem is that the *Euclid* decision is not exactly a ringing affirmation of zoning. The decision reviews the history of zoning laws and concludes that they are a sorely needed response to the problems of increasing population and urban congestion. This may be logic, but it is not necessarily law. For the legal underpinning to uphold the Euclid zoning regulations, the Supreme Court did not rely on the Constitution, but rather on the common-law concept of the public nuisance. The court said: "A nuisance may be merely a right thing in the wrong place, like a pig in the parlor instead of the barnyard." Reasoning from this homely example, the court discoursed on the repellent consequences of allowing apartments in neighborhoods zoned for single-family houses, and then concluded: "Under these circumstances, apartment houses, which in a different environment would not only be entirely unobjectionable but highly desirable, come very near to being nuisances." No wonder zoning advocates greeted this decision as being a weak reed upon which to lean.

So, in effect, zoning became a rational application of nuisance law, with the added attraction of specifying and preventing the nuisance before it exists.

At the time, many observers of the court were astounded. They tried to find the real story of what had happened. Justice Sutherland's opinion, though it contained colorful tidbits like the reference to "a pig in the parlor," was not what anybody could call an enthusiastic confirmation of the constitutionality of zoning. In fact, as the rumors began to circulate, it seemed as if Sutherland—who wrote the opinion—had originally intended to vote against zoning on Fourteenth Amendment grounds; and, furthermore, that another justice (said to be Sanford) would have stood with him. Had this original alignment stood up, zoning would have been declared unconstitutional by a 5–4 vote; more likely, if the weight had continued on that side of the balance, the vote would have been 7–2 against zoning, with only Holmes and Brandeis standing for it.

But the initial alignment did not stand. Other justices talked to Sutherland, among them the Chief Justice and former President of the United States. They talked about what unrestricted development would do to the neighborhoods occupied by people of wealth and taste. And, the story goes, Sutherland was finally persuaded. The *Chicago Journal of Commerce* commented: "The Justices do their work in Washington. Most of them live within the city limits. As they hold office for life, they regard the place of their work as their permanent home. Many of them own homes within the city and Washington has zoning . . . and Washington is benefited by zoning."

It is little wonder that many lawyers observe that a rematch of *Euclid* v. *Ambler* today would by no means be a pushover for the previous victor. One might find that five justices would be so appalled at what they felt to be the obvious damage done by zoning to the fabric of the Fourteenth Amendment that they would vote to abolish it—and to hell with all the ordinances and municipal planners.

So *Euclid* is a shaky foundation. Nevertheless, as far as definitive decisions on the legality of zoning go, it is the only wheel in town. Municipalities have been spinning that wheel ever since.

Since 1926, the Supreme Court—including the "activist" Warren court—have shown a distinct aversion for zoning cases, letting each state go its own way. Courts that have become highly sensitized to claims of discrimination in a great many forms have nonetheless maintained a steadfast indifference to allegations of discrimination by zoning. As a result, observes Richard Babcock in *The Zoning Game*, we have come to a situation involving "the treatment of zoning law as a branch of local real estate law rather than as a branch of constitutional law."

The Shadow-Boxers

The attackers and defenders of exclusionary zoning are fighting a war, but in one sense it is not all-out war. On the whole, both sides want to see zoning continued. The defender of exclusivity wants it for obvious reasons. The activist who wants to establish low-cost housing in the exurbs—along with the developer who would like to build that housing—would not want to see zoning abolished. He considers zoning a necessary tool for municipal planning. Without zoning, he feels, everything will go under the bulldozer. So the activist wants more zoning, not less; but he wants it on a regional or even national basis, not local.

So neither side wants the basic constitutional question of zoning to be held up to the light and reexamined by the Supreme Court. Each is afraid that *all* zoning might be declared unconstitutional.

But of course there is no danger of that happening—or is there? Even if a zoning case did win broad-scale Supreme Court consideration, would it not be inconceivable for such a deeply rooted institution as zoning to be tossed out? Superficial assessment would lead one to concur, but a second look leads one to wonder. The concept of "separate but equal" schools, as enshrined in *Plessy* v. *Ferguson,* was deeply embedded in the American social fabric, but it was swept away by *Brown* v. *Board of Education* in 1954, and the consequences have been vast.

We take zoning for granted. It is woven through our lives, particularly if we live in Exurbia. But it is a thread that, if pulled at its loose end by five men in black robes, could be whipped completely out of the American fabric. Would that fabric fall to pieces?

4

Battleground

One of the most interesting things about zoning is the power it puts in the hands of laymen. Exurbia's zoning commissions are made up of local citizens, who often serve without compensation. They are constantly bombarded by the pleas and opinions of professionals—builders, lawyers, planners, architects, and so forth—but it is the laymen who make the decisions.

Lawyers deride and lament this situation. They complain that the layman has too much power over land-use regulation. The people who sit on the planning and zoning commissions usually are not attorneys, nor are they architects or planners. Yet they make sweeping judgments in areas in which they have no expertise. A typical lawyer's opinion runs: "It is my view that the planning commission is a dodo. It is, as a growing body of criticism suggests, neither expert nor responsible."

The critics have a point. In most areas of the law there exist regular forums for deliberation, and widely influential precedents. For example, a decision by the state supreme court of New Hampshire regarding the implicit contract between employer and employee is read and accepted as having a bearing on a similar case in Indiana. But in zoning there is no centralized authority, no orderly dissemination of precedent, and seemingly little awareness of what goes on elsewhere. A court in Illinois declares that a local commission in a certain town has exercised its authority improperly. But this, like as not, makes no difference to similar commissions in other towns in the same state, who will blithely proceed to make judgments that are practically identical with the ones that come in for judicial criticism. In effect, each zoning case is *sui generis*. Lawyers deplore this as anarchy.

However, there is another view, frequently expressed by the

laymen who sit on planning and zoning commissions. They maintain that the attorneys who lament the lack of judicial expertise and orderly process in zoning administration are running with the hare and hunting with the hounds. Lawyers, according to this viewpoint, massage each other by moaning about "anarchy" in land use at the same time that they are making fortunes out of this same anarchy.

The disgusted chairman of one exurban planning body puts it this way: "I took on this job because I wanted to do something constructive for the town. Of course I receive no pay for it. Up to a point, I was able to stand the abuse I had to take at meetings and the abusive phone calls at all hours of the night from people who did not like a decision, or people who suspected that there would be a decision they would not like. But it's the lawyers who have made it too much to take. No matter how routine a case may seem when it starts out, you can always be sure that—before very long—there will be at least two groups of contending parties, fully represented by expensive counsel. And—no matter how the decision goes—you can be sure that the side that does not win will take it to court, and will keep it in court right up through the full extent of the possibilities. Very few of the cases during my time on the commission have been settled. The lawyers don't want to settle. They encourage their clients to play out the string. They foment litigation. And, in so many cases, the litigation they foment is not designed to win, but just to delay, to keep anything from being done."

There is no question that the practice of law in zoning cases can be quite lucrative. Today's exurban law firm may make more money out of land use than out of divorce. Furthermore, it seems equally clear that, because of the lack of precise procedure and the minuscule influence of precedent, the lawyers can almost call their own shots. The result is a spectacle of crowd-pleasing tactics and sometimes Byzantine sinuosity.

And it is not just the lawyers who live off zoning proceedings. A whole subindustry has grown up in the area. Experts and consultants are constantly being called in to buttress the claims of the conflicting parties: experts on sewage, open space, traffic, school population, and so forth.

A typical exurban zoning case involves change. The applicant wishes to build something on his land, or add to what is already there. He may want to put up apartments. He may want to put in stores.

Instantly there is opposition. The people who live in the neighborhood do not want whatever it is that the developer wants. It will "change the character of the neighborhood." And, depending upon the magnitude of the proposed change, there is a ripple effect of greater or less intensity. The immediate neighbors are the most emotional, but there are others in town who are equally unhappy about the change.

Of course, there are people on the opposing side who think the proposed change is great. The landowner, obviously; but he, too, has his partisans. If the proposal involves apartments, there are people who would like to be able to live in them, or have their kids live in them. Then, too, there are the idealists who simply believe that the "exclusionary" regulations are morally wrong.

If the proposal is for commerce or industry, it will find supporters who declare that they are sick of the rising property tax rate and that the community's tax base needs to be broadened. Some business enterprise needs to be brought in to ease the burden on the individual householder.

The case is put on the docket of the zoning commission. Everybody knows that the decision at that level will serve merely as the springboard for a tortuous and protracted process. Nevertheless, the initial action of the local board is important. It will set a tone, if not a legal precedent.

The contending forces muster their troops. At this juncture the skirmishing is as much a public-relations exercise as it is a legal proceeding. The builder, obviously, has long since retained a lawyer. (Indeed, in a growing number of cases, he may *be* the lawyer.) And the opponents of the change have also retained a lawyer. Each side gets involved in research to produce the "proofs" that will support their case.

Of course the specifics will vary, but the general thrust of the contending arguments follows a pattern that has become as stylized as knightly warfare in the age of chivalry. The builder who wants to put up, say, a shopping center, is doing it for the good of the community. He doesn't deny that he will make a profit out of it, but he does not emphasize that point, either. The builder argues that the project will harm no one and will greatly enhance the virtues of the town.

The opponents are not reluctant to talk about the effects of the project on their own lives. Neighbors claim that the proposed change will bring noise, chaos, unsightliness, and danger. Those who live farther away maintain that the builder's plan will ruin the community in two ways. It will be, they say, obnoxious in itself; furthermore, it will open the floodgates to even more detestable excrescences.

The opponents take the position that the established zoning regulations are fixed and must not be altered. The builder will point out that zoning regulations carry a provision for variances. Since this is so, the original planners must have thought that some variances would be desirable, and this particular project is of eminent desirability.

Even before the first public airing of the matter, the public-relations drums begin to rumble. The proposal is announced. The builder's PR apparatus provides releases to the local press, often with illustrations. The illustrations are architect's sketches of the projected structure.

Someday, perhaps, an enterprising museum will put these interesting renderings on exhibit. No matter what the building, the sketches present it as being of breath-taking beauty—or at least what you can see of the building is beautiful. It is one of the conventions of this art that all proposals look—on paper—as if they would be practically invisible. The plan may be a complex of fifteen stores, or a gas station, or a ten-story office building, or a hundred-unit apartment house. No matter; the preliminary drawings display it as "blending in with the surrounding " so well that one would think it perceptible only after you look very hard for it.

The opponents are not fooled by this. They have organized into ad hoc committees. The committees, under vigorous and often experienced leadership, go into action. They hold meetings, they send letters to the papers, they issue releases, they collect names on petitions, and they amass research that is designed to reveal the truth behind the developer's plan and show how the proposed project will be forever an abomination and a liability. Here is one instance where the lawyers for the opponents of change usually have an advantage. They are able to muster a lot of free and enthusiastic help. The builder must pay for all the help he gets.

Comes the time for the meeting of the zoning board at which the proposal will be offered. The rival forces gather. The contending lawyers arrive with their retinues of consultants. The builder's lawyer has retained consulting firms to look into traffic that will be generated by the shopping center, the drainage situation, the aesthetic impact of the structure, and so forth. These are entirely independent and unbiased experts, of course; nevertheless, the attorney commanding these mercenaries never seems to have to worry about their findings diverging from the case he wishes to make.

The opponents cluster around their own counsel. Many of them can be seen holding formidable sheaves of paper. These are petitions, rebuttals, and the fruits of all the research that has gone into preparing for the meeting. Veterans of these occasions know that no scrap of "research," however inconsequential, goes to waste. When you attend a zoning commission meeting, you can be sure you will get the full, unedited version.

On the dais, the members of the zoning commission chat as they wait for the proceedings to get under way. With wariness and weariness, they eye the forces arrayed before them.

There are others in the hall. Some are simply good citizens. Highly conscientious members of the community, they have not yet taken a position. They have come in the hope of hearing some facts that will enable them to make up their minds wisely.

There are fewer every time out. In many cases it is simply a matter of stamina. One can attend only so many municipal meetings without becoming maze-dull.

And then there are a few other observers. They are relaxed and smiling; they appear to look forward to the meeting with pleasant anticipation. These citizens have come just to see the show. There have always been exurbanites who treasure town meetings—particularly meetings of the education and zoning boards—as being the best free entertainment in town. Connoisseurs of suburban confrontation know what to expect. They are prepared for hours of droning presentations of minutiae as the lawyers and experts make their cases "for the record." This boredom, to the true fan, only heightens the enjoyment to be derived when the "public" takes over and begins to deliver outrageous verbal assaults on the other side. The aficionados have learned to savor the convolutions of the legal mind and the paranoiac fervor of the embattled partisans. The climax comes when the proceeding degenerates into impassioned abuse and raucous quibbling.

The meeting begins. The meeting chairman delivers a hopeless pro forma plea for fairness and moderation. Then, to an obbligato of mutterings from the other side, the lawyer for the developer launches into his presentation.

This protagonist knows that his is the unpopular side. He does not seem to care. He makes an opening speech, intimating all of the vast benefits that will accrue to the town because of the bigheartedness and expertise of his client.

Many lawyers are not loath to associate themselves personally with the cause they espouse. In other branches of the law it is unusual for an attorney to stake his personal character—as differentiated from his professional skill—on his case. But zoning proceedings are different. The developer may have retained a lawyer who has been for many years a pillar of the community, one allied with many charities and good causes. This fact is usually milked dry. The builder and the lawyer, for example, may have appeared in newspaper photographs, gazing fondly at the proposed site and contemplating the wonders to come.

There are copious visuals. The attorney has a slide show to demonstrate the beauty of the proposal and how well it "blends into the surroundings." These are, of course, somewhat imaginative renderings. The structure, to the extent that you can make it out at all, looks less like a shopping center than the second coming of the Parthenon.

Hours drag by. There are shouts of "Point of order!" People demand to know how long this is going to take. The opponents are impatient to have their chance. The builder's lawyer knows this perfectly well. He would not be unhappy if their turn came at midnight or later, when many will have had to leave because of the pressures of impatient baby-sitters and things to do the next day. The chairman asks the builder's lawyer to "please move along as rapidly as possible." He agrees, and resumes his snail's pace.

New personalities appear at the microphone—the experts to show by means of incomprehensible charts and a multitude of statistics that the shopping center will have no bad effect on traffic flow, property values, crime rates, noise level, air pollution, green space, or anything else. There are references to the places that the builder has erected in other communities. Leaders of those communities are quoted as to the merits of the establishments, and artfully composed pictures soothe the eye with visual evidence of how the developer, if he had but lived in the right era, might have doubled or tripled the Seven Wonders of the World.

At last the developer's presentation is finished—"for now." The opponents come to bat. The air of benign reason is replaced by a more combative atmosphere. These people have come to kill.

The attorney representing those who are against any change in zoning is apt to rely heavily on sarcasm, ridicule, and out-and-out attack. He is a combination of Will Rogers and Savonarola. He flays the pretensions of the developer. He trumpets that the only purpose of the development is to make money. A newcomer to this kind of proceeding might wonder how this could be such a telling point in such a capitalist crowd. Nevertheless, it is. Moneymaking is to be confined to the neighboring city. The profit motive stops at the town line—at least in an exurban zoning hearing.

The "anti" lawyer has his own experts, some of them paid, many of them volunteers. They, too, have done research. They have gone to the communities in which the builder has previously flourished. They have taken pictures, they have counted cars, they have pored over the vital statistics, and they have brought back with them anything that may bolster their argument.

But the facts are secondary. Emotion takes precedence. Speakers get up to deliver long and vehement tributes to the town as it is now. Some phrases recur again and again. One of the most popular ones is "We moved here because. . . ." Opponents of change seem to feel that whatever aspects attracted them to the town should be eternally guaranteed. An observer sometimes gets the picture of a young city family being besieged by representatives of competing exurbs, all wildly bidding to have that family take up residence in some rural paradise or other.

Doubts are cast on the motives and morals of the members of the zoning board. "I would like to know the real reasons that certain people are pushing this project."

Residents deliver paeans to the town that might make the objective observer double-check to see if he is really in the community he thought he was in. There are tributes to "gracious living," "peace and happiness," "rural beauty," and "a place for our children to grow free from bad influences."

And always there are the references, veiled and otherwise, to "them"—those denizens of the outer dark and the inner city who will enter the community through the breaches in the walls. The defender of the shopping center may point out that people would not be coming to live, merely to shop. But this does not assuage the enraged. They declaim how shopping centers breed crime. They imply that these outsiders will *not go directly home* when the stores close, but will hang around, bringing God knows what corruption and degradation to the community.

Some suburbs are declaring themselves open cities. By opening the gates—but not all the way—they hope to ease the pressure. Shaker Heights, just outside Cleveland, is trying to accomplish this without building apartments. At one time Shaker Heights was one of the great bastions of Exurbia. The name of the community carried the connotation of affluent WASP exclusivity.

That's all changed. Not that Shaker Heights has succumbed to apartments, high-rise or otherwise. It is still a town of single-family homes. However, Shaker Heights is now *integrated*. About 20 percent of its population is black, as is one-third of the student body of Shaker High. The median value of houses in Shaker Heights is estimated at $50,000 to $60,000. In the richer sections of town, houses go for three times that. The blacks do not, by and large, live in the grander areas of the community; their houses are on the other side of town, near the Cleveland line. But there are not distinct "black" and "white" neighborhoods. People of the different races live side by side.

Shaker Heights maintains itself as an integrated community by vigorous land-use management. The city seeks out white buyers for houses in integrated neighborhoods, lest those neighborhoods slide into an all-black state. This policy creates problems. A local real-estate broker sued the city, charging it with engaging in the business of real estate without a license. More serious is the ethical and social problem posed by the reverse exclusivity inherent in the practice. There are many blacks in Cuyahoga County who can afford houses in Shaker Heights and would like to live there. The local government's policy of "steering" whites into town has the effect of denying these homes to blacks. And there are, of course, a great many people, black and white, who cannot afford to move to Shaker Heights because of the lack of low-cost housing.

Nevertheless, Shaker Heights has pursued with some success its version of the "open-city" approach.

Other communities are taking a harder line. Westport offers a typical example—an effort to amend zoning regulations to permit the building of apartments.

The maneuvers and skirmishes that took place during this intramural struggle weave together a number of the threads that run through the suburban pattern of today, not only in Westport but in similar communities across the country:

The growing clout of the elderly in municipal affairs.

The protean ability of certain local citizens to quick-change into a number of guises: "concerned citizen," attorney, developer, "protector of the town's character."

The ambivalent feelings of guilt and fear experienced by many residents of single-family suburbia when they hear the word "apartments."

The exclusive nature of zoning regulations.

The growing emotionalism and polarization of the land-use debate.

Westport has a planning and zoning commission (P&Z), manned by a bipartisan body of citizens who serve without pay. During the time we are discussing, this body was appointed by the town's first selectman. Westport also has a representative town meeting (RTM). This legislative body descends from the old New England town meeting, at which every citizen participated in legislative matters. As the towns grew, the town meeting became unwieldly (although some smaller communities still have them). The RTM members are elected and serve without pay. There is one RTM member for, roughly, every seven hundred citizens of the town. These are the official bodies concerned in our story.

The events leading up to the strife had their inception two years before action began. In May 1972, the P&Z adopted a regulation that would provide for apartments in Westport. The RTM has the power to override amendments to the zoning code by a two-thirds vote. This the RTM did, rejecting apartments at that time.

A year later, the P&Z tried again. This time, the regulation was rejected unanimously.

In both cases the bulk of the opposition did not seem to be aimed at barring any apartments of any kind. No, the story was that these particular regulations were bad because they would permit apartments anywhere in town. The P&Z was told to come back with something that would limit apartments to certain manageable areas. The implication was that the consensus of townspeople acknowledged the social need for more choice in housing, but wished that their size and location would be better planned.

Few people were talking about "apartments" per se. The issue was more sharply focused than that. The urgent need—discussed in a wide variety of forums—was housing for the elderly. This grew out of the undeniable fact that Westport was growing older. The proportion of citizens who had achieved at least solid middle age had risen sharply in ten years.

The cry had been growing increasingly louder: Westport's elderly, trying to get by on reduced incomes and unable to cope with the complications of keeping up a single-family house, were being driven out of town. There was considerable sadness when a revered schoolteacher, who had taught many generations of the community's children and had been an active force in civic affairs from time immemorial, was forced to leave and take an apartment in a complex in Norwalk, on the very border of Westport. For many, this symbolized the flinty heartlessness of exclusive zoning.

Not all of Westport's elderly were badly off financially, by any means. A lot of vigorous, affluent citizens had gotten older. They had lost some spring in their step, but they had lost little or nothing in affluence, purposefulness, and acumen. The elderly in Westport had by now come under astute leadership and made up a formidable voting and lobbying bloc. It was not just that they could make themselves felt at the polls. It was simply not socially or politically feasible to oppose anything that the "elderly" wanted. This was discovered by Westport's first selectman when she advocated a lien—complete with a "means" test—that would give needy older people a measure of respite from property taxes. "No!" thundered the spokesman for the aged, "this is not what we want. It is demeaning. And besides, it is not enough." The elderly, the argument went, did not want charity. A reduction in taxes was not to be considered a compassionate measure. Westport *owed* it to its elderly. There must be no humiliating "means test."

Even in a time of economic squeeze, when taxpayers were begrudging the spending of every dollar, this was a compelling argument. A few recalcitrants objected that "elderly" is not necessarily synonymous with "poor." Many of the older citizens who would benefit most were far better off than their juniors. These carpings went unheeded.

The elderly were exerting considerable pressure for reduced taxes. They had shown their power when, in an unprecedented referendum, they had trooped to the voting booths in record numbers to defeat a school budget. Now they wanted apartments for older people.

The P&Z, burned twice by RTM rejection of apartment regulations, decided that the next effort in this direction would be based on demonstrable town sentiment. In collaboration with the Westport-Weston Community Council, a nongovernmental organization, the P&Z determined to hold a series of Future Planning Workshops. All citizens would attend, participate, and make their views known about the direction the community should take. The end result of this would be an updated town plan, a document that would embody the expressed needs of Westporters in a blueprint for the future.

But some felt that this would take too long. It was all very well to deliberate about the future of Westport, but meanwhile, what was to happen to the town's beleaguered elderly.

The time-frame was further constricted by a new development. Westport had filed an application with the state for a grant-in-aid to build low-cost housing for elderly citizens. The application was approved—if the town could meet certain specifications and a rigid timetable.

There were two immediate problems with this boon. The town had no regulation permitting apartments.° Somehow a regulation would have to be framed. Furthermore, it would be necessary to find a locale for the fifty-unit project. Eventually a site was chosen. It appeared that Westport could at least get going on one specific project that would ameliorate some of the most urgent housing needs of senior citizens. As we shall see, that appearance was deceptive.

The town "fathers" (many of them women) were, at the same time, grappling with the formulation of some kind of scheme that would permit apartments that would accommodate those who needed this sort of housing and yet not change the "character of the town."

At this point there appeared on the scene a man with an idea; a local citizen who happened also to be an attorney. His plan involved

---

° This is not to say that there were no apartments in Westport. There were—anywhere from five hundred to a thousand. But these were "illegal" apartments. They violated various ordinances. Certain citizens pointed to this fact while declaring that there was no need for new apartments, the problem was already solved. Just legalize the illegal apartments. That this probably might have the effect of destroying zoning altogether was a complication they overlooked.

the establishment of six apartment "villages" at spots along the Boston Post Road, the town's main street. The Post Road, zoned for commercial use, was bordered by shopping centers, auto dealers, stores of various types, restaurants, and gas stations. The nondescript nature and lack of beauty of these establishments had long been a source of pain for sensitive Westporters. Periodically there are efforts to "do something to clean up the Post Road." However, a number of moves to extend the commercial zoning back into residential territory in order to put up larger shopping complexes had been staved off; these notions did not qualify as "cleaning up" the area.

The "villages" would permit apartments to be built in "clusters" 1,000 feet in diameter, each cluster being anchored to a major shopping center. This would offer the elderly residents of the apartments access to stores without requiring them to walk long distances, take taxis, or ride the town's "Minny Bus" system.

It turned out that one of the "villages" designated in the plan would include property registered in the name of a client of the attorney who had proposed the scheme. He asked the P&Z to consider his proposal, stressing the urgency of doing something fast. But by now the zoning board was embarked on the project of conducting the Future Workshops, determining the real feelings of townspeople, and formulating a new town plan. Consideration of the Smith proposal was deferred until it could be handled in an orderly way, as "input" to the drawing up of the new plan.

One thing could not wait. The town had to get going on the fifty-unit project for the elderly that had qualified for state funding. So the P&Z rushed through a provision for a special permit that would allow this project to be built in the place selected, known as the "Canal Street Site." With the passage of the special regulation, this answer to the most urgent needs of older Westporters seemed well under way. The town housing authority hired an architect. Plans were drawn, and the process of obtaining the approval of relevant local and state agencies was begun.

The Future Workshops were a great success. Hundreds of people came to sessions, participated in discussion groups, and worked at amassing information and opinion. In conjunction with the workshops, the P&Z sent out a questionnaire to solicit the views of those who were not coming to the workshops. There was great enthusiasm. People who had never done anything but glare at each other were now sitting down and talking out their hopes and fears. Some of the most adamant opponents of change appeared to find that their opponents were not all unruly zealots, and that indeed there might be something to be said for certain measures of change. The most energetic proponents of change discovered that those who wished to stand pat were not necessarily a bunch of troglodytes, but people who were really concerned about preserving what they thought to be valuable standards. The Peaceable Kingdom had not come to Westport, but at least people were talking.

However, while the workshops were going on in a reasonably constructive spirit, the P&Z held one of its own regularly scheduled public meetings. The plan for apartment villages was on the agenda. At this meeting came the surfacing—like the first sight of the dorsal fin of a shark—of deeper and more violent feelings than had previously been seen.

Some representatives of the elderly supported the proposal, while others opposed it as being inadequate in scope. Others were heard from. A teacher told the group that a survey of teachers in the Westport system showed that only ninety-three lived in town, most of these forty years of age or older. The commission—and the town— were asked to consider the fairness of regulations that made it impossible for a vast majority of teachers to live in the community they served.

But the opposition to a modification of zoning was strong and articulate. Furthermore, much of it was not directed to the particular form of the regulation. The opposition was more sweeping. People were saying that they did not want apartments under any circumstances. "This is the first step down the road to overcrowded urban sprawl," declared one citizen. The theme was echoed again and again, in tandem with the assertion that nobody had proved that apartments were really needed. What about the elderly, the teachers, the policemen, and all the others who could not afford to live in Westport as presently zoned? Well, that was their problem. They could live in "illegal" apartments. Maybe the illegal apartments could be legalized. Anyway, what was so bad about not living where you worked? Look at all the Westporters who commuted to New York to earn their living.

It was now apparent that many townspeople were adamantly opposed to any apartments anywhere. But the P&Z did not consider this group representative of the citizenry. The returns from the questionnaire were showing that a majority of the respondents favored apartments. It was a slight majority, but it was a majority.

Working with the results of the workshops and the questionnaire, the commission sat down to frame an apartment regulation. Meanwhile, things were moving along smoothly with the project that would provide fifty units for elderly persons.

The P&Z came up with its proposed town plan update. The plan contained many interesting and innovative features. Main Street, a prominent downtown artery, would eventually be turned into a pedestrian mall. The municipal parking lots lining the riverbank would be replaced by parkland that would comprise a civic center. The proposed policy on apartments was of the most immediate interest. The commission proposed that certain sites fronting on the Post Road be made available for multiple-dwelling units. There were various criteria regarding location, density, and so forth. The plan would limit apartments to a total of four hundred, to be built in three years, after which the whole program would be reviewed.

When these proposals were unveiled at a meeting, there was little opposition. A relatively sparse turnout viewed the plans and drawings embodying the new concepts and listened to the presentations. There seemed to be general approval of the ideas.

Yet, the harmony was illusory. The presentation of the general plan was not where the battle was. Now the P&Z would have to formulate specific regulations to implement the idea. One of the first regulations they passed was the one that formalized their proposal on housing.

The commission's ideas on apartments varied from the "village" proposal in a number of respects, notably the requirement that parcels on which apartments could be built must actually possess certain minimum frontage on the Post Road. It happened that the client represented by the original proponent of the plan did not qualify. In other words, the attorney was receiving an affirmative answer to his "concerned-citizen" plea for lower-cost housing, but the particular client whom he represented would not be able to put up apartments.

Around this time an additional piece of information began to be discussed with interest. It turned out that the lawyer was not merely representing the owner of the property. He had, in fact, a piece of the action. Although earlier the lawyer had said, "It's his land, not mine," the truth was that the attorney and his law partner were general partners in the proposed development.

Critics noted that it was a far cry from being a concerned citizen devoted to the housing needs of the less fortunate to being a principal in an apartment development that would be permitted under the plan. The lawyer's reply was that the relevant statute did not require disclosure of the stockholders of a corporation or limited partners. He had complied with all the requirements of the law. This was not an answer that made everyone content.

However, by this time the lawyer had, as one Westporter put it, "taken off his white hat." He filed another application for his property, claiming that the "special" regulation, which had been passed to get the fifty-unit public development on Canal Street project off the ground, had opened the door to the building of private as well as public housing for the elderly.

In addition, he filed a legal challenge to the public project for the elderly, claiming that the regulation allowing the project was exclusionary. The fifty-unit complex, which had been moving ahead, came to a dead stop as legal action began. Now nothing could be done about low-cost apartments for older people until the legal snarl was untangled, and the knot threatened to grow tighter. The lawyer had come a long way from the days when he was uttering impassioned pleas on behalf of elderly citizens. Now he had thrown up a mountainous roadblock to impede the construction of anything for these people.

The suit was, undeniably, a blow. But the P&Z was reasonably sanguine about the bigger picture. The general proposal for limited apartment building had not generated much opposition. It would have to be approved by the RTM, but it would take a two-thirds vote to override, and the general sentiment was that the RTM would go along with a few scattered "nays." The RTM's study committee on planning and zoning had unanimously endorsed the regulation.

Certain other observers of Westport were doubtful. They claimed to sense the same subterranean rumblings they had felt before previous startling upheavals. It was one thing for Westporters to nod their heads in sympathy with the plight of those who could not afford $75,000 for a house and were thus excluded from the town in which they lived and worked. But now a specific regulation had been propounded. The coming of the apartments was an imminent reality. All of the dark forebodings betokened by that fact would again be stirred.

All over town the drums were beating. The telephone network was in action. Leaflets were handed out: "Do you realize that apartments will bring 1,300 people into town, with all of their children to go to our schools? We will need heavier educational spending, more police, and taxes will go up." There was no documentation.

RTM members were hearing, nonstop, from people who were suddenly alarmed. Nevertheless, supporters of the regulation still considered it a moderate action, and remained confident that it would be approved.

The big night came. The RTM meeting was not well attended. It is typical of a good many exurban public sessions, particularly on zoning, that the "anti's" attend while the supporters stay home, thinking that any sane person can see that the "right" approach will prevail. Moreover, the "anti's" always feel more fire in the belly than the "pro's."

The meeting was tumultuous. The chairman of the zoning commission outlined the regulation and offered the board's reasons for adopting it. Then the lawyer for the opponents rose. He proceeded to go through the regulation line by line, picking at a word here and a word there to show that it was unsound.

In his peroration he declaimed: "I look around and see the beaches are crowded, the tennis courts, the golf courses, the parking lots and the shopping areas are crowded. I know it sounds snobbish, but those are the good things we moved here for and we have to limit growth before they are destroyed. Apartments will just bring in more people from New York who think this is a nice place to live." Baron Walter Langer von Langendorff, who owns large parcels of Westport land and lives in a palatial home, made one of his rare appearances at the meeting. "Apartments will send our quaint country town straight to hell," he said.

Others deemed this presentation distorted, and attempted to rebut. But for those who sat back and absorbed the atmosphere, it became evident that it did not much matter what was said on either side. Any opposing argument, sound or not, would be seized upon as a rationale for rejection. Speakers were going farther in insinuation and vituperation than ever before. While the level of courtesy displayed in these forums has declined markedly in recent years, it is still relatively rare—at least in Westport—to hear allegations that members of the board are on the take. This time there were such insinuations. They accompanied the customary invocations of the integrity of the town's character, the perilous state of finances and property values, and colorful tributes to Westport as being a "rural" community. The crowd cheered raucously for opponents of the regulation and catcalled at its adherents.

Finally the members of the representative town meeting voted. The tally was thirty against, six for; more than the two-thirds necessary to overturn the regulation. There had been four members on the committee that had unanimously endorsed the proposal. Three voted against it; the other was absent.

In justifying their votes, various RTM members professed to have been immensely impressed by the "flaws" in the regulation. A member of the commission observed that the vote would have been the same if the regulation had been framed by the Supreme Court. Other people said the vote was a response to the feeling that developers, land speculators, and lawyers would find ways to circumvent and extend the regulations beyond the established limits.

In the aftermath, advocates of apartments spoke with a fire they had not resorted to before the vote. One wrote to the paper: "If I believed for a minute that this small group of elitists, standpatters and old-fashioned bigots represent the thinking of this town, I would put my house on the market tomorrow." A correspondent to *The New York Times* said, "Westport's rejection of a zoning regulation permitting apartments sends a clear message to all those who might have wanted to live there: 'If you don't have an income of $30,000 a year, we don't want you.'" Another supporter lamented, "It's hard for me to believe ... that anyone who would vote—in essence—to keep all but the middle-aged, affluent families with three children and two cars out of Westport, could really be voting his conscience."

For the moment, the standpatters had fought off the threat from within.

5

Huns Outside the Gates

"They" keep trying to breach the barricades and penetrate Exurbia. Who "they" are is never specified; but all exurbanites know the connotation of that seemingly innocuous pronoun. "They" live in the city. "They" are black or Hispanic, which amounts to the same thing. "They" are shiftless losers who would rather get welfare checks than do an honest day's work. Even when they work, what do they work at? They are not People of Consequence. They dig ditches and sweep floors.

These are the Huns who besiege the gates of the civilized citadel. They will break into our houses, rape our women, steal our money and goods. They will turn our children into dope addicts. (The fact is that our children have been doing pretty well at this on their own, but we overlook that.)

They have a lot of children, who will fill our schools and drive up our tax rates. And since we pay for schools and for town government out of property taxes, "they" will not be paying their fair share. They will not live in big houses on spacious stretches of land. They will be crowded into apartments that will instantly become filthy warrens of crime and corruption. They will offend our sensibilities and cost us money.

And it is so difficult to fight them off, for they are attacking us on three fronts: They work through the courts, they work through the legislature, and they work through a Fifth Column that is established in our midst. Yes, there are renegades inside the walls who want to open the gates and let the hordes of the city come flooding in. Some of these turncoats are motivated by the desire to make money. Other traitors seem to have no monetary interest. They are aberrations, wild-eyed radicals who seem to have no regard for the gentlemen's agreements that preserve the exurban way of life.

Exurbanites are like the hard-pressed complement of an under-manned fort, running from battlement to battlement to fire at the besiegers, and then turning to face the menace from within.

Proponents of exclusion argue that, while the affluent suburbs may be segregated, the segregation is not racial, but economic. True, these communities contain very few black residents—but this is because blacks can't afford to live in them.

So the issue, moral and legal, is drawn between *intent* and *effect*. In 1975, the Suburban Action Institute published "A Study of Growth and Segregation: Income Distribution in Municipalities in Westchester County, N.Y., 1950 to 1970." The study shows a striking and growing disparity between the incomes of those who live in the larger cities of the county and those who live in the smaller towns. Moreover, as the study notes, "Westchester is a racially segregated county. The lines separating black from white are generally the same as those separating rich from poor." Median family income for Westchester blacks in 1970 was $8,639, as against $13,784 for all Westchester families.

Between 1950 and 1970 the ten smaller and more affluent towns in the region experienced large increases in total population—but only 2.7 percent of this growth was accounted for by the influx of black citizens. The population growth of the larger and poorer municipalities included nearly 50 percent blacks.

The period of growth in Westchester's suburbs has now come to an end. Development is slowing down; building is off. The patterns are frozen. The reason for this is demonstrated graphically by the accompanying table of distribution of permitted densities in the ten northern Westchester towns.

The ten northern towns contain more than 60 percent of the total land area of Westchester County. In 1969, they contained almost two-thirds of the land in the county zoned residential, and zoned single-family residential. And they contained virtually all the residential land in the county that was zoned for single-family units on extremely large lots of two or more acres. Although these ten towns occupy about two-thirds of the county's land base and probably contain a much higher proportion of the vacant developable land left in Westchester, still they had only 10 percent of their land zoned for multifamily development.

The intent of the exclusion may be economic; the effect is economic and racial. Now, available land is in short supply, and

TABLE 1

Distribution of Permitted Densities
in Ten Northern Towns Combined, 1969

Zone	No. of Acres	% of Total Residential Acres
One-Family		
4-acre lot	26,674	16.6
2.0–3.99 acres	54,899	34.1
1.0–1.99 acres	46,250	28.7
30,000 sq.ft.–0.99 acres	14,836	9.2
20–29,999 sq.ft.	11,896	7.4
10–19,999 sq.ft.	5,048	3.1
less than 10,000 sq.ft.	497	0.3
Total One-Family	160,100	99.4
Multifamily		
2–4 units	750	0.5
5 or more units	227	0.1
Total Multifamily	977	0.6
TOTAL ALL RESIDENTIAL ZONES	161,077	100.0

Source: Economic Consultants Organization, Inc. *Residential Analysis for Westchester County, New York*, "Zoning Ordinances and Administration," Vol. 6, p. 12, Table 3

money is tight. Without drastic change in zoning regulations, the patterns of exclusion are frozen—and the cost of maintaining a residence is pegged at a level that is far out of the reach of most blacks, and increasingly out of the reach of the whites who used to be able to afford it.

For a long time Exurbia seemed to be doing well on the judicial front. *Euclid* v. *Ambler* had, after a fashion, upheld the principles of zoning. There was always the threat of a reversal, but the Supreme Court has been dependably reluctant to grant writs of certiorari in zoning cases. So attacks on the housing code were fought out on more localized fields, and Exurbia had been handling these threats.

Until the Mount Laurel thing.

Mount Laurel, New Jersey, is an affluent suburb of Philadelphia. Like its exurban counterparts throughout the land, Mount Laurel is a town of expensive single-family homes set amid enviable greenery. There are no big apartment houses in Mount Laurel. There are people who commute to Mount Laurel to do the world's everyday work: manning the counters, keeping the peace, and teaching the kids. But most of them can't afford to live in Mount Laurel. They live in Philadelphia or Camden.

Working with the Suburban Action Institute, the NAACP, and CORE, nine individuals brought a suit against the town of Mount Laurel, alleging that the town's zoning regulations were discriminatory. As is the custom with land-use cases, the suit wended its way through various venues and wound up in the state supreme court of New Jersey. Early in 1975, that body delivered its decision. The ruling went against Mount Laurel. The court said that the single-family zoning in the town was contrary to the state constitution. Nor was the decision narrowly focused on the specific details of the suit. The court referred to every such municipality. It cited the provision for the "general welfare" in support of the proposition that towns like Mount Laurel must make available "an appropriate variety of choice in housing." It said, in effect, that suburbs must assume a "fair share" of the present and prospective regional need, and make up land plans that will accommodate—and attract—families from all social and economic levels.

The decision—unanimous—was unprecedented. Whether it is a "landmark" is another matter. Its proponents hailed it as the big breakthrough. "This will do for housing what the *Brown* case did for school integration."

Opponents, naturally, take a different view. Exurbanite stalwarts in other towns declared immediately that the New Jersey supreme court was a "notoriously" liberal court. There was no reason to assume that other state courts would obediently swing their helms and turn into the wake created by *Mount Laurel*. The *Wall Street Journal* lamented that soon Princeton would look like Paterson, unless sanity intervened. (It is the misfortune of certain New Jersey communities—Paterson and Paramus, for example—to be held up as the awful examples of what Exurbia will be like if the sanctity of zoning is violated.)

Skeptics predicted that *Mount Laurel* would take many years to have any effect, and that lawyers would accrue great fortunes as they argued over the meaning of terms like "appropriate variety" and "fair share." However, there is a shortcut, and Governor Brendan Byrne of New Jersey appeared to be taking it by offering state goodies to municipalities that brought their practices into line with the spirit of the decision.

Then there is Petaluma.

Petaluma is a town of about thirty thousand, thirty miles north of San Francisco. Some may know it as the scene of the annual hand-wrestling championship competition. The Petalumans are past the stage of fighting to keep apartments out of town altogether. The question in Petaluma is whether the town can set limits on growth.

The town passed an ordinance (called a "no-growth" regulation) that placed sharp restrictions on building permits. The issue went to court. Local courts ruled that Petaluma could not pass such a law because it placed unreasonable limits on the rights of citizens to live in communities of their choice. The issue went to a Federal Court of Appeals, which threw out the lower court ruling and reinstated Petaluma's right to restrict growth.

The Petaluma plan was not designed to limit the town's population to those who could afford high-priced housing. It contained provisions for a percentage of low- and moderate-income housing. However, the regulation fixed an overall ceiling of five hundred units per year.

Builders and real-estate people had opposed the Petaluma plan. They found themselves allied with civil-liberties groups and champions of the poor. The civil libertarians denounced the scheme because, they said, it violated the constitutional right to travel and live wherever you please. Those concerned with poor people felt that the town would, by limiting growth, evade its fair share of the responsibility for bearing the social and economic burdens of the region.

The town fathers were joined in alliance by organizations usually considered to be at the liberal end of the spectrum: the Natural Resources Defense Council, the Environmental Defense Fund, and the Sierra Club. The members of these groups were worried about the preservation of the environment, and were willing to go along with restrictive regulation to maintain it.

The freedom of action—or the right of self-preservation—of the municipality was posed against the freedom of action of property owners and people who might want to live in the town. The mayor of Petaluma upheld the city's right to "decide for itself what it wants, so that it can plan orderly growth, protected against urban sprawl," while providing adequate facilities to keep pace with growth.

The Federal Court of Appeals found that, in this case, there was not enough restriction on the right to travel or low- and middle-income housing to support the opponents of the regulation. But the decision was more general in that it declared "the federal court is not a super zoning board"—thus continuing the hands-off posture of federal courts in land-use cases. The court said, furthermore, that zoning power was a function of the state, which delegated it to municipalities. If actions like the Petaluma plan had a bad effect on the surrounding region, it was up to the state to do something about it. This would appear to support the decision of the New Jersey supreme court, which threw out Mount Laurel's zoning as being unresponsive to regional needs.

During the years 1974 to 1975, there was other action on the legal front. Eastlake, Ohio, a suburb of Cleveland, passed a law stating that any change in a land-use ordinance must be approved by 55 percent of the voters in a citywide referendum. But this did not stand up. The supreme court of Ohio threw it out, declaring it to be in violation of the due-process clause of the Fourteenth Amendment. The court's opinion ventured into social commentary, saying that the local law would have the effect of "building walls against the ills, poverty, racial strife, and the people themselves, of our urban areas." In October 1975, the U.S. Supreme Court agreed to consider this case.

In Delray Beach, Florida, a farm workers' group wanted to build a low-cost housing project. The town refused to supply water and sewer facilities. The U.S. Court of Appeals decided that the refusal was racist.

The attorney general of Pennsylvania moved to withhold state recreational funds from the community of Upper St. Clair, a suburb of Pittsburgh, on the basis that its zoning laws kept out lower-income families.

The Suburban Action Institute filed a suit on behalf of a number of individuals, challenging the zoning laws in New Canaan, Connecticut, an affluent town with a population of about twenty thousand and a zoning code requiring large lots for building purposes. In August 1975, a federal district judge dismissed all the charges that the New Canaan regulations violated the Constitution or civil-rights legislation. The decision agreed with the contention of the town's attorneys that none of the plaintiffs had ever owned land in New Canaan; nor could they show that anyone had ever refused to sell them land. Their exclusion, said the judge, was due to "the economics of the area housing market" rather than to an unconstitutional discrimination.

In July 1975, the U.S. Supreme Court ruled—5–4—that inner-city residents lacked standing to challenge the zoning laws of Penfield, New York, a suburb of Rochester. The court said that it was the housing market, not zoning, that kept blacks and poor people out of Penfield.

The city of Hartford, Connecticut, sued seven neighboring suburbs, asking that they be denied $4.4 million in federal funds available through the 1974 U.S. Community Development and Housing Act. The basis of the suit was that the zoning laws of the suburbs were restrictive. In October 1975, a U.S. district judge issued a temporary injunction barring the towns from receiving or spending the money, which is provided by grants from the U.S. Department of Housing and Urban Development (HUD).

The basis of the Hartford suit was that the towns were not using the money for its primary purpose, low- and moderate-income housing. The suburbs, claimed the city, wanted the funds for roads, parks, sewers, and other public facilities. A HUD spokesman stated that such grants can be used for nonhousing projects—as long as the municipality has a plan for providing lower-cost housing. This action was the first of its particular kind. Other cities were watching it closely as they pondered similar actions.

In New York State, the NAACP sued the Long Island town of Oyster Bay, charging that zoning laws prevented blacks from living there. Blacks, said the NAACP, constituted less than 1 percent of the town's population. In 1975, the NAACP dropped the suit, saying, "Recent Federal court decisions raised the problem of whether we could ever reach the substantial issue of exclusionary zoning." The supervisor of Oyster Bay hailed the withdrawal of the suit as "a great victory for home rule." He saw it as "proof that proper planning to maintain our suburban character cannot be labeled discriminatory or unconstitutional."

In April 1976, Jimmy Carter made what came to be a celebrated remark about government's responsibility to refrain from destroying the "ethnic purity" of neighborhoods. His principal opponents at that time, Henry Jackson and Morris Udall, immediately jumped the peanut-grower from Georgia. This, they exulted, was the finish of Carter—his counterpart to George Romney's notorious "brainwashing" remark, after which Romney sank from sight as a presidential candidate.

The euphoria of Carter's rivals lasted for two days. Then it emerged that Carter had said something that was very popular with a lot of people, notably suburbanites.

Then, on April 20, 1976, the U.S. Supreme Court ruled unanimously that federal courts can order the creation of low-cost public housing for minorities in a city's white suburbs—even if those suburbs have not been found guilty of racial discrimination.

This ruling (Hills v. Gautreaux) was by no means the definitive decision that opponents of discriminatory zoning were hoping for. It was keyed to special circumstances existing in Chicago ten years back, when the suit was begun, and its wider applications appeared dubious. Nevertheless, it was another crack in the wall. However, Gautreaux was quickly followed by several United States Supreme Court actions that upheld exclusive zoning. One significant decision came in June 1976, when the court ruled, 6–3, that it is constitutional for a city to submit rezoning applications to a referendum of the city's voters.

The case involved a builder who wanted to put up a high-rise apartment in Eastlake, Ohio, an Erie shore community forty miles northeast of Cleveland. The city charter called for a referendum (the assumption being that, in this instance, the voters would say "no" to the apartments). The Ohio Supreme Court threw out the provision. The United States Supreme Court reversed the Ohio court. The referendum requirement stood. Since more than half the states have some sort of provision for referendums on local housing, the ruling has widespread implications. It was bad news for those who have been looking to Washington for staunch support in opening the suburbs.

A week later the United States Supreme Court declined to hear arguments on challenges to zoning regulations in two California communities, one near San Diego, the other in the Santa Clara-Santa Cruz area.

In what may have been an even more significant action, the United States Supreme Court decided, in effect, an important zoning case before hearing the case. This case concerned Arlington Heights,

Illinois, a suburb of Chicago. A federal judge had ruled that, by refusing to rezone a parcel of land for an integrated housing project, Arlington Heights had violated the Fourteenth Amendment. Some hopeful anti-zoners were betting on Arlington Heights. They considered it to be "Mount Laurel" on the highest federal level. The case was scheduled for argument before the United States Supreme Court during the 1976 spring term. The Court put the case off to the following term; but, in a footnote to another decision announced in June 1976, the justices declared that, in this and other cases, it was not enough to show that the *effect* of the zoning is discriminatory. Complainants would have to show that the *purpose* of the regulations is discriminatory.

Lawyers can make a case on the effect of zoning laws, but it is immeasurably harder—virtually impossible—to show that the laws were passed with the deliberate intent of keeping certain people out. As it so often happens in zoning, the court had given with one hand and taken away with the other. In sum, supporters of exclusive zoning had good reason to believe that the major threat would not come from the highest judicial level. Their opponents were somewhat discouraged. However, the anti-exclusion people were, in turn, encouraged by the success of the "Hartford approach," under which the suburb sues to keep the city from receiving federal money. Other suburbs around the country, for example those near Buffalo, were busily instituting similar actions.

The exurbanites are growing more and more mistrustful of their state legislature as a bulwark against urbanization. They feel outnumbered in the state capital. Exurbia has money, energy, and articulateness; but the cities have the votes.

In 1974 and 1975, there were continuous alarms in the posher suburbs of Connecticut as urban legislators in Hartford popped bills into the hopper, bills designed to damage what one local editor called the "holy icon of local zoning." State legislatures across the country were involved in similar proceedings.

Some of the measures proposed by Connecticut lawmakers were blunt in their attacks on zoning. One bill stated simply that all towns that have zoning provisions must "provide for apartments for the elderly and for low and moderate income families." There were no specifics. The sponsor—who appended the ritual disclaimer that his bill was not antisuburb—said that the omission of specifics was deliberate. "They can put them anywhere they want."

Then there was the Urban Development Corporation (UDC) bill.

This would set up a body bearing the responsibility for promoting "the safety, health, morals and welfare of the people of the state through the provision of an adequate supply of safe and sanitary accommodations." The state Urban Development Corporation would be entrusted with the power to issue bonds and notes to raise money for housing construction.

So far, the exurbanite might say, so good; who could be against the pious premise of the legislation. But then came the kicker: the location of the new housing that would be erected by the agency. There was no room for it in the middle of Hartford, New Haven, Bridgeport, Waterbury, or the other larger cities in the state. The housing would have to go somewhere, and where else but the suburbs?

So the bill contained, in addition, a provision giving the state corporation the power to condemn land and to *override local zoning regulations*.

There was considerable support for the bill. Frank O'Hara of the Connecticut Coalition for Open Suburbs expressed it typically in saying that the suburbs must do their part and share the burden of the cities.

Of course the representatives and spokesmen for the suburbs did not see it the same way. It would "sound the death knell for small towns." It would "destroy the foundation of constitutional, democratic self-government in Connecticut." It would force into the suburbs "low-rent housing in a density that could not be absorbed.' It would "obliterate local control." It would "kill our way of life.'

This was not, of course, the first time that such legislation had been introduced. Over the years there had been malcontent city representatives who had talked about breaking suburban zoning. These individuals were written off as politicians who were posturing for their constituencies. Their bills never got out of committee.

It was widely predicted that the UDC bill would die in committee as the others had. Some suburban legislators assured the folks back home that this would be the case.

But there was a new sharpness to the atmosphere. Legislators who supported the measure were able to say to their suburban brethren, in effect, "We are really doing you a favor. If this does not go through, there is far worse in store." One state senator declared, "A new day is dawning, and these towns cannot see that, if communities persist in their protective zoning laws, the courts will mandate their participation to fulfill general housing needs."

A suburban politician attended a hearing on the measure and was shocked at the weight of its backing. He was particularly dismayed to find that organized religion seemed to be out in force to break his town's zoning. Among those pushing for the bill were the Connecticut Council of Churches, the Ministry of Social Concerns (Bridgeport diocese), the Office of Urban Affairs of the Archdiocese of Hartford, the American Jewish Committee, and Christian Community Action.

In a close contest, the bill got out of committee. Opponents were confident that the measure—somewhat modified, but still containing the ominous teeth embodied in the power to override local zoning—would be beaten.

They were surprised and dismayed when the bill passed the state senate. They were dumbfounded when, in the final hours of the session, it was passed by the general assembly.

Now all that stood between Exurbia and the gaping maw of urbanization was Governor Ella Grasso. Grasso had never appeared to be an enemy of local zoning, but it was true that, in her sweep to victory in 1974, she had failed dramatically to win the votes of many of the posher suburbs.

At last, after a delay that was agonizing for Exurbia, Grasso vetoed the bill. Suburbia was saved, but only momentarily. Antizoning legislators, full of defiance and fight, began preparing similar bills to be put in at the next session.

Exurbanites watch the courts and state legislatures warily. Few are aware of rumblings on yet another front, and, with regard to the peace of mind of these embattled souls, it is probably just as well.

Most suburbanites suspect that the federal government does not place a high priority on their continued well-being. The minority who were for the land-use bill, up for consideration in 1975, were confirmed in their suspicion.

This was a measure that would provide federal money for states that were willing to establish systematic procedures for classifying land according to industrial, environmental, agricultural, or other uses. A government agency that would have access to detailed information on land supply and needs would be set up to administer the program. There would be five categories of critical concern:

Environment: shorelines, beaches, and historical areas.
Key facilities: airports, highway interchanges, recreational areas, facilities for energy development.

Utilities: facilities for regional benefit.
Large-scale developments.
Land sales or development projects.

States could participate or not, as they chose.

Ostensibly, none of this has anything to do with zoning. However, opponents of the measure—including building trade unions, the U.S. Chamber of Commerce, and various right-of-center groups—claimed that it did, indeed, have everything to do with zoning. One spokesman for the opposition declared that this was the first step toward federal zoning of private property. Congressman William M. Ketchum (R.-Calif.) said, "I have been considering this destructive bill for months. . . . It remains a frightening piece of legislation that brings the federal government into the backyards of every American household." William J. Randall (D.-Mo.) said, "This legislation is so bad that it simply should not be debated. It could ultimately mean federal control over every piece of land in America, to the detriment of individual property rights." (Again the dichotomy: It is okay for a town to tell an individual what he can do with his property, but it is not okay for the federal government to do this.)

Morris Udall (D.-Ariz.) led the fight for the bill. His forces attacked opponents as wanting to preserve a system in which there was little check on the "local appetite for development." Proponents derided the claim that the bill was the opening wedge for national zoning. They insisted that it had no reference to zoning. "The opponents of this bill," said Representative Alan Steelman (R.-Tex.), "have attempted to make a frog out of a prince."

For the defenders of the status quo in Exurbia, there were paradoxes and pitfalls. The basic idea of the measure was protection against the voracious developer—and the exurbanite is all for that. However, the exurbanite is emphatically against anything that substitutes a regional approach for the total control of land use by local government. Those suburban representatives who were attuned to the implications of the bill's provisions saw immediately that if a state were to go along with the program, regions of that state might be planned in an orderly fashion, but that regional planning would likely involve heavy pressure for the breaking of zoning codes in the most exclusive municipalities.

There is, in Washington, a local-government lobby. Udall was able to maintain the support of this important group by permitting amendments guaranteeing rights to local authorities even after state land-use commissions were formed.

But this did not assuage the fears of exurbanites who were following the bill. They were worried about the precedent. Once the doors were opened for regionalization, no matter how many safeguards were incorporated in the specific legislation, the future looked dark. Bills and laws can always be amended. Moreover, there was another factor that made the amendments added in committee of questionable value. We shall come to that in a moment.

The peril to Exurbia lay not so much in the wording of the bill itself, but rather in what people thought it meant—and that includes judges. True, the defenders of the land-use legislation said it had nothing to do with local zoning, but the opponents kept saying it would destroy local zoning. If that cry were repeated often enough, it would come to constitute a hidden clause in the bill. If legislators thought they were voting on the merits of local zoning, then their action would have a profound effect in this area.

Well, one might ask, how real was the danger? After all, hundreds of bills are introduced in Washington, but would one that endangered the homes of the fattest cats in the country be seriously considered?

The threat was by no means illusory. Land-use bills, similar in essence to the 1975 version, had passed in the Senate twice, in the Ninety-second and Ninety-third Congresses. The bills had not passed in the House of Representatives either time. In 1974, one had fallen seven votes short on a procedural ballot.

What was providing the impetus? There were many powerful forces backing the legislation. Many people were disgusted by random development and urban sprawl. The environmental lobbies had become extremely potent, and had shown their power by providing the votes to defeat legislators whom they deemed antienvironment. Planned conservation of the country's diminishing resources and natural beauty had become an issue that was not quite akin to supporting motherhood, but which had a ring of "goodness" and "honesty" about it. Senator John V. Tunney (D.-Calif.) said, "The days have passed when our supplies of air, water and land could be regarded as infinite resources." Tunney added: "In our push for prosperity we have made much of our air unbreathable, much of our water undrinkable, and we are on the way toward making much of our land unlivable." Senator Henry M. Jackson (D.-Wash.)

described the measure as a "building block to build order out of chaos so that we can proceed with a program in which we can say in advance what areas we need to set aside and what areas should be used for development. We must have development and we must have conservation. That is the whole thrust of this legislation."

Conservation and planning are big items to many of the people who provide votes, money, and invaluable campaign assistance to "progressive" legislators. However, the seductions of the land-use legislation were not confined to politicians considered to be left of center. While subsequent events have to a considerable extent blotted the fact from memory, Richard M. Nixon once assigned top priority to land-use legislation. In January 1974, Secretary of the Interior Rogers C. B. Morton testified before the House Interior Committee that he favored the Udall bill. The support of the Nixon administration pulled along many Republican lawmakers.

One may wonder why the Nixon administration placed so much emphasis at one time on land-use legislation. Close observers attribute this phenomenon to the efforts of one man: John D. Ehrlichman.

Before getting into politics, Ehrlichman was a successful zoning lawyer in Seattle. His experience convinced him that there would have to be a comprehensive law to control urban growth. He worked successfully to persuade Nixon. A congressman says, "John Ehrlichman was the big advocate of land-use planning in the White House. The fact that they supported the bill was purely the result of his presence. After he was gone, the sole preoccupation of the White House was survival."

In the cataclysmic closing days of his tenure, Nixon performed an about-face and turned against the bill. This was embarrassing to many who had gone along with him, notably Morton.

So the land-use legislation had a lot going for it. It had come close in 1973, even closer in 1974, and now, in 1975, it was up again. The Ford administration was giving it no more than benign neutrality; but it looked like a good bet this time. Opponents conceded that the bill would become law—if it managed to get out of committee.

So the House Interior Committee became the arena. Lobbying was intense on both sides; several of those involved remarked that they had never seen such arm-twisting.

On May 14, the bill came to a crucial test and survived, but the vote was close, 22–20. On July 15, land use came up for the big moment, in a committee room overflowing with spectators. The activity had become more feverish and the pressures heavier during the preceding days. Representative Roy A. Taylor (D.-N.C.) said that the bill had drawn more grass-roots opposition than any he had seen in his fifteen years in Congress.

The vote was taken. As the environmentalists and planning advocates groaned in anguish, it went against the bill, 23–19. The land-use bill was dead in that session. From the perspective of the exurban blockhouse, this front was quieted; suburbia was safe from regionalization by Washington—at least for the time being.

But nobody thought the issue was dead forever. There would be other congressional sessions, and the specter would rise again.

Here's where it stands.

There is unlikely to be any sweeping, definitive resolution of the question of exclusive zoning by the United States Supreme Court. While land use will become a more prominent political issue, there is small chance of a federal law that comes anywhere near settling all the issues.

The conflict will be further localized and sharpened. Antizoners will increasingly base their legal efforts on statutory rather than constitutional grounds. Cities and suburbs will confront each other in court. Present trends indicate that the suburbs will be faced with a series of "trade-off" decisions; yes, there are ways in which they can limit growth and development that they don't want—but in doing this they may well cut off their supplies of federal and state funds for badly needed programs. Legislatures in states with big urban populations will consider drastic anti-zoning measures.

The fighting will not be confined to the staid areas of the courtroom and legislative chamber. There will be activism and extremism. There will be confrontations like those that accompanied the school desegregation and busing disputes.

And the pressures on Exurbia will grow and grow.

6

Man Here Wants to Open Up the Suburbs

When idealism clashes with self-interest, there is always an intangible factor weighting the scales in the direction of idealism. The zeal of the person who is fighting for what he thinks is right provides a moral force that is not enjoyed by the individual who is digging in to protect his self-interest.

Exurbanites who are struggling to preserve exclusive zoning are up against some skillful and energetic opponents who have taken on the opening of Exurbia as a holy cause. The determination of the standpatters is strong, and their resources are considerable. Many of them are able to convince themselves that they are on the side of God, and vice versa. Others, however, as they think it through in the stillness of the night, come face-to-face with the notion that their efforts are devoted to maintaining a favored means of personal existence rather than to some larger cause. When the doubts creep in, determination can turn to desperation, and desperation is not the motivation of winners.

The reformers have no such qualms. Like Tennyson's Galahad, their strength is as the strength of ten because their hearts are pure.

Paul Davidoff is one of the country's most vigorous and effective zoning reformers. Like many of his confreres in the movement to open up Exurbia, he lives in an affluent suburb, Larchmont, from which location he commutes to his job in New York City as executive director of the Suburban Action Institute (SAI). This organization operates largely in the area comprising New York, New Jersey, Pennsylvania, and Connecticut.

From a modest office on lower Park Avenue, Davidoff and a small staff mount operations on a number of fronts: initiating lawsuits, presiding over studies, mailing out releases—constantly pushing for a change in attitudes and practices. Davidoff, a tall, relaxed man about forty, does not conform to the conventional image of a wild-eyed ideologue on the march. Resting his long legs on a cluttered and battered desk, he talks calmly of the institute's goals and methods. He is fully aware of—and utterly indifferent to—the abomination with which he is regarded by suburbanites who want the Good Life to go on the way it has in the past.

Davidoff says of SAI, "Our goals are to seek to alter American urban growth policies in such a way as to give recognition to the contribution that the suburbs can make in solving immense problems of large national problems of poverty, discrimination and lack of opportunity." As Davidoff sees it, the suburbs have been enabled to ignore these problems while the cities have struggled with them. They can't be solved without the involvement of the suburbs. SAI is intent on bringing about that involvement.

The Suburban Action Institute is funded largely through foundation grants. Occasionally it takes on government contracts, for example, a survey of suburban patterns, called "A Study of Exclusion," conducted for the Commonwealth of Pennsylvania. Early in 1976, its staff consisted of three full-time employees and a general counsel who works out of a private office.

Davidoff has a law degree, but he does not practice. (SAI's legal work is handled by general counsel or special counsel retained for particular proceedings.) He is a teacher—presently a professor of planning at the University of Pennsylvania—who started a graduate program for urban planning at Hunter College in 1965 and moved from there into the field of advocacy planning. He was, he says, "deeply upset" by the 1966 Housing Act, which set up the Model Cities program with, as he saw it, the purpose of rebuilding ghettos and strengthening patterns of exclusion.

The institute, and Davidoff, rose to national prominence after the *Mount Laurel* decision, in which the New Jersey supreme court handed down the first ruling by a state supreme court explicitly outlawing discrimination against minorities in the suburbs. The Suburban Action Institute did not bring the suit—it was brought by the Camden Regional League of Services—but was deeply involved in its furtherance.

Davidoff is committed to the legal route to changes in zoning that will eliminate exclusion. His organization holds great hopes for the "Hartford approach," in which a city takes legal action to keep federal funds from going to neighboring suburbs as long as those suburbs persist in carrying on what SAI views as highly restrictive practices. He is far less enamored of the legislative channels—for example, the increasing thrust in state legislatures to pass laws permitting override of zoning. Commenting on the New York Urban Development Corporation law, which contains such a feature, Davidoff says, "It's questionable how far it can be used. The governor has not found ways to override. I never liked the UDC override thing because it leaves intact exclusionary zoning except where the state wants to override it. I don't think that's the right answer."

What is the right answer? Davidoff says, "What is being practiced in America is outright discriminatory segregation. The towns are acting in such a way as to deny minorities the right to live in these communities. Whether or not they wish to live in them is a separate issue. But the effect is there, and we should rid ourselves of it. What it has done is to pollute the suburban society by segregating its schools, its systems, and its entire communities."

There is another factor in the wariness with which Davidoff and other reformers contemplate the possibility of change by legislation, or via a sweeping U.S. Supreme Court decision. Davidoff is a professional planner. Planners believe in zoning; it is their primary tool for the control and direction of orderly growth. They do not want to see zoning eradicated or limited beyond the limitations that they would apply to it. The fact that zoning is based on the concept of nuisance law—and anticipatory nuisance law, at that—does not bother Davidoff. "The theory is that nuisance law alone would not work, because it would have to wait for the investment to be made and the nuisance created before you could stop it. So anticipatory nuisance law makes sense. It is what Justice Holmes called the cheap way to regulate rather than to acquire. But regulations should establish standards to protect health and safety, and that's it. The problems with zoning have arisen as communities have gone beyond the minimums and established *levels of quality* for the community. Private market operations should work in a private market. We have no objection to a man buying four acres or a hundred acres and living on them as he wants. What we object to is translating the means appropriate for a private market to a public market where the effect is directly discriminatory."

The discrimination arising from zoning practices is difficult to prove because "racial discrimination is the consequence of economic discrimination. One has to show the disproportionate effect of exclusionary discrimination on black citizens." The fact is, says Davidoff, that many suburbs discriminate heavily against middle-, moderate-, and low-income families. The discrimination is economic in origin but racial in effect "because there aren't many blacks who are not middle, moderate, or low. But whether it's enough to arouse a court is questionable." So he looks for other avenues of attack than those that rely on such measures as the Civil Rights Act.

Won't inroads on the potency of restrictive zoning cause changes in the "character of the community"? "Of course," says Davidoff. But this is not necessarily bad. Moreover, it is not up to the community to decide whether it is good or bad. "I think it's good spiritually, morally and constitutionally that a community stay within the law."

The best chances for change through court action lie, in Davidoff's opinion, with actions that are taken on statutory rather than constitutional grounds. "Where Congress has acted and created civil rights, the court will uphold those rights. Where we run into difficulty is in cases which attempt to expand the concept of constitutional rights. There the tendency of courts has been to narrow rather than to broaden." So his disposition is to go into federal court on statutory grounds, like those of the Fair Housing Act of 1968.

Davidoff is scornfully amused at the spectacle of fervid conservatives appearing as the leaders in the fight to preserve exclusionary zoning. "I mean, here you have all these conservatives in the suburbs using as much public law and control as they can for their own private ends. They can't make a philosophical case for it. In general what happens is that self-interest overrides philosophy. They want to protect their way of life and property values, and they use whatever means are necessary. In my first class in planning school, Charles Abrams remarked that it was not surprising that the heavy supporters of zoning in this country and England included Herbert Hoover and Neville Chamberlain. Dean Jefferson Fordham of the Penn Law School used to refer to this as 'Ivy League Socialism.' Overregulation and extreme restriction have no place in the practice of conservatives."

Zoning, says Davidoff, "is essential to preserve the community amenity. It's a proper device for regulating growth in the community." It should not be destroyed. "We wish it be inclusionary rather than exclusionary. We want to bend it, to change it, to alter it so that it is no longer abusive. We think it can be done so that communities can create zoning ordinances that protect social and environmental amenities while at the same time preserving the rights of all citizens of the area."

"We're not going to win this fight overnight," Davidoff admits. "It's going to take longer to get people to accept the idea that they should live with other Americans than it did to get them to accept the idea that their children should go to school with other Americans."

How does he feel about what he is doing? "I don't know whether I feel good or bad. I continue working at it and hope it will succeed. I'm still naive enough to think that the public will respond to this. I believe in the American system—although there's so much around me that says this is foolishness on my part. My students and others at the university are far more cynical. But I've chosen to work directly within the system rather than outside the system. I believe that by opening up opportunities and by offering choices that permit us to be more explicit about what we're doing, we have a chance to improve. We'll see."

Davidoff is certain of the rightness of what he is doing and confident that he is getting someplace with it. The direction and force of developments in zoning give him good reasons for confidence, although there is the danger that reactions against exclusion will go farther and in different directions than those he favors. The antirestriction activists have been working to build a considerable head of steam. This they have done. Whether they can fully control the channeling of that power is yet to be determined, and depends to a considerable extent on the extent and nature of the defenses carried on within a profusion of exurban barricades. Those outside the gates want in. Successes in the courts and the legislatures have encouraged them to expect that victory is close at hand. They have their own ideas about the completeness of that victory.

Not unnaturally, the Paul Davidoffs of this country are regarded in suburbia with attitudes that range from fear to loathing. They are revolutionaries; they are "do-gooders"; they are Socialists; they are busybodies; and if they live in Exurbia, as Davidoff does, they are traitors.

One thing is certain. The activists cannot be ignored. It is said that, toward the end of the 1946 baseball season, the members of the Brooklyn Dodgers at last realized that Jackie Robinson was likely to be brought onto the team the following spring. The Dodgers got together to voice their unhappiness, and to hint at various counter-measures that they really thought would preserve the whiteness of major-league baseball. One observer reports that Dodger manager Leo Durocher looked at them with a faint smile and said, with relish, "He's coming, boys, and you can't stop him. He's coming—and he's hungry and he's good. And there are a hundred more behind him."

There are few exurbanites today who are able to ignore the reality that "they are coming," and that the assault on exclusion is being pursued with skill and dedication along a multiplicity of approaches. Confronted with the ability and the accomplishments of people like Paul Davidoff, the suburban standpatter can no longer look forward even to living out his lifetime in affluent seclusion, let alone preserving the pattern of exclusion for future generations.

7

Do They Want to See Us Broke?

On the morning of November 4, 1975, Westporters opened their copies of *The New York Times* to find a long story under the headline WESTPORT AND ITS NEIGHBORS IN A LONG-SIMMERING FEUD.

The story, written by Michael Knight, a *Times* reporter who often covers Fairfield County news, began: "Westport, Conn.—The usually well-hidden but sometimes bitter animosity between this affluent community and its less wealthy neighbors broke into the open for a few moments last month. Then it disappeared from view again, leaving only polite smiles to mark the place where the apparent tranquility of suburbia had been disturbed."

The article referred to two incidents. One was the reaction of people in Bridgeport to the appointment of a Westport educator as Bridgeport's superintendent of schools. "How could anyone from a lily-white town like Westport relate to the needs of our school system, which is 68 percent minority?" asked the head of the city's NAACP. "This is where they get their day workers and their maids to keep their houses clean, fix their cars and take care of their children. We don't need anybody from Westport with their Great White Father attitude coming in to run our school system." There were other references to the attitudes of poor people in Bridgeport toward the neighboring suburb with the adjusted median income of about $30,000 per year. (The Westport school official later withdrew, and a Bridgeporter was given the job.)

The second incident was the inception of a movement in Norwalk, Westport's urban neighbor to the west, aimed at cutting off federal community development funds for Westport because of Westport's refusal to permit low- and middle-income housing. A Norwalk legislator was quoted as saying that the city had to spend its paltry revenue-sharing money on housing for the elderly while Westport spent it on tennis courts. "And then they look at you like

74

you crawled out from under a rock when you say you live in Norwalk, where they think the schools are full of hoodlums."

Mr. Knight's story reviewed Westport's battle to keep out apartments. It included some of the livelier statements made at that time by Baron von Langendorff, a perfume tycoon, who lamented that apartments would bring in "outsiders" who would build "shanties," thus destroying Westport's "rural" charm.

Westporters were characterized as snobs who regard Bridgeport as a wasteland where everyone is on welfare. The story was given visual punch by a photograph of the "Nanny Bus"—a fuming old coach that lumbers from Norwalk to Bridgeport and back all day, carrying black people from ghetto areas to their jobs as domestics. The term "Nanny Bus" is an artful coinage designed to contrast with Westport's "Minny Bus" system. Westport obtained federal and state subsidies to install a fleet of air-conditioned Mercedes-Benz buses that shuttle commuters to and from the train station and, during the day, ferry Westporters around the town. Most of the noncommuting riders are youngsters who would otherwise be hitchhiking, using the family car, or be transported by their mothers. (When a capable and aggressive group of Westporters pushed through the Minny Bus plan to fruition, many urban planners were disgruntled. They complained that the funding was not set up for the purpose of offering luxury transportation to Exurbia, but rather to provide better bus services for the cities. No one could blame Westport for taking advantage of the opportunity, but it did not enhance Westport's popularity in certain areas.)

While the article wound up by declaring that the perceptions of each other held by the three communities were by no means accurate, the sting was undiminished. Westporters were surprised, hurt, and angry. Some muttered that the timing of the piece (Election Day) was somehow part of a "plot," although who was doing the plotting and what it was supposed to accomplish were unclear. One of the two local newspapers denounced the *Times* story as "thirty-six column inches of drivel . . . shabby . . . shoddy . . . the worst kind of yellow journalism . . . patently biased."

A few troubled Westporters expressed the thought that Mr. Knight's story might not be pure drivel. One wrote:

I agree with you that Michael Knight's New York Times article was not a model of investigative journalism. I further agree that it was cowardly to paint a rather sensational, lengthy and poorly documented picture of urban-suburban bigotry, only to take it all back in the last paragraph, when most newspaper readers have stopped reading.

In spite of all this, I am terribly afraid that Michael Knight may still be right about us. We do not have to conduct people in the street interviews to know that we have turned apartments down three times, that armies of maids are bused into Westport's Post Road, and that several years ago, while Project Concern was being debated, the opponent's anti-busing slogan was, "If you like Bridgeport kids so much, why don't you go live in Bridgeport." The amount of bigoted hate mail received by one Westporter who vocally supported Project Concern filled a wastebasket.

Of course, most of us could answer, "We are willing to have apartments. It's just that we haven't seen the right plan yet." Or, "What's wrong with importing black maids; they are glad for the work." Or, "I'm no bigot. I just don't think it would be healthy for those poor black kids to see our community and then have to go back each night to the slums."

I'm familiar with that kind of talk. I don't believe it is honest talk. I ought to know. Some of my best friends are Bridgeporters.

And another:

I disagree with your editorial that Michael Knight's critical article about Westport in *The New York Times* of 4 November 1975 did Westport a disservice.

On the contrary, it did us a distinct service, because it has prompted us to examine ourselves and to review our attitudes as a community, toward our neighboring communities, particularly toward Bridgeport and Norwalk. Any citizen who prompts his fellow citizens to look at themselves and the values by which they live does his community a service. Such a citizen fulfills an important function in a free society: he prevents social and moral complacency. He pricks us to a vital, ongoing examination of our collective worth as a community. Constant re-examination of ourselves is our strongest protection against complacency.

One may not agree with Mr. Knight's characterization of Westport as an affluent community concerned primarily with the perpetuation of the good life. One may not agree with Mr. Knight that Westport has traditionally opted for its own comfort, safety, style, and convenience over those same qualities in its neighboring communities. One may not believe that Mr. Knight's concept of the typical Westporter represents all Westporters, or even the majority of Westporters. One is always free to disagree. However, there are some things which Mr. Knight says about Westport which ring true in my ears, and he has caused us to look at ourselves as the objects of other people's perceptions. To see ourselves as some people in Bridgeport and Norwalk may see us can be upsetting, indeed; but it can be a potentially healthy experience, if we do not shut our eyes.

When Socrates questioned the values by which his fellow Athenians lived and operated as a community, they accused him of disservice, of impiety and innovation. So in 399 B.C. they gave him poison to drink. Self-righteous as Socrates may seem, he viewed himself as a responsible citizen of good will whose contribution was to question social values and thus to produce a dialectical self-examination in his community.

One can reject Mr. Knight's view of Westport and still appreciate his contribution to this community by making us take a fresh (and unexpected) look at ourselves. Frankly, I like Westport a great deal. My wife and I freely chose to live in Westport; we were not transferred here. I am very happy that my family lives here. I believe that it is a good place for us to live and for our children to grow up in. I am also glad that Michael Knight cares enough about the community to cause it to look at itself. No harm can come from self-review.

But most Westporters seemed to feel like the author of the following apologia pro sua exurbia:

Westport has been "my town" for more than 38 years. It has never meant, to me, a place where one simply hangs one's hat.

It has meant my home and my family and warm friendships and fine tradespeople and good government and rewarding experiences in the cultural and sociological development of its character. With pride and prejudice and first-hand knowledge, I claim for it a distinctive quintessence of citizen responsibility, conscientiousness, and wholesome respect for human rights and dignities.

Therefore, it was a shock to read the recent article in *The New York Times* which devastated the integrity, the ethics and the moral attitude of Westport.

You, the Editor of the *Westport News*, are to be commended for your swift and potent editorial rebuttal to the attack. Was the *Times* piece the work of someone who simply hangs his hat in Westport or was he fed his material by typical transients? Was it a quick critique written off the top of the head after one or two cursory conversations with a few malcontents?

If Westport has one fundamental weakness it is that it does harbor certain Johnny-Come-Latelys who set themselves up, in lightning-fast time, as authorities on the mores and the morals of the community, inevitably to the detriment of it.

It has always opened its arms (and more power to it for its tolerance and sense of fair play) to people who move in—often with a chip on their shoulder—and commence to create havoc with zoning, schools, budget, town services and citizens' rights, and then, their own self-interests or shoulder-chips satisfied, move on. (On to another community, another crusade?)

Somehow these vocalizers always get the media's ear and a plastic instant-image of the town emerges.

The unfortunate impact of the *Times* article is that it deliberately fabricates a snobbery in Westport that does not exist. It appears to be planned class-against-class mischief-making. The old hackneyed rich vs. poor, big house vs. little house demagoguery.

A lot of exurbanites are becoming hardnosed. They are responding to the drumfire of criticism in ways that manifest a diminution of couth. For many Westporters, the last straw snapped when a state agency threatened to cut off funds for sewers because of the town's "all-white image" and "exclusionary policies." It was, of course, the housing issue again. When, in 1975, Westport's local government rejected apartments for low-income families, the action sent out reverberations that seem to echo back in myriad ways.

The facts are that the Connecticut Department of Community Affairs advised Westport that sewer funds were being held up because of local housing policies. The department declared: "The civil rights impact of the proposed project and civil rights issues in general have not been satisfactorily considered by the town."

Up until that moment, Westporters had not, by and large, thought of a sewer line as having any "civil rights impact." Of course the sewers would serve single-family homes, but what of that? These exurbanites were worried about drainage problems, not civil-rights problems. When your septic tank is backing up, you want a sewer, not a lecture on your responsibilities to urban neighbors.

Nevertheless, the state was getting tough—and it appeared to have the power to put some teeth into its threats. Numerous suburbanites have developed a hard shell. They are relatively impervious to criticism. They don't care that much what a malcontent in Bridgeport or New York or Chicago or Los Angeles says about the way they live their lives. But when they threaten to keep us from having sewers, to many of us it is too much.

Predictably, the Letters to the Editor column in the Westport paper bristled with outrage and defiance. One tormented Westporter offered the following comments, printed under the headline WOULD THEY RATHER WE WERE BROKE? I include these remarks at some length, because they are particularly representative of a growing attitude in Exurbia.

Of all the towns to pick on, Westport should be at the end of the list. Our town is wide open to anyone regardless of race, creed or religion. All one has to do, who wishes to move here, is to pick out the place that's for sale or rent, meet the terms and conditions set forth by the owner, put up your money and move in. Period. It's as simple as all that. So what objections do [they] have to the method, the American way of obtaining housing? I'd like to hear from them.

Regarding federal and state officials who see [Westport's] rejection of multiple family dwellings as an indication of the town's unwillingness to open its doors to less privileged classes, all I can say is that they must be suffering from mental constipation.

Actually [they] can't get it through their thick skulls that Westport is not a low-income area. We who live here made many sacrifices to get here.

Most of us came here the hard way. We worked hard to improve ourselves and our way of life.

Now these officials want to give so-called underprivileged people an opportunity to live in Westport at the taxpayers' expense, hand them on a silver platter this style of life and housing by increasing their welfare payments and subsidizing their housing.

What incentive is there for the so-called underprivileged, both young and old, if you hand it to them? It's the likes of those government do-gooders who have destroyed the moral fiber of our people and undermined our kids' desire to better themselves.

If it is socially undesirable to live in Bridgeport (I don't know why, because more than 160,000 people live in Bridgeport) and socially undesirable to live in Norwalk (another 80,000), then let those unhappy people understand that we have no objection to having them be our neighbors and friends. But we object with a passion to paying their tabs—and we are not going to be forced into doing it. No way.

Furthermore, we should tell it like it is! That we are not interested in strengthening our ties with minority groups and organizations, including Norwalk Economic Opportunity Now (NEON), the South Norwalk Community Council, and the Bridgeport Spanish community newspaper, nor in getting in touch with the federal Department of Housing and Urban

Development about grant programs for subsidized housing for lower income families. Who do these people think they are? In Russia they call them Commissars—here they are called Commissioners.

In summing up, there is no reason to abide by their unreasonable recommendations. We govern ourselves, and Westport has done a pretty good job to date. Let Norwalk and Bridgeport handle their own affairs. Why get sucked into problems they can better handle and, moreover, are responsible for?

As for subsidized housing for Westport they can start sending checks to about 25 percent of the present residents of Westport who are struggling to make ends meet today.

The letter expresses some attitudes that infuse Exurbia, but which many exurbanites do not feel free to express quite so bluntly. For example, "Our town is wide open to anyone regardless of race, creed or religion. All one has to do . . . is . . . put up your money and move in. Period." True, of course, but according to those outside the gates, not enough. "We are precluded," they say, "from enjoying your town's wide-openness; precluded by our poorness. Moreover, we are poor because of our otherness from you, and we are kept poor because you maintain that otherness."

Another example: "Westport is not a low-income area. We who live here made many sacrifices to get here." The outsiders reply: "The sacrifices you made to get there are nothing to the sacrifices we make every day merely to stay alive in squalor. We live with a whole other order of sacrifice which is beyond your ken. We are no longer willing to make sacrifices on such a different level. Let us begin to equalize the sacrifice. Since we have nothing more to give up, the equalization process must take place on your side."

The Westporter states: "We worked hard to improve ourselves and our way of life." The outsider answers: "For you, 'working hard' meant managing to stay in college for four years and managing to look impressive enough behind a desk to continue to draw a fat salary. Have you ever cleaned a house for money? Have you ever scrubbed the floor of a plating plant? If hard work is equated with living in your town, then we work hard enough to qualify."

The Westporter: "Now these officials want to give so-called underprivileged people an opportunity to live in Westport at the taxpayers' expense, hand them on a silver platter this style of life and housing by increasing their welfare payments and subsidizing their housing." From the city comes the answer: " 'So-called under-privileged?' Well, leaving that aside, we ask who is being subsidized. You take the money out of the cities where we live; you let us come into your town to do your dirty work; but, when the sun goes down, we have to get out. We are subsidizing *you;* and we are sick of it."

Another point the exurbanite makes: "What incentive is there for the so-called underprivileged? . . . It's the likes of these government do-gooders who have destroyed the moral fiber of our people and undermined our kids' desire to better themselves." The answer: "We appreciate your concern about our 'moral fiber.' We happen to be a little dubious about *your* moral fiber (although we are not hypocriti-cal enough to tell you that we're worried about it). Anyway, if being ignored and/or screwed by people like you builds moral fiber, then by this time ours must be so strong that we are paragons of virtue. It is time for us to share this advantage with you."

"We are not," says the outspoken exurbanite, "interested in strengthening our ties with minority groups." "Right on!" exclaims the denizen of the city. "At least you are telling us how you really feel. But we have news for you. We are not interested in 'strengthening our ties' with you, either. We don't give a damn about 'ties' with you. All we want is a better place to live. You want to keep us from having that. We won't let you do that to us anymore."

Perhaps the most important question is the one carried by the headline that appeared above the suburbanite's letter: WOULD THEY RATHER WE WERE BROKE?

After all, say many sober observers, it doesn't do the inner city any good to destroy the suburbs. A Norwalk newspaper columnist, Irving Taub, cautioned the zealous against exerting punitive mea-sures. "Should federal funds not be forthcoming to Westport and even if Westport is forced to pay for its own sewage problems by itself, it would not create the housing which is generating so much concern with Norwalk officialdom."

In the same vein, many people—committed to neither side—are troubled by the ploy resorted to by the city of Hartford in suing to keep federal funds from going to neighboring suburbs that do not permit low-cost housing. One legislator laments the fact that the city has "cast a cloud" over the "spirit of mutuality" that previously invested efforts to work out city-suburb problems. Another com-ments on the picayune nature of the suit. He points out that the court action would deprive one of Hartford's neighbors of $25,000.

"You can't build many houses for $25,000." The mayor of one of the sued towns says: "I believe we were making a great deal of progress on a voluntary basis and I certainly hope we can sit down and talk out our differences, but it's awfully hard to do that when you're being sued."

Another suburban politician points out, reasonably, that even if the city were to get all of the money earmarked for the suburbs—and that is a dubious assumption—the sum would hardly make a dent in the city's massive problems. And as for the additional housing: "I really don't see how it's going to help them. If we build a hundred units and a hundred people move out of Hartford, then a hundred more are going to move in." The magisterial *New York Times* observed that "Hartford and its surrounding towns have been working together on regional plans for common problems" and that the effort "will inevitably, and unfortunately, be ruptured by this confrontation." The *Times* goes on to comment: "Nor does Hartford's action do anything to help the aging suburbs that are already suffering some of the same problems of deterioration as the city's core."

Reasonable people keep asking the same logical questions: What good does it do to tear down the suburbs? Can that really help the city? What do they want from us? One exurbanite cites Abraham Lincoln: "You cannot bring about prosperity by discouraging thrift. You cannot strengthen the weak by weakening the strong. You cannot help the wage earner by pulling down the wage payer. You cannot further the brotherhood of man by encouraging class hatred. You cannot help the poor by destroying the rich. You cannot keep out of trouble by spending more than you earn. You cannot build character and courage by taking away man's initiative and independence. You cannot help men permanently by doing for them what they can and should do for themselves."

Exurbanites ask the reasonable questions over and over again.

They are missing the point. The point is not the building up; it is the tearing down. People who have nothing are too far gone in misery to believe that much can be done for them in their lifetimes, and too steeped in justified cynicism to pay much attention to the reasonable pronouncements of the "haves." But they can derive the satisfaction of seeing Exurbia and exurbanites reduced; and for many this will be about as much satisfaction as they can expect out of existence. So they echo the rejoinder of a Hartford politician: "What

I'm saying is, fine, you invite me to dinner and you give me a few crumbs and nice conversation, but that's the extent of your friendship. Then when it comes down to the bottom line, when it comes down to acting, the action never takes place."

So the answer to the question "Do they want to see us broke?" is a resounding *Yes*. Maybe they can't render us as broke as they are, but at least they can pierce the barrier of what they see as our snobbish exclusivity, and that they are determined to do.

8

Exurban Education in Extremis

Education in the affluent suburbs is full of paradox. Exurbanites see their schools emptying as enrollment dwindles, but they don't want to let kids from outside attend their schools. Exurban parents are appalled to discover that spending a lot of money does not mean their kids learn to read, write, or add, but they recoil in horror from suggestions that educational spending be equalized. They demand that their educational systems be restored to excellence, but they consistently vote down school budgets.

An examination of some of these conflicts may give us a better idea of what's gone wrong with this aspect of the Good Life.

Connecticut ranks second among the states in per-capita income. (Alaska is first.) Connecticut, in 1975, ranked forty-seventh in the amount of state support for education. But of course Connecticut's suburban areas contain some of the most highly tooled and expensive school systems in the United States. By and large, the money to support education in Connecticut comes from local property taxes— 73 percent as against a national average of 48 percent.

Under the formula operating in Connecticut in 1975, the state contributed a flat $250 per pupil, no matter where that pupil went to school. That is not sufficient to keep a child in school these days. So the local community, through its own taxes, put in the rest of the money. There was no ceiling on how much a community could spend if it were willing to vote the taxes.

The result—in Connecticut as in a great many other states—is a considerable variation in expenditures per pupil between one community and another. It can, and has, varied by as much as $400 to $1,600.

For some years there has been a tendency to look askance at this system. A rich town can spend a lot of money on its schools because it has a lot of money to spend—which is the case because the residents of the town are wealthy, own desirable property, and can pay high taxes on it. A poor town or city simply does not have the tax base to approach the amount spent per pupil in Exurbia.

This, say the critics, is the worst possible way to fund education. Not only does it tilt the scales unfairly toward students who live in the richer communities, it perpetuates the "have/have not" equation by depriving disadvantaged youngsters of the education they need to better themselves. In the long run, say the critics, this does not even make economic sense for the wealthier towns. The residents of these towns will just have to pay higher social costs (welfare, and so forth) to those who are thus deprived.

This point of view is gaining wide acceptance. The property-tax method of funding education has come under attack in the courts and in the legislatures. In some states, courts have ruled it unconstitutional. This is the situation in Connecticut, where, in December 1974, a superior court judge declared the system in violation of the state constitution on two counts. The judge found that the inequity deprived some children of "equal protection" and that it also resulted in the state's evasion of its duty to provide "free public education." The ruling was appealed, but without waiting on any ultimate disposition by the courts, the legislature got busy.

Nowadays, whenever a legislature goes into action on a matter concerning relationships between the city and the suburbs—be it housing or education or taxes—it is bad news for the exurbanite. The equal-education case was no exception. The bill that came out of committee was quickly dubbed the "Robin Hood" bill. It proposed to cut state per-pupil grants in half, allotting $125 instead of $250 per pupil to "wealthy" towns, and to distribute the funds left over to communities considered to be more in need.

The purpose was, obviously, to "equalize" education throughout the state. Once again the alarm bell sounded in the suburbs. The proposal was "outrageous," it would have "disastrous" effects on towns like Westport; it was a "crassly conceived grab" by urban legislators, impelled by their hunger for reelection.

The suburban opposition to the equalization measure was articulated in various ways, but two general lines of argument emerged. They are interesting in that they appear to cancel each other out.

One line was the predictable "that's-their-problem" response. According to this reasoning, the suburbs should be free to spend whatever they please on schools. Some communities may be able to afford less, but that is their tough luck. Nor, according to standard exurban thinking, is it simply a matter of luck. The implication seems to be that the "poorer" towns and cities could lavish more on the education of their children if only they had the will and the industry to do so. If they lack the money, let them find ways to make the money. The proposition that inferior educational facilities tend to perpetuate the inability to afford better schools may or may not be valid, but it is not anything for the exurbanite to worry about. This viewpoint is summed up in the words of one Connecticut suburbanite. "Communities like Darien have decided that no expense is to be spared in child education, and tax residents accordingly. Simply stated, Darien pays for what it wants. Other communities may wish for more expensive education, but are unwilling to pay the price. Unwilling, not unable, is the basic problem."

This line is usually accompanied by a statement like the following: "The economically disadvantaged do have the same right to expensive education as their more affluent neighbors—but not at the expense of those neighbors." The last is a quotation from one of the numerous reactions to the "Robin Hood" bill that have festooned Letters to the Editor columns. It is interesting in its bold conceptualization of the "right to expensive education," and it expresses very well a popular attitude in Exurbia. The British novelist Peter Dickinson once described a character as having "compassion for all human suffering whose alleviation would not seriously affect her standard of living."

There is a further line of argument advanced by exurbanites who wish to preserve the status quo in educational funding. This formulation involves a kind of paternalistic lecturing directed at city-dwellers, stating that equalization of school financing is a will-o'-the-wisp; that it will not make the situation any better. This is a refinement of the old "money-does-not-buy-happiness" ploy. An editorial in a Westport newspaper puts it this way: "Nor has there been any mention of any studies that indisputably prove that more money necessarily improves education. Theoretically, one can assume that a child in Westport where per pupil costs now hover near $1,800 should be obtaining a much better education than one in a town where per pupil costs are $568 per pupil, but, as the old song goes, 'it ain't necessarily so.' "

Many suburbanites would agree with the above. They are disillusioned with educational experimentation. They were taxed for elaborate school buildings and installations that do not seem to be paying off. They go white at the lips when they calculate the tax bite eventuating from the latest proposed school budget, and, increasingly, they vote it down.

Those who say that money does not buy education have a few heavy intellectual guns on their side. They cite Christopher Jencks of Harvard to cast doubt on the efficacy of more spending. Mr. Jencks has been arguing for some time that the things that educational dollars buy—experienced teachers, smaller classes, technological airs, and so forth—cannot be shown to improve student achievement. The names of other scholars spring to the lips of those who want to keep the school budget down. James S. Coleman of the University of Chicago now says that student achievement is a matter of family background.

In any event, here is Exurbia, arguing on the one hand that it is entitled to spend whatever it wishes to spend on schooling, and arguing on the other hand that spending money is not the way to assure good education. The dichotomy sheds an interesting light on a growing question in the suburbs—that is, whether it is worthwhile fighting for educational autonomy at all.

In the affluent areas of Connecticut, those who are battling to keep open local options on school spending are strongly concerned with exurbanite lethargy. The "Robin Hood" bill was fought to a standstill in the 1975 session of the legislature. The state board of education came up with a substitute proposal, less onerous in its actual provisions, but nonetheless one that tends in the direction of equalization of funding. When a hearing was held in Norwalk on this proposal, not a single Westporter attended. The absence of a significant turnout led numerous partisans of the status quo to utter dismal predictions that educational equalization would come, and come soon.

Another factor that gives impetus to the drive for regionalization of education is the disparity between the use of school buildings in Exurbia and in the cities.

In the area of school population, Exurbia is growing old. A school population that ten years ago was a pyramid with its broad base in the lower grades is now a reverse pyramid, top-heavy in high school, diminishing in elementary school. It is happening because exurbanites no longer have big families.

So, stagnation of growth and a declining birth rate in Exurbia are emptying some expensive and beautifully appointed school buildings. What to do about them?

The case of Mamaroneck, New York, is typical. In 1969, school enrollment in Mamaroneck reached its peak: 6,400 students. Then it began to decline, and all projections indicate that the decline will continue without reversal.

Meanwhile, taxes have been going up, and most of those taxes go into education. What's the answer? Logic dictates: Close the schools. So a study committee in Mamaroneck recommended the shutting down of two of four elementary schools in the district, which includes the villages of Mamaroneck and Larchmont. Those "drastic steps" were necessary to avoid unacceptable tax increases, while preserving "the present levels of quality for students and property values for homeowners."

For many children, of course, this means no more neighborhood school. Opposition coalesced immediately and powerfully. "It is not busing that we are concerned about," declared the opponents of the plan, "it is the end of quality education."

And so the battle is widened, a battle that is being replicated across the country. The exurbanite is faced with a distressing choice of trade-offs, none of which appears satisfying. They can keep the schools open, enjoying the ambiance of the neighborhood school, but what will happen to the tax rate? They can acquiesce to the financial logic of closing schools, but then what happens to the dream of quality education? The future offers no hope of rescue; the projection for Mamaroneck anticipates a continuing birth rate of just over half the rate of twenty years ago and virtually no building of new homes.

Stirring within this situation is a latent factor that will inevitably generate additional pressures on Exurbia. Contemplate the picture. In the inner city are crowded and antiquated schools, giving their students less than adequate education. The adjoining suburbs have lavish school buildings, playing to far less than capacity, being converted to other purposes, or—more often—closed down altogether to reduce the burden on the suburban householder.

There will be many who will draw the obvious conclusion: Why not bus the kids from the city to the suburban schools? The city will pay its way. The tax load on the exurbanite will be eased, and the suburban child will be able to continue attending his neighborhood school.

Will this proposition meet with general acceptance in Exurbia? Don't bet on it.

9

Back to Basics

"I didn't come out here," says an anguished exurbanite, "because I wanted to be an elite snob. I don't care that much about fresh air. The commute is killing me. I did it for the kids. If it weren't for the kids, I would have stayed in the city. But in the city you have to send the kids to private schools. Out here the public school system was supposed to be the cream of the crop. My kids would get the best education possible. So I came out here. And now look at them!"

And now look at them. As disillusioned suburbanites see it, their kids are rebellious, undisciplined, and antagonistic. This might be borne, but what is worse is that they are uneducated. It seems that Johnny from Exurbia cannot read (or add) any better than his counterpart in the ghetto.

This is infuriating to the exurbanite who wants his children to achieve. How can they achieve—even to the point of getting into a decent college—if they haven't been taught anything. The exurbanite who has always told himself that he "did it for the kids" feels that all he has done is a waste. Nor is this all. The result-oriented achiever, who winds up in the wealthier suburbs and pays the steadily mounting property taxes that go largely into the education budget, is outraged when he contemplates the bottom line. As a business proposition, exurban education looks to him like a loser. His town is paying, say, $1,500 per pupil (as against, say, $600 in the adjacent city), and yet the product is badly flawed and not too marketable.

The December 1975 issue of the education journal *Phi Delta Kappa* reported on a Gallup survey of public attitudes toward education. The ten issues that concerned a cross section of Americans most about their schools were (1) lack of discipline, (2) busing, (3) money, (4) lack of good teachers, (5) school and class size, (6) drugs,

(7) poor curriculum, (8) crime and vandalism, (9) lack of adequate facilities, (10) lack of pupil interest.

The poll showed a sharp rise in public antipathy toward "progressive" education, which nowadays is frequently equated with "permissiveness." The prominence in the listing of vandalism, drugs, crime, lack of discipline, and pupil apathy are all facets of this mood.

Americans have gone sour on education. This feeling is in no way confined to Exurbia. The disillusionment is, however, reflected in the affluent enclaves in a particularly ugly way.

Looking at the above list from the viewpoint of Exurbia, one can detect the items that are the most abrasive. Exurbanites are now discussing discipline with the same fervor exhibited ten years ago in talk of college acceptance. It's no longer a matter of the kids achieving peak scores to get into Ivy League schools. It isn't even a matter of struggling through to graduation. Exurbanites are alarmed that their children will destroy the educational plant; or, if the younger generation fails in this, that they will cause so much damage that constant repair becomes an unbearable tax item. Today, when the school administration of a suburban town comes back to the municipal government for annual supplemental appropriations of hundreds of thousands of dollars just to fix things broken by vandalism, it is no longer a matter of minor concern.

As for the availability of good teachers, Exurbia is discovering that, even though it pays more, it does not seem to get much more in ability. Teachers are no longer Exurbia's pets. They are unionized, militant, arrogant, unresponsive to the wishes of parents, and their labor-management contracts frequently make it impossible for them to be replaced, even if the administration is of a mind to replace them.

Once Exurbia was the spearhead of progressiveness in education, and exurbanites were proud and happy about this. It is always nice to be in the forefront, and the good feeling lasts just as long as leadership is producing results that appear to justify the money and effort.

Alas, progressive education is now a bad word in the suburban archipelago. Parents say their kids can't read, can't write, can't add, and can't think. And they attribute these defects to the mindless experimentation and frivolity of those entrusted with the educational burden. One parent (who has felt obliged to place her children, at considerable expense, in private schools) declares: "Our schools are producing functional illiterates who cannot organize material, cannot write coherent sentences and have not mastered the rudiments of grammar, paragraphing, punctuation, and spelling. This situation can be laid at the door of English teachers and the contentless English curriculum. A child cannot do what he has not been taught to do." The sentiment reverberates through dinner parties and PTA meetings. Every time *Newsweek* or *Time* publishes another of their articles on "Why Johnny Can't Read," exurbanites nod angrily in agreement.

One unhappy Westport resident laid it out this way:

Our forebears saw quite clearly what was needed in education, and for generations, the Three R's were the foundation upon which other solid disciplines were built. Our modern educators, in reacting against some excessive practices, began making innovations—both in disciplinary and teaching methods—some to the good, though carried beyond their reasonable ramifications. In the process, traditional disciplines in their pure forms were altered, bastardized, or simply taught less. . . .

The academic disintegration of American school children seems to have paralleled the increasing preoccupation with liberal, so-called humanitarian, and "individualized" methods in education. The crusade to eliminate rote learning, far from producing well-rounded, or scholarly, graduates, has produced instead boys and girls ill-equipped for higher education, for professions and grades, and more broadly, for life in the modern world.

Children of educational permissiveness are apt not to be their own masters, for they will not have been taught that both practical accomplishment and the achievement of lofty ideals require a firm foundation of basic knowledge and the well-established habit of orderly application to a given task. School is not optional, and its standards must not continually shift to accommodate low achievers. Basics don't change, even in a changing world, and those changes that do occur justify stability wherever attainable.

The "new math" is taking a pounding.

It is distinctive. It is easy to joke about or get mad at. And its concepts and its language are so alien to veterans of the "old math" that it has become a primary target for criticism.

Exurbanites who are eager for their children to get a good education and achieve great things in the world know that mathematical aptitude tests are a formidable hurdle in the path of educational progress. Therefore it is natural for them to become upset when the child is failing math and, indeed, cannot seem to be able to solve the simplest problems. The situation becomes even more frustrating when Dad or Mom tries to help. They find that they cannot even begin to speak the jargon.

So, the exurbanites blame the schools, the inventors of the "new math," the teachers, and the whole trend toward innovation in the schools.

They do not receive much reassurance from the teachers. Instead, they discover that they are being denounced as the big reasons for Johnny's lack of ability to add.

In 1975, the fraternity of math teachers studied itself and found itself blameless. In a study prepared for the Conference Board of the Mathematical Sciences, and sponsored by the National Science Foundation, it was concluded that declines in math test scores are not caused by faulty teaching or by the "new math" itself. The "new math" is basically sound, the mathematics teachers were reassured to hear. Lack of achievement by pupils could be laid at the door of "societal pressures."

Indeed, the team that conducted the study went further. The very label "new math" was an affront and constituted one of the "societal pressures" that were leading toward poor results. The report told parents and educators: "From this point in time, use the term 'new math' only as an historical label for the vague phenomenon or the very diversified series of developments that took place in school mathematics between 1955 and 1975."

Otherwise, the name "new math" was declared *verboten.* Teachers were advised to talk, instead, about the "present mathematics program" or "contemporary mathematics teaching."

This injunction is not likely to have a magical effect in enhancing the delight of suburbanites with the way their children are being taught to add, or in making them philosophical about a 350 score on a college board mathematics aptitude test. For one thing, the suburbanite may not be able to thread himself, like Theseus, through the mazelike intricacies of "contemporary mathematics," or grasp the mysteries of "sets," but he knows the product of a public-relations man when he sees it. And the idea of solving the problem of unhappiness with the "new math" by not calling it "new math" smacks more of PR brainstorming than of rigorous scientific research.

The anxious parents are further maddened when—in response to their suggestion that the schools go at least part of the way back to "basics" and teach computational skills—teachers tell them that these skills are declining in importance and will soon become no more functional than the vermiform appendix. Why? Because of the invention of the mini-calculator. That is what they are being told. The Mathematics Conference Board declares that, with the increasing availability of hand calculators, it is more important that a pupil know when and where to use a given arithmetic operation than to be able to actually perform the operation. This is the type of statement suburban parents would expect to see in an advertising campaign for calculators; they do not expect to hear it as an answer to their anxiety about their child's inability to add and subtract, and they are driven to frustration when it is the only answer they receive.

It is galling to discover that your child is practically illiterate, particularly when you may be paying as much as ninety cents out of your property-tax dollar for schools.

For many exurbanites the news of illiteracy is long delayed. Their children speak quite fluently (although not to their parents), are frequently on the telephone, and seem quite capable of carrying on communicative, though distressingly obscene, conversations.

The son or daughter goes away to college, having managed to gain admission someplace. This is not an occasion for discovering the kid's writing proficiency. Communication is carried on via long-distance telephone (collect). But at last it becomes necessary for something to be conveyed in the form of a letter. And the exurbanite is appalled at the misspelled and ungrammatical screed he receives from this product of a vaunted educational system.

In 1975, the National Assessment of Educational Progress, a federally financed project, reported the information that today's youth can't write. The report stated that the writing of thirteen- and seventeen-year-olds was less coherent and more awkward than the writing of counterparts sampled four years previously. This was not news to any parents who had observed the atrocities that their child had been laboriously scratching on paper.

Similar reports are becoming an everyday occurrence. At great expense, underwritten by tax money or foundation grants, an august body utters a pronouncement relating to the deterioration of learning in the United States. The pronouncement contains no news for anyone who has been paying any attention; it is, however, couched in words that progress with the stateliness and pace of the Great White Fleet of 1904.

Then—and this is also a commonplace—the difficulty is attributed to "societal developments" rather than to any deficiency in concept or ability on the part of educators. The report on writing skills followed this pattern. A "writing specialist" attributed the decline to the fact that society places more emphasis on the spoken than on the written word. "Business and personal communication depends primarily on the telephone," he asserted. (This is another predictable element of such pronouncements. Technological developments are cited as causes or ameliorating factors. Kids don't need to be able to add because now they can have pocket calculators. They need not be able to write because they can talk on the phone.)

Finally, and this is again predictable, the report finds nothing to indicate that the schools should go "back to basics."

Indeed, there is good reason to believe that—at least in the area of writing—there is no way that the schools could go "back to basics." By and large, teachers cannot write. Many of them are as illiterate as their students.

And this situation seems to have become imbedded in the system. Late in 1975, the Stamford, Connecticut, board of education passed a regulation that said, in effect, that teachers should be able to spell and compose reasonable sentences. Those who could not would receive remedial help. Teachers who were hopelessly unable to use language in writing would be weeded out.

To many, this seemed a modest proposal; not to the teachers' unions. The Stamford Education Association declared that the board's action was "humiliating, demeaning, and degrading." The union called the regulation an attempt to "punish the many for the alleged inadequacies of the few." (A school board member had learned about teacher illiteracy much as parents learn about the illiteracy of their children. He had received an incoherent letter from an English teacher in the system.) The union denounced the board for having "publicly embarrassed our city," and demanded that the regulation be repealed.

People who choose exurban existence know that it is expensive, but they console themselves with one thing: education. If they remained in the city, they would have to send their kids to private school to get a decent education. At least in the suburbs they will enjoy the benefits of a public educational system that is the equal of any private school.

Sad experience is teaching many exurbanites that this is but a dream. Their children are not learning in the local public schools; indeed, they seem to be deteriorating intellectually and morally. So, for discipline and tuition, private education becomes the only answer.

St. Luke's School, in New Canaan, Connecticut, takes pupils in grades six through twelve. Traditionally it drew its students from cities, notably Stamford. Lately, however, the influx of students from the suburbs has risen sharply. In 1975, for the first time in many years, St. Luke's reached its full enrollment capacity. The average tuition at St. Luke's is $2,600. When one is paying a large tax bill to support a supposedly superb public-education system, the private-school answer constitutes a galling extremity. But this is what is required.

What do the private schools offer? Primarily it is an emphatic return to basics. Randy Brown, headmaster of St. Luke's, expressed the school's philosophy at some length. Inasmuch as it represents what the suburban striver wants for his kids and is not getting, the statement is worth quoting at some length.

The St. Luke's School Philosophy of Education

STRESS ON FUNDAMENTALS

I guess the one part of our educational philosophy that has gotten the most publicity is our return to a more fundamental form of education. At St. Luke's, we do not experiment for the sake of experimentation. There was the time in this country when the "three R's" were stressed in secondary school education. Then, over the last decade or so, often curious innovations were introduced into the classroom.

The result of these innovations has been a generation of high school graduates incapable of expressing themselves in writing, and who have difficulty with the simplest arithmetic. . . .

We are determined to enable our students to deal effectively and comfortably with the English language, and to effect basic mathematical computations that engage the principles of addition, subtraction, multiplication, and division.

Perhaps these objectives appear to be too limited and simplistic. It is my own view that there can be no loftier goal in American secondary school education. The tragic truth is, that, every June, all across this land, tens of thousands of young men and women are granted secondary school diplomas, when an alarming percentage of these young adults can not write a simple English sentence, and they can not add, subtract, multiply, or divide. It is not their fault. They have been cheated. We do not intend to cheat our students.

Simply stated, all we have done at St. Luke's is to return to the same kind of education that proved so successful in previous generations. Why this type of schooling was ever dropped in the first place baffles me.

STRICT DISCIPLINE

At St. Luke's we have a strictly enforced dress code. To some, this may sound archaic, but I have found that there is a direct relationship between the way students look and the way they behave. A sloppy appearance seems to breed a sloppy approach to learning. To avoid this, no boy or girl is allowed on campus unless he or she conforms to our dress code. Quite frankly, except for a small number of girls, we have experienced few problems in this area. By and large, most of our students actually seem to take pride in the way they look.

We have also virtually eliminated class cutting. Most of our students want to attend classes. Those who do not, quickly learn that our reaction is immediate. Their parents are informed as rapidly as they can be reached. If this does not dissuade them, we reserve the right to expel anyone who cuts seven classes during the school year. Thus far, we have not had to go to this extreme. . . .

One of my greatest feelings of accomplishment here at St. Luke's is to see a boy or girl who rarely attended classes at his or her private school and who was marked as "impossible to motivate," actually become an enthusiastic member of our school community. In fact, I think motivating the "unmotivatables" has been our primary area of success.

Our student body at St. Luke's represents all social and economic backgrounds. I believe this is essential if we are to prepare our graduates for the world beyond the academic walls. Many people conceive of private schools as catering to the financially elite. In my opinion, this would defeat a major purpose of secondary school education, which should be that of teaching students how to get along with people from all walks of life. After all, that is what America is all about.

I recently asked one of the boys in our junior class what made St. Luke's better than his previous school. "The teachers give a damn," he replied. I guess that sums it up better than I can. . . .

These are some of the answers I have for those who wonder why St. Luke's is doing nicely in a generally depressed market. The one remaining question is, I guess, will we continue to thrive in the years to come? I sincerely believe we will, if we maintain the integrity of our purpose. And we will.

There was a time when your typical exurbanite would have dismissed all this as old-fashioned and square. Now it represents the educational standard to which he is trying to rally. Maybe it is an illusion, as the efficacy of high-dollar public education was an illusion. But the growing pull of the illusion, if it is one, is another demonstration of the spreading feeling that a lot of things are rotten in the suburbs.

10

A Few Black Kids on a Bus . . .

Bridgeport is about twenty miles from Westport. In terms of money, society, attitude, and style of life, the distance might be measured in light-years.

The following is the story of one modest effort that was made to bring the two communities closer together.

Bridgeport has a large black population, low median income, heavy crowding in the inner city, much poverty. Westport enjoys the opposite situation in these categories. According to the 1970 census, there are 156,542 people living in Bridgeport and 27,318 living in Westport. But the area occupied by Westport is larger than that of Bridgeport by four square miles.

In 1968, the inner cities were seething. Martin Luther King's murder precipitated bloody riots. The Kerner Commission reported that the country was splitting into two societies, one black and one white.

That year Westport entered into an agreement with Bridgeport to study ways in which the wealthy town could help the city educate some of its children. A specific proposal emerged. Westport boasted a lively and well-planned summer-school program for younger children. A number of Westporters suggested that forty Bridgeport kids be invited to attend summer-school sessions in the morning and the popular beach-school program in the afternoon.

There were precedents. In 1966, an experiment called Project Concern had begun in the Hartford area. This involved inner-city kids attending suburban schools. State and federal grants covered the costs of the host schools, and the city paid for the buses. City children would attend school in the suburbs only where there was room for them. There was no provision for busing suburban children to the city.

In Westport, the Inter-Community Camp, a private organization of liberal orientation, began a program to be attended by Westport children, who would pay their own way, and children from Bridgeport and Norwalk, whose tuition would be covered by various grants.

The Westport proposal to bring Bridgeport children to summer school appeared on the agendas of the board of education and the recreation commission. Instantaneously, the town's grapevine began to throb. Soon, critics of the plan had surfaced to circulate petitions in opposition to the idea.

On the evening of May 13, 1968, a tumultuous meeting took place. The Westport town boards with jurisdiction over the summer-school plan sat before nearly a thousand townspeople. Speakers denounced the idea of bringing city problems into the idyllic precincts of the town, and of cluttering up Westport's "crowded" beaches with outsiders. Proponents of the program attacked the opponents as selfish and narrow-minded. Terms like "bleeding heart," "do-gooder," "Socialist," "bigot," and "racist" were hurled around the auditorium with abandon.

The Westport recreation and education boards approved the plan unanimously. The black children came in for the summer program; they have been coming ever since. Yet this was merely a skirmish. The battle lines were drawn, but the opposing forces were to wait two years before going into all-out action.

In 1970, the superintendent of schools in Bridgeport asked Westport to consider "the placing of some urban children in suburban elementary schools." The Westport League of Women Voters undertook a broad-scale education drive, laying out the facts of the program at meetings and neighborhood "coffees." A small but highly visible faction in the League of Women Voters was against the idea, and was garnering considerable publicity for its stand.

Now Project Concern was becoming a hot political issue. Westport usually voted Republican. For many years the board of education had been dominated by Republican majorities, although few people considered the board to be highly political. Republicans worked well with Democrats on educational policy, and with few exceptions, votes were unanimous. The general thrust of the Westport education board was moderate and nonpartisan.

By 1970, this changed. The Westport Republican town commit-tee had moved to the right. Under extremely conservative leadership, the Republicans had nominated for the board of education a citizen whose far-right stand differentiated him sharply from the tradition of Republican moderates. In the election, the Democrats who had concentrated on this seat won many independent and Republican votes and elected a Democratic majority. Now the five-member board was splitting 3–2 on many substantive issues. This new spirit of ideological partisanship was to be sharply in evidence throughout the maneuverings over Project Concern.

At this time an Urban Coalition Task Force was studying the means by which suburbs in the area could cooperate with cities. The request of the Bridgeport superintendent had urged that Westport not wait for the results of this study but bring some Bridgeport kids to Westport schools right away.

On March 30, 1970, the Westport board of education met, and a Democratic member moved that the board go on record as favoring some kind of face-to-face involvement between Westport and Bridgeport children within the next school year. The Republican members protested bitterly, and after a night of procedural wrangling the motion was withdrawn—with the proviso that it would be raised at the next meeting.

The subject became the focus of agitated debate. The Republican board members said that there were numerous alternatives to Project Concern, that it was limited and unable to achieve the "presumed objective," and that nothing should be done until the Urban Coalition Task Force study was completed. Project Concern was called "tokenism," and its supporters were accused of "steamroller tactics."

In Westport the ad hoc committee is as handy a weapon as was the rock to our Stone Age forebears. An anti–Project Concern group sprang up. In the grand old tradition, it bore an acronym, BEST, standing for Bipartisan Education Study Group. During the week of April 9 this committee rushed out questionnaires to registered voters. The questionnaire could scarcely be called objective; it was constructed to make it nearly impossible for the respondent to say anything positive about Project Concern. A little less than half the forms were returned; of these, 90 percent expressed opposition to immediate action on the program.

At the next board meeting—a heavily attended and highly charged session—the board voted 3–2 for a somewhat ambiguous resolution that referred the question back to the Urban Coalition

Task Force but also pledged action no later than the end of the year. The strongest proponents of Project Concern were disgruntled, feeling that this was foot-dragging. The anti's saw it as another gimmick to shoehorn busing into the town; they began to circulate petitions calling for a referendum on the issue.

The Urban Coalition Task Force study was presented to the Westport board of education in November. The members of the task force—local citizens—had spent the summer listening to community opinion and arguing with each other. At the public meetings a wide range of opinions was aired. Some liberals opposed Project Concern because it did not go far enough. Others questioned the educational theory that inner-city children would learn better if they studied in suburban schools. Still others offered alternatives they felt to be more suitable means of intercommunity cooperation.

The alternatives were virtually ignored. The debate ranged over Project Concern and the idea of busing in Bridgeport youngsters. Quite a few opponents declared that the outsiders would be depriving Westport kids of a full share of educational benefits, even though the city children would come only if there were room for them. Some of the most conservative elements in town were joined in a surprising alliance by black leaders from Bridgeport and other cities. These black representatives were intent upon gaining control of their own school districts and were thoroughly opposed to any other plan. While many felt that the race question infused the entire proceeding, the subject was actually mentioned on few occasions.

The report of the task force was a compromise. It contained a list of possible programs, by no means confined to education. There were proposals for adult seminars, a theater group, and so forth. However, wherever Project Concern stood on the list, all involved knew that it was the number-one item that would be considered by the Westport board of education.

On November 30, the board met to consider the proposal. The Westport school administration opened with a specific recommendation in favor of Project Concern (although that term was not used). The number of children to be involved was not vast; twenty-five Bridgeport students would enter a Westport elementary school the following February, and fifty more would move into two other elementary schools six months later.

This meeting, and the one that followed it, brought into play all the themes that had been sounded throughout the year. Those in favor insisted that Project Concern was a modest proposal indeed, and the least that could be done in the way of cooperation. The opponents attacked from many angles, but laid particular stress on the symbolic aspect of the plan. Maybe there was nothing wrong with just bringing in a few kids from Bridgeport—but this would be only the beginning. It was the camel's nose under the tent flap.

On December 7, the board voted 3–2 to begin Project Concern. The next day, thousands of letters went to Westport voters proposing that the chairman of the board of education be subject to a recall election.

For the next month, Westport was intensely absorbed with the question of whether or not the Democratic chairman of the board of education should be kicked out of her job.

Recall is an extreme measure usually confined to the purpose of getting rid of public officials who are guilty of malfeasance or nonfeasance. The Westport town charter stated simply that a petition for recall should state the grounds for recall. Many said that the device was improper and illegal in this context. There was no precedent; the town had never had a recall election before.

On December 29, opponents of Project Concern presented a petition containing the signatures of 29 percent of the community's voters. It asked that an election be scheduled.

Some substantive questions about the validity of the petitions surfaced. People claimed that their signatures had been solicited on the basis of a referendum on Project Concern. Though in actuality this was so, technically such solicitation was a violation of the charter. Also, it appeared that some petitions had been left in bars around town to accumulate signatures, again in contradiction of the statute.

The advocates of recall circulated a second petition, incorporating changes designed to obviate the problems that had cropped up with the first batch. They quickly obtained the requisite number of signatures.

Opponents of recall had gone to court and obtained a temporary injunction against the special election. On March 31, a superior court judge made the injunction permanent, ruling that the recall provision in the Westport town charter did not apply to members of the board of education. The state supreme court refused to review this.

So the recall effort was defeated, not at the polls but in the courts. The opponents of Project Concern felt cheated. The upholders of Project Concern were glad that the decision had gone the way it had, but they were not jubilant over their victory.

Some Westporters looked to the town election in November 1971 as the "referendum" that had been aborted by the court. The pro–Project Concern Democratic candidates for the school board won, but the issue was clouded by the entry into the election of a third force, the Conservative Action Party. Although the Republicans ran hard-line candidates, the Conservatives felt that they were not far enough to the right. The third party polled 13 percent of the vote, more than the winning margin for the Democrats.

Project Concern has continued in Westport. Seventy-five Bridgeport children still come in to Westport schools. Surveys conducted in 1975 showed that the program had lost some popularity; 65 percent of the polled Westport teachers said the program was a "valuable experience" for children, down from 85 percent the year before and 88 percent two years back. As for Westport parents whose children were in Project Concern classes, 48 percent responded favorably in 1975, 22 percent were negative, and 30 percent were neutral. A year before, 57 percent had been favorable and only 18 percent neutral. The Bridgeport parents continued to indicate overwhelming support for Project Concern, saying that it was improving their children's schoolwork and that their kids were making friends in Westport.

Westport has continued the program without much fuss.

This was not, however, the case in Westport's neighboring town, Wilton, a community that is smaller and even more exurban in income and attitudes than Westport.

Wilton entered a Project Concern arrangement with Bridgeport at about the same time Westport did, although the number of students involved was smaller. The program was approved without the bitter and ugly imbroglio that enlivened the Westport scene for so long. Residents of Wilton were inclined to bask in the self-generated glow of enlightenment and look patronizingly toward their Westport neighbors. When the plan had been in operation for a couple of years, a straw poll of Wilton residents showed that they favored it by more than two to one.

But as Project Concern continued in Wilton, things began to change. Residents discussed the fact that Bridgeport was not paying any more money to the Wilton system than it had at the beginning even though costs had gone up. In response, Bridgeport educators said that Project Concern was not costing Wilton any money because the Bridgeport kids filled only seats that were empty in the suburb's schools, while Bridgeport provided cash plus two teachers and two teacher's aides.

Then the Wilton board of education brought up a point of educational philosophy. Perhaps it would be better to involve more city students in the program, but not keep them around so long. There were other objections. Wiltonites who had expressed no objection to the program at the time of its inception now declared that they had been given no clear idea of its full scope. The implication was that, somehow, somebody had pulled a fast one.

The basic problem with Project Concern in Wilton was that children have a tendency to grow older. The crux of the difficulty was seven students from Bridgeport, all of them boys, all of them black. These boys were nearing the end of eighth grade. The next year they would, in normal course, enter Wilton High School.

No public word was uttered about the racial (or one might say racial-sexual) aspects of the situation. Nevertheless, as Wilton seethed and its board of education deadlocked for months over whether to continue the program, Bridgeport school officials implied that race was indeed the issue, and that the overt objections—which they considered frivolous—were masks.

Some manifestations of the Wilton attitude were particularly irritating to the Bridgeporters. For example, certain residents of Wilton advanced the argument that, since the city youngsters had been so superbly educated in the suburb through grade eight, they could now return to Bridgeport and become leaders in "their own" schools.

Bridgeport saw this as patronizing. One of the city's school officials declared: "It might surprise Wilton to learn that we are fiercely proud of our school system. That we have a high percentage of college entrances. And that we don't consider it the optimum educational experience for our children to go to school in the suburbs." He condemned the "Lady Bountiful" attitude that he perceived in the affluent suburb, and maintained that the program, in conception and in execution, was beneficial to both communities.

After months of argument, the Wilton education board at last resolved the dilemma by means of what it apparently thought to be a Solomon-like judgment. The seven boys could be accepted in Wilton High School, but this was a special provision for the seven only, made in consideration of "the relatively short notice" they would have on a switch of systems. But henceforth, all Bridgeport kids would get off the Wilton bus after the eighth grade.

To the astonishment of many in Wilton—and to the dismay and embarrassment of some—Bridgeport responded by terminating its Project Concern relationship with Wilton altogether. Among the Wilton opponents of the program, there was no public jubilation, but on the basis of private observations, it was reasonable to suppose that the Bridgeport decision did not constitute too heavy a blow. Indeed, one might even say that it came as something of a relief.

A young woman who had gone through the Wilton system voiced her reaction. "For twelve years I attended school with kids just like me, whose parents worked hard and made money so that their children could have everything they ever wanted. I didn't learn to live with children from backgrounds different from my own, for Wilton's student body, then as now, was absurdly homogeneous. Instead of visualizing the Project Concern program as a favor to the 'poor, disadvantaged' Bridgeport students, Wilton citizens should have been thanking Bridgport for giving the students of Wilton the opportunity to enrich themselves and learn to relate to children of entirely different backgrounds, to share ideas and themselves. Wilton has sold itself short, and lost something very beautiful and productive."

Events since 1970 have not provided much encouragement for those who were most energetic in promoting Project Concern. At the time of the battle over Westport's participation, the people who were in favor of the program continually cited the "Coleman Report," a comprehensive study made by the sociologist James S. Coleman in 1966. Then, Coleman was a champion of busing. One of his most widely quoted conclusions was that school integration could reduce the gap between black and white children by 30 percent.

Today, Coleman has, to some degree, muted his enthusiasm for the educational aspects of such plans as Project Concern. In an interview in *The New York Times Magazine* (August 24, 1975), he admitted that he had somewhat overstated his case. Asked about the celebrated "30 percent improvement," Dr. Coleman said, "In view of subsequent studies, that 30 percent figure, if ever I used it, was an overestimate. Some of the studies do show some positive effects—not strong effects, but positive effects. I think the sum total of evidence suggests that school integration does, on the average, benefit disadvantaged children. The benefit is not very large, not nearly as great as the child's own home background."

Coleman has come to believe that emphasis on school segregation "has led us to neglect questions of residential segregation, which are really profound, the strongest remaining source of actual discrimination in this country."

So today the opponents of Project Concern can claim that its educational benefits are questionable, and they can cite the author of the seminal research on the position for support. Those who based their support for Project Concern primarily on educational grounds do not have a strong comeback. However, Coleman's current thinking is not without difficulties for suburban standpatters. If they now cite Coleman as an authority, they must also cope with his emphasis on de facto residential segregation. There are not many exurban adversaries of busing who wish, at the same time, to open up housing opportunities for blacks and poor people in their communities.

The significant issue pits exclusion against urbanization—with the muted drums of racism beating in the background. The black children from the inner city symbolize regionalization to the exurbanite, and the connotations of regionalization are vast and ominous: high-rise apartments, crime, dirt, crowding, ugliness, and, yes, interracial friendship and sex between teenagers.

The experiences of exurban towns with programs like this are most important for what they tell us about overall relationships between the exurb and the city. The fact is that, from the beginning, a large number of Westport citizens wanted nothing to do with Bridgeport, even in terms of a strictly limited program. In Wilton the program was more widely accepted initially; opposition arose as some of its implications became clearer. Specific issues of theory, scope, and money were the weapons and the rationalizations; the underlying motivation of the violent opposition was fear.

On the exurban side we see fear, the desire to be left alone, and the attitude that the "outsiders" be left to stew in their own juice. On the city side we see suspicion, touchiness, and resentment. These are not auspicious omens for cooperation between the exurban haves and the city have-nots.

There is one more important threat running through the Westport struggle over Project Concern that repeats a pattern surfacing throughout the exurban archipelago. At one time exurbanites were proud of their school systems, felt fortunate that they could enroll their children in fine schools, justified their strivings for success and exclusivity on the basis of opportunities for their kids. This is no longer the case. As Exurbia grows older and children grow up, reality replaces expectation. And, as the expectation was bright, reality is dark.

There was a time, in Westport, when Project Concern would have had far smoother sailing than it did in the early 1970s. This was the time when the school establishment was supreme. Of course there were always grumblers, but they were in a distinct minority. They were dismissed as ill-adjusted malcontents. Whatever the school administration said, went.

By the time Project Concern became a reality, this was no longer the case. Wesporters who had revered their schools were astounded at the virulence of the attacks on the system, and particularly shocked at the opposition of some who had previously been solid supporters of everything educational.

But the battle over busing-in the Bridgeport kids was only the beginning of the assault on the educational establishment in Westport.

11

The Day They Pulled the Plug
on Education

In Westport, Bedford Junior High School is the place to go on election night to hear the returns. At around 8:00 A.M. on June 4, 1974, the curious began to gather. This was not a run-of-the-mill election. The town had just voted on a referendum proposal to cut $800,000 out of the $13-million school budget.

At one end of the Bedford gym the budget-cutters huddled in little groups, grim and defiant. At the other end the budget-supporters greeted each other, chatting casually. There was concern but not panic. After all, there had been threats to the schools before, but they had always been repelled. This was a serious threat, but the pro-educationalists were willing to wait and see how it came out.

The chairman of the board of education was not chatty. He had little doubt about how it would come out. He had spent part of the day standing, incognito, on voting lines, listening to conversations ("My God, I can't buy gas for the lawn mower, and they want to raise the taxes five mills. And what are we getting for it?") The chairman was under few illusions; education was about to take a bad beating. In Westport, as in other exurban towns, the concept of quality education is marked by four criteria: modern, even lavish, buildings and facilities, concentration on preparation for college, innovative educational practices, and (above all) generous spending of tax money.

Beautiful school buildings can be as embarrassing as a massage parlor hostess at a state dinner. In recent years Westport has erected some strikingly designed structures, but there have been problems with delays, acoustics, insecure window glass, and oddly cramped interior facilities. Traditionalists regarded the free-form edifices with sour derision, and passions were inflamed by the numbers on the price tags.

Education in Westport is geared to the youngster who will go on to college. The guidance department is heavily involved in college selection and admission. Certain students enjoy an advanced-placement program enabling them to take college courses and thus get a head start. Vocational training is not a big item.

"Far-out" is a subjective term. The educationally sophisticated have always hooted at the notion that Westport was a leader in progressive education. One could always point to a school system in Pasadena or Briarcliff that boasted a much more innovative program. But to nonmavens, Westport education seemed pretty futuristic. Revised reading curricula, "new math," individualized instruction, electives, relaxed discipline, and student participation in the setting of high school policy—all struck a lot of citizens as ego- and career-building ploys for the faculty rather than sound educational approaches for the kids.

Creation, expansion, and innovation cost a lot of money.

Westport voted and spent the money. From the mid-1950s the town's per-pupil expenditure ranked third or second in the state. The budget proposed in 1974 would peg that figure at $1,800 per pupil—paid for by property taxes. This would elevate Westport to number one in Connecticut in educational spending.

There are always people who oppose spending money. For many years there had been grumbling in Westport. What is wrong, people kept asking, with square brick buildings that *look* like schools? Whatever happened to the good old three R's? Why do the schools seem to pay a lot of attention to the very bright kids and ignore the others? And, above all, how can we keep on spending money for fancy education when we can't afford it?

All of this complaining was old hat to Westport's dominant educational establishment. The exurbanite wanted to know that his children were getting the best—and that meant the best educational apparatus that money could buy. The exurbanite mother, well educated and purposeful, was interested in educational programs and determined to maintain them. The bill was high, but they could afford it. True, there were, no doubt, people—older, ill educated, less gifted—who were having trouble paying their taxes. But these people were not visible, did not come to meetings, did not write letters to the papers, and did not organize. The malcontents would have to understand that Westport was a unique place. One of the important things that made it special was the school system. Good schools cost money. Those who did not want to pay the price could move elsewhere. One exurbanite spoke for many. "The old-timers complained about the taxes. My God, they've all made a pile on real estate. If it weren't for us they'd still be growing onions on their land. And if we didn't have decent schools, who the hell would want to buy their land?"

On sporadic occasions when the school budget was challenged, Westport's educational establishment swung into action with the efficiency and industriousness of army ants repelling a raid on the nest. The school administration issued "cut lists": ominous descriptions of the educational benefits that would have to be abandoned if the cut were sustained. The Westport PTA Council and the school PTAs held meetings to denounce the irresponsible effort to cripple quality education. Teachers sent, via their pupils, handouts to voters' homes. Ad hoc associations were formed (Westporters for Better Education) to buy advertisements in the local papers and to apply pressure on town officials. In the end all would turn out well. The education money would be appropriated, and Westporters would be assured that their vaunted educational system would continue untrammeled. There would be unrest in certain quarters, but it could be ignored.

For 1974–75 the Westport school administration asked for $13 million, up $1.8 million from the previous year. The figure would make up 63 percent of the entire town budget.

At this point a new group—Taxwatchers of Westport—surfaced and began to talk of a referendum. Educators retorted that the referendum provision in the town charter had never been intended to apply to anything like this.

The Taxwatchers circulated their petitions. They needed sixteen hundred signatures within one week; they had more than twice that number within three days. A few educators grudgingly admitted that they were somewhat impressed by the unprecedented efficiency with which the operation was conducted. However, there was still no widespread alarm.

The familiar machinery went into action. Pillars of the establishment came forward to certify the folly of budget-cutting. Teachers chatted informally with students about the ideals of education. The newest of a long line of organizations, Save Our Schools (SOS), sprang into being. PTAs met in urgent session. The administration promulgated a list defining the horrors that would ensue from a financial slash: closing of the oldest elementary schools, curtailment of interscholastic athletics, no more cheerleading, elimination of the dream programs, and so forth. The board of education accepted the cut list, announcing that it was irrevocable.

Telephone wires began to hum. But this time the time-honored techniques for "Saving Our Schools" did not seem to be working. Soon SOS activists were discussing, *sotto voce*, the reactions they had encountered. Many former "friends of education" seemed apathetic and occasionally even hostile about entering the lists once again. The typical reaction: "I guess I'll vote against the cut, but those people do have a point." More and more, partisans of the education budget wondered if 1974 might conceivably be a different ballgame.

Of course times were tough—but in an image-oriented town like Westport it is possible to think that things are better than they are. Behind the facades, there was muted desperation. A lot of commuters no longer had jobs to commute to. Delinquencies on property taxes had reached a peak. Real-estate brokers received daily the opportunity to sell high-priced homes, but there was no one to buy. Westport's one-person welfare department—which most people did not know existed—was swamped with cases, many from areas of seeming affluence.

There were other changes. Westport was getting old. In ten years the over-fifty group had risen more than 10 percent in its share of the population. Those between twenty-five and forty—traditionally the most energetic educationalists—had declined by about the same amount. For the first time, fewer than half the adults in the town had children in the school.

Westport had developed a considerable floating population—corporate nomads who were assigned to three years in Kansas City, three years in Aruba, three years in New York, and so forth. These temporary citizens took the present excellence of the school system for granted, but showed a marked lack of enthusiasm for the raising of current taxes for future educational benefits. The New Neighbors club reported that, in contrast to past patterns, newcomers were more interested in the social and recreational advantages offered by the town than in the schools.

In 1974, there were about 6,400 students in Westport schools.

Ten years before, there had been almost exactly the same number. But the upward shift was dramatic. In 1964, 54 percent of the children were in the elementary grades, 22 percent in junior high, 24 percent in high school. Now the number of elementary pupils had dropped to 41 percent. Junior high students had risen to 29 percent of the total and 30 percent were in high school.

For those children and their parents, educational innovation was no longer a bright promise. They had experienced the experimental programs, the electives, and the relaxed discipline. Some parents were happy, but a good many were not. They expressed their unhappiness in various ways, but it always came down to the same thing. They had expected their children to learn certain basic things. The kids had not learned them. For one Westporter, a longtime supporter of all things educational, the moment of truth came when her son—a freshly graduated product of the system—interrupted a meeting she was conducting to ask genially, "Hey, Mom, how do you spell 'success'?"

There was another important difference. The opponents of the budget were no longer the disorganized and inarticulate losers of former years. A retired publisher had taken the helm of the Taxwatchers, who by now had built a commodious tent. Into it they were beckoning not only the old-timers, the cranks, and the chronically impoverished, but every voter who had a grievance against the school system. Nor did the budget-cutters rely on the traditional voting strength of the town. Their hardworking organization reached and enrolled a multitude of new voters: the elderly, the disaffected, and the submerged. On the eve of the referendum, the town registrars worked until 1:00 A.M. to enroll 377 voters.

June 4. Eight-thirty P.M. The results began to come in.

For the educationalists it was disaster from the moment that the first machine was opened. The final tally was 6,743 in favor of the budget cut, 3,794 against.

Why had they voted against the budget? The reasons were mixed. Money, of course; some citizens were no longer willing or able to authorize an extra pennyworth in taxes. Disinterest; a Westporter who had been willing to shoot the works when the children were in elementary school took a more remote view when the kids had outgrown the system.

But there was more. Bitterness; the system had labored and

brought forth products with mouselike reading and computation skills. Hatred; there had always been outsiders who stared somberly through the window at the exurbanite feast. The schools were the playthings of the haves; now was the chance to break their toys.

And through it all was a thread of biased nostalgia. "Kids didn't do these things when I was young." "These things"—liquor, drugs, sex, rebellion—"must have been put there by the schools." The educators might say, with merit, that schools were different today because the kids were different, not the other way around. But a lot of people could not see it that way.

The victorious Taxwatchers quickly demanded that the "politically inspired" cut list be junked; embittered educationalists urged that the board stick with its Draconian proposals to maintain "credibility" against the next onslaught. There was no formal revision—but within a couple of months, certain "must-cut" items (athletics, cheerleading) began to creep back into the picture. One elementary school was closed—but the declining lower-grade population had dictated its closure in any case.

Some programs were eliminated or cut back, and the teaching staff was reduced. But a newly militant teachers' union would not abide this. Issuing pronouncements reminiscent of the 1930s, the teachers prepared a thirty-eight-item list of demands, including a 25 percent pay increase, control over class size and other matters of policy, and ironclad seniority. To a good many Westporters, a teachers' strike seemed to be moving from the status of remote possibility to near-certainty.

The superintendent of schools insisted that his job was to identify and meet educational needs, not look at price tags. He emphasized his determination to continue to do his job, with the hope that somehow the community could be brought to a better understanding of its system. As a beginning, all citizens—parents or not—were urged to visit the schools during Westport Education Week. Attendance was not overwhelming.

There were new assaults on the "permissiveness" of the system. An "old Westporter," who had long since qualified as one of the town's most colorful and outspoken characters, rose at a meeting to assert that he did not like to see school-age children "walking the streets," and that some unspecified thing must be done.

Dissent and division were not confined to the ranks of the

vanquished. The chief Taxwatcher had always maintained that he was interested in saving money, not in telling teachers how to teach. But others who had marched under his banner were not so modest in their aims. A new group, Westport Community Action for Responsive Education (WE CARE), surfaced to proclaim its determination to become involved in the full scope of policy making and curriculum setting. This organization manifested obvious similarities and affiliations with like groups throughout the country.

And from the state capital in Hartford there was heard the ominous thudding of a distant drum. The Commission to Study School Finance and Equal Education Opportunity stated that the "public school finance system is inequitable and inherently unequal" and that the "current system of financing public schools by local property taxes is harmful and inadequate." Westport educationalists attempted to sound the tocsin for banding together to fight off this assault on local control of education; but they found a lot of people who had become heartily sick of "local control."

And the kids? Well, they seemed to be the one group in Westport that had not fought in the battle of the budget, June 1974; least scarred, most affected.

12

Gray Eminence Begins to Tilt the Scales

People don't die the way they used to.

In 1900, 4 percent of the American population was over sixty-five. In 1975, more than 10 percent of Americans had passed that milestone. The country is getting older.

This, of course, is wonderful. Everyone wants to live longer. We revere our elders, and we want them to remain with us on this earth for a full and fruitful span of years. Indeed, though we do not think about it so much, we ourselves are growing older. It will not be long before we can be classed among the elderly. In fact, many of us are there now, although we neither realize it nor acknowledge it.

Today, people don't just live longer. They retain a greater measure of vitality well into what used to be thought of as senescence. They continue to have aspirations and demands on life. The truth is that often the elderly want and expect more than they did when they were younger. In Exurbia, their power to obtain it is growing.

In a democracy, numbers, purpose, and cohesion spell clout. "Gray Power" is upon us. Senior Americans know what they want, and they have the votes and the thrust to get it. One of the most significant results of this development is the 1971 revision of the social security laws that assures members of the aging generations of more than four times what social security pays today—but which may well deplete the cupboard to such an extent that today's twenty- to thirty-year-olds may find it scantily stocked, if not bare.

At the municipal level, "Gray Power" is having potent effects. Senior citizens are able to use their ballot-box clout to reward politicians who act in their interests and to punish those who act counter to their wishes. The phenomenon is evident everywhere, but it emerges with particular strength in places where the elderly congregate. The "sun belt" is becoming a focus for the keen attention of political demographers. In Arizona, where the sun shines bright on many citizens of riper years, the 34,000 residents of Sun City voted down school bond proposals for the neighboring community of Peoria, population 7,000. The county board of supervisors had to step in and separate Sun City from the smaller and younger community so that Peoria could float bonds to support its schools.

Another piece of news from the same area casts some doubt on the Norman Rockwellian picture of beaming grandmother and grandfather types who yearn to lavish their affection on the young. At a retirement community near Sun City, one of the original members moved out. This citizen sold his home to a family that had young children. The community passed an ordinance forbidding children under eighteen within the boundaries of the town. The Arizona court of appeals upheld this ordinance. The war between the generations is turning from cold to hot in many places; the turn is particularly marked in suburbia.

"Gray Power" is exhibiting muscle all over. In Monmouth County, New Jersey, the defeat of school-funding proposals is directly attributed to bloc voting by older citizens of the area.

Miami Beach is perhaps the most egregious example of the voting clout of the elderly. The median age is between sixty-two and sixty-seven. The citizens go to the polls. A former councilman, swept out of office after opposing some measures desired by his senior constituents, remarked that 92 percent of them vote and the other 8 percent would if they could get out of institutions. Here there is no question of school funding. The senior citizens want rent control, low-cost housing, free or reduced bus fares, free hot meals, recreation, exercise classes, congenial jobs, a doctor on every ambulance. They demand services of all kinds, and they get them. "Let's face it," says one older Floridian, "we have nothing else to do but vote. It's an outing for us." Such "outings" in Florida have doubled the homestead exemption for the elderly from $5,000 to $10,000 and introduced a "mobile home bill of rights" and probate reform challenging some rights of children in their parents' estates.

Associated Press reporter Kay Bartlett observes that public transportation has become a pet project of the seniors. Many communities have adopted reduced fares for the elderly. In 1972, the

Pennsylvania legislature voted to subsidize bus companies if they permitted those sixty-five and over to ride free. Colorado has voted to permit groups of five or more senior citizens to ride school buses.

The National Council of Senior Citizens—one of the largest of the elderly organizations—boasts 3.5 million members. Ms. Bartlett quotes from a speech by its executive director, William R. Hutton: "I can remember—back in the early days of political action on the part of senior citizens—when we could cool our heels in the waiting room of a senator or congressman. We would wait for hours in hopes the legislator would pass through and we could plead our case in a quick standing visit or a fast walk down the hall.

"That's all changed now. While all of Congress is surely not beating a path to our door, it is uniquely satisfying to hear constantly from legislators via letters and telephone visits—asking where we stand on particular issues, asking how a certain proposal or piece of legislation might affect the elderly, asking our advice." Nowadays, as they approach their golden years, Americans can look forward to the exhilaration of belonging to a political bloc for fun and profit. There is nothing like knowing that you will be on the winning side—not to mention the opportunity to bring a little more gray into the lives of all of those who are younger than you are.

It was not until about 1973 that the elderly residents of Westport began to achieve their potential as a political force. When they did at last begin to exert their weight, the effects were notable.

These senior exurbanites, like those in similar communities, zeroed in on three objectives: reduced school expenditures, low-cost housing for senior citizens, and a break in property taxes. The seniors of Westport marched side by side with neighbors who were worried about taxes and disillusioned with the local school system to win an unprecedented referendum that knocked $800,000 out of the education budget in 1974. In the great Westport panic over the incursion of apartment houses, one exception was made. A fifty-unit senior-citizen project was okayed.

The school budget issue was not one affecting primarily the elderly; they banded with other groups who, for various reasons, wanted to cut educational spending. The low-cost housing for older people was, by its very nature, applicable to those who needed it. There was little likelihood that any wealthy senior citizen would sell his $100,000 home to move into one of the new units.

But the tax-relief fight was something else again. Here the thrust was toward across-the-board favorable treatment purely on the basis of advanced age, whatever the financial condition of the beneficiaries.

The elderly of Westport demanded tax relief. This was not the most propitious time for the town's government to contemplate a reduction in the tax base. The economy had gone sour. Unemployment in Westport was above 10 percent and climbing. Many other residents were trying to get along on severely reduced incomes. Defaults on tax payments climbed in startling measure.

Nevertheless, there was general agreement that something should be done. The town administration formulated the proposition that there should be tax relief for those "in need of it." The chosen instrument was to be a "lien"—a tax-free loan to be repaid to the town upon transfer or sale of the property or upon the owner's death.

Reaction came fast. Spokesmen for the elderly denounced the plan in the strongest possible terms. They leveled their blasts at the notion that tax relief was to be given to those "in need" of it. There was to be none of this "in-need" nonsense, the spokesmen declared; everyone who had achieved a ripe old age was to be given a tax break with absolutely no strings attached. Age was to be the only qualification. One leading tribune for the elderly described the provision as an insult to all of the fine senior citizens who had contributed so much to the town. Another spokesman stated: "Their tax payments over the years have earned them the right to first-class treatment." Yet another rejected the lien as "demeaning." (There were many citizens who would have found a tax-free loan from the government anything but demeaning, but alas, these persons did not fall within the age requirements for relief.)

It is worth noting that the most energetic and vociferous opponents of the lien were senior citizens who most definitely did not fall into the description of "the most downtrodden minority in America today." These members of Westport's elderly contingent live in very large houses and drive very expensive cars. The years have touched them lightly indeed, particularly in the pocketbook. And without speculating on motives, an objective observer would certainly come to the conclusion that across-the-board, no-questions-asked tax relief would be of greater benefit to these individuals than to those who were less well off.

The lien provision went through. The spokesmen went into action, appearing before gatherings of the elderly to tell them that they were being insulted. This had its effect. Applications for the relief in its present form were surprisingly low.

At the same time that Westport was going through its travail, a neighboring Exurbia—Weston—was contemplating its own version of aid for the elderly. Here the formula was much more pleasing to elderly activists: straight tax relief for one year. However, some of the hard-pressed Weston town fathers, looking at their strapped municipal budgets, dared to enunciate words even more onerous than "lien." They talked about a "means test." After these daring citizens had suffered considerable lambasting for their Scrooge-like attitude, the idea of a means test was dropped.

But in Westport the fight continued. The town administration stuck to its insistence on a tax-free loan rather than outright tax remission, pointing to its efforts in all other areas to keep town expenditures cut to the bone. The board of finance backed up the administration. But there was still one recourse left to the elderly crusaders: the community's legislative body, called the Representative Town Meeting (RTM). The members of the RTM were subjected to an all-out pressure campaign. Typically, one opponent of the provision called the relief plan a "niggardly bill . . . a real cheap situation." He told the representatives that they must not "throw us a bone with a string."

There were some defenders of the lien, even among the elderly. One resident said: "It is degrading to the elderly that their emotions are whipped up by self-appointed spokesmen who appear to believe that the elderly cannot think rationally for themselves to the point where reason and cool-headed arguments fall on elderly deaf ears."

The ears of the members of the RTM were not deaf. By a close vote they eliminated the hated lien provision. Westport was now in line with most other Exurbias in acknowledging "Gray Power." There were few who felt that the clout of the golden-agers would make itself any less felt in Exurbia as time went on.

13

The Collapse of the
Exurban Family

The Good Life has never been so easy as it appeared to those who were striving for it. There always seems to be a little more house than one can afford and a little less fun than one is entitled to. To the generation of exurbanites who came in the post–World War II wave—and who are now well into middle age—the full fruits of existence in Exurbia have always been more a matter of hope than of realization. Exurban life was a complex of concentric circles. You arrived, you moved into your dream house, and you began to raise a family. You had so much going for you—and yet it seemed, right from the start, that you were located in an outer circle of satisfaction. So— without being sure what was there—you pushed toward the next innermost circle. Having reached it, you were still not happy—so it was necessary to push inward again.

Then comes the realization that there is no innermost core of perfect happiness in the suburbs. It usually comes slowly, and not without a fight. You see it happening, for example, among boat owners. Boatmen are always trading up, or planning to trade up. They never seem content with the vessel they own today; they are scheming to acquire another one for tomorrow, with the assurance that *that* one will be it.

And, of course, suburbia has been growing older. The corporate hotshots of the 1950s and 1960s are finding that they haven't quite made it to the summit—and that it is harder, not easier, to maintain a foothold at their present position on the steepening slope. These are people who have played in the major leagues; and the major leagues are brutal about age. There are always younger and hungrier guys coming up from below—and when you're through, you're through.

People who have lived comfortable and insulated lives have difficulty adjusting to—or even understanding—hardship. A lawyer who represents indigent citizens in civil cases comments: "My black clients from the city are hardened and streetwise. They have the instinct for survival. When trouble comes they react with resourcefulness and even surprising good humor. Getting evicted is old stuff to them."

It's different with the formerly affluent: "One woman had spent twelve years living in a large house on three acres. Then came the divorce and her husband's remarriage. She could get no money out of him, and so moved into a local apartment. She got a job, but it did not pay much money. She has not been able to pay the rent—apartment rents are high in this area—and now she's being evicted. She can't believe it. She says, 'Do you mean they can evict me even though I have young children? Even though I am doing my best to pay?' I try to explain that the law makes no distinction between those who are doing their best and those who waste their money. She doesn't understand. Another woman, in a similar situation, is being put out of her house. She is pregnant. She cannot believe that the law is not somehow different for her. I talked with a man who had—until he was fired two years ago—made fifty thousand dollars a year. He has run through most of his resources, but he does not want to give up his house. I told him that he is not eligible for welfare. He said, 'Are you telling me to go out and steal?' To him, moving to a smaller place would be an admission that he is washed up. Furthermore, he has the idea that if he does not live in the big house he will never get another job commensurate with his status and abilities. Frankly, he probably will not get such a job ever again, although it has nothing to do with the house. Logic has nothing to do with it. These people are panic-stricken and incapacitated. They say, 'But I have to stay here. The kids are in the schools here, and, after all, it's such a good school system.' They are hooked on affluence, and need it even when they are no longer affluent."

The exurbanite who is broke often considers moving away as the absolute last resort. He or she can't afford the Good Life, but cannot conceive of any other. Within the affluent suburbs there is today a substructure of people who are trying to get by on food stamps and welfare allowances amounting to about fifty cents a day. On this they attempt to maintain the old amenities and, in addition, keep up a front. In the end they are ambushed by the realities of the suburbs.

Typically, a woman who was separated and trying to make it on her own insisted on staying in her exurban house—which was the only thing left to her after the breakup. The mortgage payments were high. She was able to get a job. There was, of course, no public transportation, so she had to drive to the job. One of the economies she resorted to was allowing her car insurance to lapse. She had an accident and is now being sued. Her license has been suspended. Unable to drive to work, she has lost her job. She needs help, but she does not fall into a category for which there is any particular sympathy or channel of help. It is hard to imagine what she will do.

A public-service lawyer in a suburban community describes the following case as typical. Jimmy is now sixteen. He grew up in Exurbia. His parents are divorced. Each has remarried. For a while he lived with his mother in Fort Lauderdale, but he did not get along with his stepfather. So Jimmy returned to the town in which he had lived all his life. For a while, he slept in the houses of school friends, until their parents kicked him out. Then he moved into an overcrowded house with a group of parentless kids, boys and girls. Jimmy had been smoking pot since he was twelve, experimenting with harder drugs since he was thirteen. He was picked up three times for shoplifting. Now he is a resident of a halfway house run by a local church.

Jimmy's father has no interest in him. His mother now has young children by her second marriage. She does not want Jimmy, either. He has been persuaded to reenter school, but his status with regard to the local school system is questionable. Is he a valid resident of the town? He needs some money, but he does not qualify for state welfare, since he is neither aged, nor disabled, nor a parent of dependent children. The cloudiness of his legal status has held up his qualification for town welfare. (This being an "affluent" community, the provision for local welfare is tiny.) There is no doubt that Jimmy is abandoned, but is he a "liberated minor"? In some respects the law views him as an adult (he has a driver's license). In some respects he is still a child. Exurbia abounds with cases like Jimmy's.

Here are some observations on the Good Life from the point of view of two people who have a special concern with what is happening. One is director of guidance for a school system in an affluent town:

"The kids I see are kids in trouble. Their troubles grew out of a network of problems, many of which are particularly evident in a town like this one.

"You begin with the alcoholism. There has always been a lot of drinking here—it's no surprise at all that the kids begin to do it. Then there is divorce and separation. Families are falling apart, and, as they do, the school is expected to become a surrogate parent. The calls we get from parents are not centered primarily on academic concerns. We hear, 'Would you keep an eye on him and see if he is clean, if he is getting enough to eat, if he has the proper clothing?'

"One new feature is what is happening with women. Many have just gone off into a new lifestyle. They are losing connection with the kids—and the kids feel it. I have always felt that, when the pill came out, we then saw how much people really love kids.

"We seem to be reaching a situation in which everything is futility. Parents just can't cope. The fathers aren't there, were never there. Now you have the women who aren't there, or who are there but who wish they weren't there.

"Parents don't seem to be able to come to grips with the great strains under which their kids are trying to grow up. One of the toughest things for parents in a town like this one—and it's surprising because these are sophisticated people—is to realize the extent to which the issue with the kids is *sexuality*. Kids have grown up to feel that they have a great deal of sexual freedom at a very early age. They don't know how to cope with it. Boys in particular. They have been conditioned to feel that they have to have sex at, say, age fifteen, and that they have to be terrific at it. There's the machismo element, the pressure to perform. Suddenly you have healthy kids coming in to counselors asking, What's wrong with me? Am I impotent? Am I a homosexual? Why can't I have an erection, why can't I have intercourse?

"And then the girls are on the pill from very early on. They have the license to perform, and that turns into the pressure to perform. This reaches down into the sixth and seventh grades.

"How much should we ethically share with parents about VD, about abortion, about all the rest of it? Counselors who are fully able to handle a wide range of problems are constantly finding themselves out of their depth. Parents want the schools to take care of it—but at the same time they don't want to hear about it.

"Just as the parents in this town crack under stress, the kids do too, and in much the same ways. Drugs are still big. I mean hard drugs. Pot has become institutionalized. What is newer and increasing is the drinking. Hardly a month goes by when we don't rush a kid to the hospital to have his stomach pumped out.

"The parents have troubles of their own. When they hear about these things the reaction is apt to be unreasonable anger and very little help. So we are compelled to try to deal with a lot of the problems ourselves.

"These kids have been neglected and overprotected at the same time. It's in the nature of the community. The kids go off to college and immediately run into trouble. There's an enormous drop-out rate in freshman and sophomore years. We see this isolation from the real world in so many ways. One of the standardized intelligence tests has a question about going to the store to buy a loaf of bread. The kids can't cope with it. They haven't the foggiest notion of what is involved.

"Family life in a town like this insulates kids and yet at the same time presents them with a tremendous range of choices which they don't have the maturity to live with. And it's going to get worse. The divorce rate will keep on skyrocketing. I guess, from my point of view, I don't see the suburbs as a particularly successful mode of living."

Now, a suburban clergyman who spends much of his time counseling those who come apart in the beautiful countryside:

"The strains have always been intense. I'm not sure they're increasing so much as that people are losing their ability to cope.

"Suburban families invite trouble. We have a community in which there is not a constellation of support built into it—old friends who help to keep you in line because you care about what they feel about you and who know more about you than you might like them to know. This lack grows out of the mobility, the transiency of people in social groupings; we don't look to others for support in the ways that people in other communities have done.

"When people here get into trouble, they are likely to turn in on themselves rather than share their trouble with others. I find people who are going through divorce and who haven't told anybody about it yet. The decrees will become final next week, and nobody knows about it yet. What a load of pain to carry by yourself. Divorce doesn't happen because one of the partners suddenly shacks up with somebody else; it happens because there's been trouble for a number of years.

"And people don't stay together for the sake of the kids anymore. We came through a period when we tried to do everything for our kids. Now we are in a period in which the basic thing is, When you want to do it, *do* it. You've earned it; take it. So parents are neglecting their children to find their own satisfactions. Part of this is our response to psychiatric insights; we have a right to pleasure; if you feel angry, express it, if it feels good, do it. Kids feel and act this way, but this is not a kid's attitude. It is one they have picked up from their parents. We now feel that our puritan ideals have repressed us all our lives, and all of a sudden we say, 'Hey, it isn't so bad to feel good.' And it's not—until, as often happens, it explodes out of all proportion.

"As this happens, families—which were not in good shape to begin with—collapse. The man who has spent fifteen years building the corporate spot looks around and discovers that his family has learned to get along without him.

"It's been building for a long time. Husbands and wives in this community will go ten, fifteen years with no sex life at all. That's all right for a while; everyone is doing his thing, maintaining the image. Then they say, What am I getting out of all this? My wife or husband doesn't communicate with me, my kids don't need me, we don't do anything socially, so I guess I can let it all go.

"Men in a town like this don't usually ask for help. Women come for help, men seldom do. Sometimes, if things work out, the man will come in later. Basically the man has already defined his role for himself and he maintains it. Women used to see themselves in one role; now they are adopting other roles. They say, I'm worth something. I'm not going to go down to the church or the community council and volunteer; I want to be paid. And often there is no market for their services; this becomes a point of anger or a put-down, one or the other. There's no place to take it out except at home, and what you are doing at home is not that good.

"We have not developed the Good Life. The job and the home and the community have not all worked together; they haven't learned how to work together, and they've got to. Add to this a real gut-level economic unrest, and you have a lot of people who are scared. They don't think things are going to get better. They want to take their profits and satisfactions now in whatever way they can get them.

"This is not to say the Good Life can't work here. I see it working in some families, and it's beautiful. It happens because people work at it. They have set priorities; they have defined their lives, instead of having them defined for them. They say, Yes, the job will take a lot of time, but we can make things work if we plan and think it out together. But so many people haven't given any thought to it.

"The worst by-product of the strain is drinking. If there's one thing I would like to wipe out, it's the drinking.

"There are so many lonely people here, and we think drinking will ease our loneliness. Many married people are lonely. And more and more there are unmarried people who are lonely.

"If I could order things, which I cannot, I would set up an orientation course, an introduction to suburban life. Here people would learn about the strains, and the isolation, and the need to communicate with one another. They would think about priorities, and the work that it takes to live successfully and happily in this atmosphere.

"People would attend such discussions as a matter of course; they would not wait until things fall apart. It would serve as an early-warning system, to detect the point at which the strains between corporation and community are beginning to become too great.

"The Good Life is possible in the suburbs. There are many advantages. When things go well, they go very, very well. But the risks are high. When we don't recognize the risks, we let the life go to pieces. And then things can become very, very bad. We have a lot of people here for whom it has turned very, very bad."

14

Trouble in Paradise: Policing Exurbia

The policeman in an exurban town is not an exurbanite; he doesn't make enough money to live in the community he polices. But he gets to know the exurbanite in a very special way. He is a frequent visitor to the big houses on the spacious plots of land, but he does not come as a guest.

In surveys concerned with needs for social services in two typical exurban towns, the problems mentioned most frequently by police officers were alcoholism, marriage problems, and parent–child problems, particularly as a result of lack of parental attention. More often than not, these problems overlap, interact, and feed on each other.

Most exurban police forces have received special training in crisis intervention, with particular emphasis on the settling of household fights. They have plenty of opportunities to use this training. The peak times are the weekends, especially Friday and Saturday nights.

In one town, characteristic of many, it will happen this way. A call comes in; there is a disturbance in a house on a street where every house stands on at least two acres and is valued at a minimum of $100,000. The call does not come from a neighbor. There are no neighbors in Exurbia. Someone in the house has uttered a disjointed cry for help into the phone.

Two patrol cars are dispatched. Each car contains one officer, and the local police know that it will take at least two policemen to handle the problem.

The policemen arrive. They find the Johnsons having an evening at home. Alice Johnson, thirty-six, is locked in her bedroom, screaming through the door. Roger Johnson, forty, is outside the door. His fists are bleeding. He has smashed through half of the upper panel of the door. Bill Johnson, fourteen, crouches in front of his father. Bill's shirt is torn, there is a bruise on the side of his face. He holds a knife.

One policeman, Officer Nagy, takes the knife away from Bill. The other, Officer Phillips, moves between Roger Johnson and the bedroom door. He half-guides, half-pushes Johnson into an adjoining bedroom. Nagy identifies himself and asks Mrs. Johnson to open the locked door.

Alice Johnson is bleeding slightly from a cut over the eye. None of the three is seriously injured. Nagy wets a towel and wipes away the blood.

In the other bedroom, Roger Johnson, who was momentarily cowed by the uniforms, has regained full volume. He shouts at Officer Phillips: "Who the hell are you to come busting in here? This is my home! Get the hell out of here! By God, I'll file a complaint about this...." And much more. Johnson lurches toward Phillips and starts a roundhouse swing. The policeman evades the punch. The momentum carries Johnson, staggering, to the bed. He sits down hard. Johnson cocks a bleary eye at Phillips and yells: "You can't do this to me! This is police brutality!" Phillips speaks in a low, soothing voice. Gradually, Johnson subsides. He begins to talk. "Not my fault.... You don't know.... That bitch in there.... They don't understand what I go through.... Up to my ass in bills.... Everybody on my back all the time.... Got to get away from it some way...."

Mrs. Johnson is telling her story to Officer Nagy. Roger Johnson came home on the commuter train Friday night. He had had a few drinks in the club car. The Johnsons went to a dinner party. Johnson had a number of drinks before dinner, and some after dinner. When they got home, he had more to drink. There was an argument. It started over Johnson's drinking, then broadened to cover neglect of his family, his late hours, and his interest in other women. Johnson accused his wife of spending money like water and not giving a damn whether or not he worked himself into a grave. Bill Johnson, awakened, tried to intervene and was told that he was a rotten snot-nosed kid. Johnson turned on his wife and accused her of playing around while he was sweating out his job; a job, moreover, that he did not know how long he could hang onto. Alice Johnson went to bed; Johnson stayed downstairs and had some more to drink.

Saturday morning, Roger Johnson was quiet. Nothing was said about the night before. Johnson went out, as usual, to play golf. He returned at five o'clock. He had been drinking.

The Johnsons had been invited to another party, and they went. Johnson got drunk. He was assisted into the car, and Alice Johnson—none too sober herself—drove home. In the Johnson house the battle of the night before started again. This time Johnson hit his wife. Bill Johnson threatened to kill his father if he touched his mother again. Johnson brushed his son aside and went after his wife. She locked herself in the bedroom and called the police.

The officers continue to keep the parties separated. Their objective is to cool the situation and avoid making an arrest. Sometimes the officers may suggest to the domestic disputants that they get some counseling help; many suburban policemen are trained not to try to provide counseling themselves but to know about the services available in the town and suggest some alternatives.

This particular problem is more serious. Officers Nagy and Phillips have phoned headquarters and described the situation. Something like this has happened at the Johnsons' house once before. The policemen on the scene sense that the problem will flare up again—with, perhaps, extremely serious results—unless they either arrest Roger Johnson or bring an experienced counselor onto the scene immediately. Nagy and Phillips do not make the decision. This is done at headquarters, where the duty officer considers the possibilities. Several of the psychiatrists in town are available for emergency duty, but they have been worked overtime. The pastor of the Johnsons' church is also available; and lately he has spent a great deal of time coping with the mundane problems of his flock. The duty officer calls the pastor; the pastor wearily rolls out of bed, dresses, and drives to the scene. Officers Nagy and Phillips return to patrol.

But the Johnson imbroglio has taken an hour. Neither officer has been on patrol during that time. And this brings us to another problem.

The case load of exurban police departments has risen sharply in the past couple of years, in some cases close to 50 percent. A lot of work is the kind of crisis intervention that Nagy and Phillips have just finished. It usually does not result in an arrest; indeed, one measure of the policeman's success in such a situation is the avoidance of the necessity for an arrest. This takes intelligent, well-trained policemen.

Exurban policemen, like their urban counterparts, feel that they are overworked and underpaid. The frustration of the exurban police is exacerbated by the fact that they deal with adults and children who are, by comparison, enormously wealthy. Nagy and Phillips make about $15,000 in a town where the median family income is $28,000. One lives in the neighboring city; the other lives in one of the many "illegal" apartments that proliferate in Exurbia as legal apartments continued to be zoned out. When Officers Nagy and Phillips see the more affluent members of the community on police business, they do not see them at their best.

The union movement among suburban policemen, as among other municipal employees, is growing stronger. These policemen spend their days and nights surrounded by the appurtenances of money—multiple new cars and big houses and swimming pools and enormous liquor bills. They see the squalid realities that frequently lie behind the facade, but this does not keep the policemen—understandably—from wanting a bigger share of the pie.

On the whole, suburban police forces have shown a considerable sense of responsibility in going after more money. They are tough bargainers, but they look on the strike as a last resort. There are other available job actions, some of them quite imaginative. Early in 1975, the police force of Westport was embroiled in a contract dispute with the town. The officers and their families picketed town hall. Then they hit upon an interesting job action. They agreed—in defiance of the appearance regulations—to grow beards. The results were bizarre, but in many cases surprisingly imaginative. The beards of a lot of the younger men, in particular, were most becoming. Westport—a community that prides itself on its artistic heritage—found itself with a force of Velázquez noblemen in uniform.

Suburban policemen feel not only underpaid but overextended. The mounting need for intervention in drunken brawls in the homes of the wealthy takes cops off patrol. And when policemen are pulled off patrol, things happen. Police chiefs in Exurbias across the country agree that burglary and vandalism are on the rise. Some of the burglary is carried on by "professionals" who come in from the surrounding cities. But much of it is attributed to homegrown products: youngsters who grew up in the town and now live on their own. They don't work regularly, they may well be on drugs, and they need money. So they rob to get it.

The conditioning starts early. Kids shoplift for kicks. The excitement of this begins to pall, so they turn to vandalism. Mailboxes are a particularly tempting target. In a town where most houses are set back from the street, and remote from adjoining residences, the mailbox is easy prey. In one town the raiders destroyed more than a hundred mailboxes within a couple of hours.

From mailboxes the next step is breaking and entering. Youths will look for an empty house; day or night, it does not matter. There are no neighbors to see what's going on. Whether the house is occupied can often be determined by a phone call. Then, into the house. They rip through, breaking everything that can be broken. And since there is fine merchandise for the stealing, they steal it. The kids at this stage don't know what to do with the loot. They can't take it home; they don't know any fences. So they leave it in the woods. In Exurbia the woods may be full of ruined television sets, silverware, paintings and appliances.

The youngster grows older. He leaves home, perhaps to wander around the country, but then he goes back to the hometown to become part of a sizable floating population of young people who "hang around." He lives in a room somewhere; that kind of housing is illegal, of course, but it is not controlled. And now he is into stealing on a profit-oriented basis. He becomes more organized; he is introduced to the conveniences of the friendly fence. Fences abound in Exurbia and the nearby cities. Most of the things that are stolen in a town are fenced elsewhere, but not always. Not long ago an exurban woman—whose house had been hit twice within three months—went shopping to replace some of her treasures. Visiting a store in the center of town, she was somewhat startled to find, on grand display, most of the things that had been taken from her house. The retailer was arrested for possession of stolen goods. This was on a Tuesday; the next day he was out on bail. On Friday yet another robbery victim was staggered to see her household valuables on sale in the very same store. The police arrested the dealer again. By now they hope they have a pretty good case against him. But this is the exception. Most of the loot ripped off by the sons and daughters of Exurbia is disposed of with far more organization and skill.

Many of these young burglars steal to get money for drugs. Drugs are still around in Exurbia. The novelty is gone, but there are plenty of kids who got into hard drugs and have not gotten out. There is still dealing, but today it seems to exist on a personal basis, not wholesale or even retail. Westport kids get on the train to New York, get off in Harlem, and barter stolen loot on the street for drugs.

As for marijuana, exurban police rarely go out to arrest people for possession. Pot comes into the picture more often as a collateral issue. When a youngster is picked up, let's say, on a traffic charge, and marijuana is found, the charge is expanded to include possession.

Some parents felt relieved when the word spread that alcohol was replacing drugs as a thrill. This was more normal; this was the American way. A martini-belting suburban father was not inclined to get too upset over his boy's having a few beers. After all, beer is better than heroin or LSD; and the old man could even look upon the practice benignly and perhaps nostalgically, harking back to the drinking bouts of his fraternity days. Drinking still seems, to many exurbanites, more like a rite of passage than a serious problem.

But don't try to sell this point of view to the suburban police officer who has just finished rounding up three strong sixteen-year-olds for being drunk and disorderly in public. Alcohol is bad news to the suburban cop, no matter what the age of the consumer. And it's not getting better. The police can put the pressure on the owners of local bars; but the tavernkeepers and bartenders plead the obvious difficulty of constantly demanding proof of age. As the permissible drinking age has been reduced to eighteen in many towns, the actual drinking age goes down into the junior high school echelons—and often below that.

It often seems that Exurbia is awash in alcohol. In many towns it is routine for police to observe the commuters debouching from incoming trains. There is usually a handful of lost drunken souls wandering through the parking lot, looking for their cars. The policeman's job is to intercept these people before they get behind the wheel, call home for transportation, send them home in a cab, or if necessary, provide free taxi service in the police car.

Nor are these the only problems that erode the time and patience of the police force. To take just one other example, merchants in even the most affluent suburbs are being deluged with rubber checks. Some are passed by professionals. More and more, however, the delinquent is a local citizen, perhaps a pillar of the community. Under the stress of the sluggish economy, the charge account is becoming a ticking bomb for the exurban storekeeper. He simply cannot permit customers to run up tabs of $500 or $600 as they did in the old days. The rate of default is too high. So the merchant asks for immediate payment. Mrs. Exurbanite writes a check, innocent of the knowledge that there is not enough in the account to cover it. Or, she knows full well that there is not enough money in the bank, but she writes the check, anyway, hoping that somehow something will turn up.

Merchants will ordinarily allow considerable leeway to customers, especially older customers. They feel that, after all, there is little choice. The money is not there, but maybe it will be. However, when an individual's checks bounce consistently, the merchant will go to law. And at this point the police are involved to the extent of considerable routine: paperwork, waiting time, and court appearances.

It's occurring all over Exurbia. The police are finding that the residents of the community, whom they formerly had to protect from crime, are increasingly becoming their customers. They may not be criminals—but they generate a lot of police business.

The suburban police professional has long since become an excellent practicing pyschologist. He attributes much of his increased case load to the terrific stresses—emotional, social, and economic—under which the exurbanite lives.

But, whatever the reasons, the policeman in Exurbia finds that his job is getting a lot harder; and there is little to indicate that the tendency will reverse itself.

15

Abdication of the Matriarch

Exurbia was a woman's world; so much so that it is easy to overlook the degree to which women—accepting and playing a particular role—made the idea work.

The male exurbanite was, for practical purposes, only minimally a part of it. It existed *for* him, but he did not live in it. He only slept in it. He lived in the job he commuted to.

It was Mrs. Exurbia who was making it tick. The accepted vision showed her floating serenely down the idyllic day, driving the kids, doing the shopping, checking on the maid, attending the meetings of volunteer activities that she ran and that helped to keep suburbia going.

Perhaps Mrs. Exurbanite was never truly happy in the role; but she played it, and played it well. Her functioning was central to the maintenance of the concept of the Good Life in the suburbs.

Now what? Here are some shards of the old image of the suburban matron, culled at random from a year of reading and observation.

A letter to the editor: "Until it has been scientifically proven that women are NOT the equals of men, we women will have to keep pushing and striving. The odds have been so great against our being accepted as real human beings with options to do anything we choose to do—and believe it or not that includes getting married and bringing up children—that we can't afford to flag."

"Assertive training is the step beyond Consciousness Raising; it helps to do something about what is wrong," said Dr. Barbara Powell, a behavior therapist. "Women are brought up to be submissive and passive; to depend first on their family and then on their husbands. The majority of women who take Assertive Training find they are not functioning as well as they would like to; people take advantage of them; they can't refuse unreasonable requests; they can't say 'No.' "

Part of a statement issued by the action committee chairperson of Westport-Weston NOW in response to a proposal for expansion of the Westport YMCA: "The structure of the present YMCA places male facilities downstairs with men and boys separated and female facilities on the third floor, with women and girls together. We question the use of United Fund Monies if there is any evidence of discrimination whatsoever."

A letter: "What's it all about? With us libbers, it's issues that count—issues designed to give women full equality before the law. We work to try to attain passage of the Equal Rights Amendment, to equalize credit and housing opportunities for women, to establish day care centers so that women who need or want to work can have adequate child care, to see that affirmative action contracts are enforced, to fight for equal pay for equal work, to secure a comparable balance with boys in athletic programs for girls, to improve conditions for women in prisons, to change the negative image of women which the media too often creates, etc., etc., etc."

A letter from a male exurbanite: "For too long has the silent army of devoted wives and mothers, who do a grand job of maintaining a home properly, been overlooked by the news media in favor of the noisy minority which holds that 'fulfillment' for women can only be obtained outside the home. I am fortunate to be married for over 40 years to one of that silent army. For two and a half World War II years I was absent, and afterwards my business kept me abroad six months each year for twelve years. Yet during these absences she kept the father's memory and influence bright. In our three children's schooling days she handled three school-related volunteer jobs, yet let nothing prevent her from being at home when the children returned from school."

Four young women ran into considerable flak when they insisted on joining Westport's volunteer firefighters. The president of the local Uniformed Firefighters observed: "If women hang around the building, the wives [of regulars] aren't going to like it."

The New York Times (September 1, 1974): "The wasting away of Avon Products, Inc., on the stock market ticker is one of the grimmer tales of woebegone Wall Street."

Doris Sullivan writes in the *Bridgeport Post*: "Members of the League of Women Voters are apparently taking over the town government [of Westport] and some local old-time politicians are convinced that things will never be the same again."

From the record book of the Class of 1950, Wellesley College (reported by Carol Ray Berninger in *The New York Times*): "Connecticut housewife: 'I'm still trying to find out what I'd like to be when I grow up.' "

Linda Wolfe *(Playing Around: Women and Extramarital Sex)* declares that there is an epidemic of adultery among American housewives.

The first woman sheriff in the history of Fairfield County, Connecticut, promises to change the image of her office by becoming a lobbyist for the interests of the citizens of the county.

A Westport woman, concerned about sexism in school materials, says: "By raising children as equals we do not mean to create unisex people. Rather we want them to explore and develop their own individuality without the limitations and expectations of sex-role stereotyping. Children should have the freedom to choose a life where they may become capable, happy, warm human beings that are persons first—and males and females second."

Dr. Ida Davidoff, Connecticut psychologist and family counselor, observes that 75 to 90 percent of Connecticut women who go to internists have psychosomatic disorders.

An unhappy Californian laments: "But if boys are boys and girls are boys, where is any place for beauty, charm, grace, gaiety, tenderness, inspiration, gentleness and refinement? Girls were such a nice idea. God, could you come up with something else to take their place?"

Advertising agency head Lois Geraci Ernst launches her new campaign for Prince Matchabelli's Aviance fragrances. A thirty-second television spot opens in a kitchen to show an attractive matron clad in jeans and apron. Over striptease music the woman sheds her apron and rubber gloves and tosses away a soap pad, singing throatily, "I've been sweet and I've been good, I've had a whole day of motherhood." The scene changes to the bedroom, where she sprays on the product while singing, "But I'm gonna have an Aviance night!" Mrs. Ernst ("As far as I know, *Ms.* stands for manuscript, and I'm a wife") anticipates that women's libbers will find the commercials objectionable, but declares, "Sex is here to stay."

The publishers of *Ms.* try to respond to growing criticism that the magazine has gone soft on women's issues.

Susan Brownmiller *(Against Our Will)* observes that, while rape can still be said to be a big-city crime, "the rape rate in suburbia is noticeably rising."

Dr. James L. Framo, professor of psychology at Temple University, Philadelphia, says: "What I'm hearing more and more of in marital therapy is that husbands are afraid of their wives and their wives are stunned to hear it." Dr. Framo goes on: "Based on what I see in therapy, it is hard for me to relate the subjugation of women to reality. The concept of power loses its meaning within the family." He finds that men feel increasingly awkward. "They are confounded by language problems. They are afraid to use the word 'girl' for 'woman.' Their speech and behavior has become stilted and unnatural. We have come to the point in our society where we don't know the word for 'manhole.'" He adds that he sees far more women who want to leave their husbands and families than vice versa.

The Tracers Company of America reports that runaway wives are now twice as numerous as runaway husbands. A private detective says: "I get more inquiries from guys looking for their wives. I think a lot of women are bored and feel tied down. They're hitching up to that wagon of Women's Lib. They think there's more to life than hassling with kids and housework." A lawyer comments: "Because it's becoming acceptable for a woman to live without her children, because there's less social stigma attached to it, a lot of these women are voluntarily giving up their children. When I started practicing law sixteen years ago, it never happened."

A Harris poll reports that more women are working than ever before. Among more affluent families, says the report, a woman is not thought to be fulfilling herself unless she is productively employed on a job.

Writing in *Connecticut* Magazine, Gladys Walker quotes the forty-seven-year-old wife of an executive who had made her eighth move in sixteen years: "I knew it would mean the good old Welcome Wagon all over again and getting that damned bowling ball out. It's the only way you can get to meet people in New England. I'm getting too old for all this."

The woman decided to get a job; but found that she was trained for nothing. Her husband teased her "about wanting executive wages in exchange for unskilled labor and he was right. That's when I gave up and everything has been downhill since."

Some women won't play the role anymore. Others can't play it. Still others are trying to play it—but their hearts are not in the performance. And it's all having a profound effect on Exurbia.

About half of the women over sixteen in Westport are in the labor market; the figure was 41 percent in 1970, and all indications are that it has grown by at least 10 percent since then.

Some of it comes as a direct result of inflation and economic difficulty. It simply takes more money than it used to to live in the affluent suburbs, and many of the men who have been the traditional high-rolling providers of the Good Life are not making that much more. A considerable number are making less, or indeed nothing at all. So the exurban housewife goes to work as a matter of financial necessity.

But there is a lot more than economics behind the current attitudes and aspirations of women in Exurbia. Once the suburban mother who went to work for pay felt guilty about it. She felt, whether it was true or not, that her friends looked down on her.

The major role was motherhood. Well-educated—and often professionally trained—women who married successful men and moved to the suburbs were motivated by the assurance that they could be very superior parents. One woman says: "It was my role, and I loved it. I loved getting the house in shape and going to the beach with the kids. We were proving that we could make a profession out of raising children and doing housework. We were convinced that you could handle drudgery and rise above it all and not wind up like your own mother. We were fully extended in that job, but we were appreciated. For one thing, we all had great regard for the opinions of psychiatrists, and then the psychiatrists were coming down four-square behind the idea of the importance of a full-time mother. You could not help feeling that you were doing something important."

That's all gone now. First, as the kids grew older, women shifted into the area of volunteer work. For some, the activity was a means of using skills and education to do things that needed to be done in the community. For others—particularly those whose marriages began to show cracks that would lead to the ultimate fissure—it was a necessary anodyne. A multitude of suburban communities got a lot of free mileage out of the energies thus made available.

One woman—on her own with children for twenty years, although not actually divorced until the mid-1960s—tells how it went with her.

"When it started, I could not believe it was happening. My competition was buxom, empty-headed little broads who really galled the hell out of me because they were so stupid. I kept saying, 'What's so great about them? What's wrong with me?' I had always been a bright, pretty little girl, and I was doing all the things you're supposed to do to be a perfect wife. So I hung in there until I couldn't anymore.

"After the breakup I had no particular desire to remarry. The Parents Without Partners idea bored me. I was not willing to shack up for company—I had beaux, but I was discreet about it. Just one at a time, and no suggestion that it was going anyplace.

"I didn't know anybody. This was a town, then, where your friends were husbands and wives, people you met because the kids were going to school together. My kids were in boarding school because I was unhappy with what was happening to them in the public school system. I needed money, but I wasn't qualified for anything. I spoke four languages, but I couldn't type.

"So I went into community work to keep myself sane. I know people around here think I'm forceful and tough. I'm not. I die every time I have to get up and talk to a group. But doing volunteer work was the only thing for me to do, and I thought that I might as well be good at it."

Capable women who used to work hard for suburban communities, without pay, are just not doing it anymore. The satisfaction is going out of it.

The experience of the woman whose words appear next contains many elements typical of those which have helped to make volunteer public service a not-so-rewarding way of spending one's time and energy. The speaker has worked in various public posts in an exurban town, spending the last few years on the zoning commission, of which she became chairman.

"Things did not always go smoothly, but there was always an atmosphere of courtesy in the old days. This started to change in various ways. For one thing, there's the lawyers. It became so that every decision we made resulted in a lawsuit. Lawyers were just using our hearings to warm up for the court cases they make their money from. I have become a good friend of the man who serves subpoenas. I've gotten at least a dozen in the past few years. The pressures on citizens who serve on sensitive town bodies are growing enormously, and the town does not provide us with adequate legal counsel. We're out there all by ourselves.

"And the people who appear before us—those who are directly involved and those who have, or think they have, some interest in a matter—are getting worse. In one recent case some people moved into half a dozen houses in a new subdivision. The contractor promised them a paved road. Then, for various reasons, he was not making good on his promise. The people blamed the town, and in particular they were taking their frustrations out on us. They were obnoxious beyond belief. At one meeting the builder and one of the residents started hitting each other with their fists. I had to evict people from the hall. Meanwhile, these newcomers to town were keeping up a campaign of abusive phone calls and vituperation through the press that became almost unbearable.

"People who volunteer to do important work for a community should be able to take criticism. I don't question that for a moment. But the kind of abuse that one has to take from so many disgruntled people today—and the kinds of vicious attacks that we get from local newspapers which happen to disagree with the elected administration—well, these things seem to go beyond what one should have to take. The press then stirs people up further. They would call me at all hours, insisting that I do something immediately about whatever problem they happened to be concerned about. You do a job without pay because you feel someone has to do it and then you are treated contemptibly.

"I'm not a woman's libber. I can see that the woman's movement is making people think that they should not volunteer. But this idea will spread because of the way the community uses its volunteers. No one ever offers a compliment, but they are so quick to make a nasty phone call or write a nasty letter. Who will volunteer under these circumstances? It will soon be a crisis. They will have to pay people to do what we have been doing, and where will the money come from?"

There is a kind of woman volunteer, much more prevalent today than in the past, who still derives kicks from volunteer service, but whose services are not always of enormous benefit to the community. Even the most seemingly affluent suburbs need a wide range of social services, and these needs are not always recognized. Westport, for example, is a place that boasts a very high median income and is replete with large houses and symbols of money/status. Nevertheless, a recent study turned up 890 people in the town who were subsisting at below the official poverty level. To be poor anyplace is bad enough; to be poor in a place like Westport is true misery. And it is all the worse because the really poor person is, for all intents and purposes, invisible.

This situation is made-to-order for the Jargon Lady. This is a volunteer who derives tremendous satisfaction from power, not because that power can be used to help the community, but because it boosts the ego. Such people—and given the nature of suburban voluntary service, they are usually women—are as bureaucratic as the most case-hardened Washington functionary and as fluent in gibberish as the most accomplished foundation grantsman. To the Jargon Lady, all programs are "on-going"; all proposals are to be "finalized" (although little actually does receive finalization); all good works are aimed at enhancement of the "quality of life"; talking with people is "group process"; "facilities" are always "utilized"; and so forth.

An aggressive Jargon Lady can amass a great deal of power in a community that is hungry for what seems to be capable volunteer assistance—this is increasingly so as the supply diminishes. The result of her ministrations is little concrete accomplishment, and further erosion of the willingness of other women to take on responsibilities.

There are many variations in the situation of the exurban woman. One point emerges clearly. She is no longer gung ho for the motherhood role; nor is she nearly so likely as before to do volunteer work. Once she might feel guilty about taking a job; now she feels guilty and apologetic if she is not working at a demanding, paying job.

The effects of this development can be felt in many ways—in the family, among the kids, in business. One paramount effect is that a source of skilled and energetic—and, perhaps most important, *free*— help is drying up. Exurban communities, already in trouble on expenses, will have to find paid workers to do what used to be suburban woman's work.

16

Lib in the Suburbs

The scaffolding that used to support much of the exurban approach to life is collapsing. Piece by piece, it is slipping down an incline. At the end of that incline is the women's movement.

Not all, or even anything close to a majority, of suburban women are activists for feminine rights. Some enroll in its ranks. Some accept a few of its objectives and reject others. Some are infuriated, but grudgingly admit the existence of the conditions that have brought women's lib into being.

Few are totally unaffected by it. Those—and there are many—who gravitate only a short distance down the slope are nevertheless changing their viewpoints as a result of the existence of the movement. They may be shocked by the outspokenness of their militant sisters, but they can feel themselves drawn to the degree that they at least begin to question the lives they have been leading.

A suburban clergyman who spends a lot of time counseling families in trouble observes: "Women's liberation is very necessary. At the same time it has thrust a good many people into ways of thinking that they are not always able to handle. Women achieve personhood without having the backgrounds or the tools to deal with the problems that go along with it."

More and more exurban women seem willing to take a chance on the problems of personhood. They may move along slowly, far behind those in front, but they are moving.

The following are excerpts from an interview with a feminine activist in Exurbia. Once this woman fitted into the mold of a suburban housewife—a successful husband, a growing family, a bright and active mind devoted to filling the time left over from family things with good works performed on a volunteer basis.

It's different now. The expression is vigorous and sometimes

144

rough, but we must remember that the day when *How to Win Friends and Influence People* was a bestseller was a long time ago. Now it's *Winning Through Intimidation*. Most suburban women do not go all the way with either the viewpoints or the actions that this woman espouses—but they often grudgingly admire the energy and daring, and they are edging in this direction.

Q. Why would women who live in nice homes in affluent suburbs become activists?

A. All women, regardless of how good their positions seem, are oppressed. To begin with, look at the train station in the morning. Obviously, most of the people who get on the train are men. Women are not expected to have good jobs or to accomplish important things. Recently I heard a woman described as being "very well paid." She is making $25,000 a year, which to a man is nothing. We think of women as we think of blacks. Our expectations of blacks are that they will live in the ghetto and be responsible for a lot of crime and be on welfare. Our expectations of women are that they are going to live in a nice house, have someone come and clean it, raise children, go to PTA meetings, and get all of their kicks out of their husbands and their kids. And, incidentally, all of the PTA mail comes addressed to the man, when it's always the woman who goes to the meetings and does all the work.

Q. What is NOW doing about all this?

A. Every man and woman in the country has been affected by the women's movement. We operate on three levels. We sponsor consciousness-raising groups as a basic beginning. We're trying to get women to change their heads about themselves. We have to do this to counterbalance all the antiwoman propaganda that we have all grown up with, I mean the presumption of woman's sexuality, their enticing nature, and so forth.

Then we take public action, for instance writing to the newspaper about the school labels being addressed to men, that sort of thing. Some of these things seem like nit-picking, but we have to act on them.

We also put on public programs—say, a panel of gynecologists—to ask them how they feel about women and to show them how—inadvertently, perhaps—they may have been going along with sexist practices.

Q. What are you saying to women when you raise their consciousness?

A. Well, we're *not* saying to every woman, "Don't volunteer, don't be a mother, don't get married." We're not saying those things, but that's what the world is hearing. The women's movement is a matter of facilitating choice. What we are saying is that there are other choices than the ones you have been given—many, many other choices. We are showing that you *can* be unmarried, that you *can* be paid for what you do, that housework is shit and should be shared by men and women. We're not putting down the woman who thinks otherwise; we're just saying that you ought to know, for your own sake or at least your daughter's sake, that there is another way to live.

Q. Are you reaching women?

A. Yes. We're very poorly organized, and we don't have time to write a lot of letters and do a lot of things. But we have seven consciousness-raising groups going, and they close out at fifteen. They meet every week. And we have other groups, some involving men. So we are reaching a lot of people in this community. But we have a long way to go because what we want is to shake the entire establishment.

Q. Doesn't the movement do harm to some women by making them unhappy with their lives?

A. I'll take myself as an example. I seemed to have everything; I had every reason to be happy. And yet I knew that I was very deeply unhappy. Since there was no reason, it seemed, for me to be dissatisfied, I blamed myself for my unhappiness. I did all kinds of things, but I was still miserably depressed, without any reason at all that I could understand.

I began reading women's movement stuff—Germaine Greer was the one who started me off. And then I was filled with anger and completely unable to talk about it. You know how we are at parties around here, we will talk about all kinds of controversial stuff, but I was completely unable to talk about this because it was me.

It's not that the woman feels satisfied and then finds out there is a women's movement and says, Oh my God, I ought to be unhappy. What happens is that the woman says, Oh yes, my life is wonderful, but I don't feel right about myself. So she goes to a consciousness-raising session and finds that everybody else feels like that, too—and that's one of those great feelings.

Q. What do women do when they discover themselves in this way?

A. Many things. For example, one woman has just decided that she does not want to be married anymore; she is living with a guy in a monogamous way, but she never intends to get married or have children. She has gotten very involved in working in the area of animal liberation. Many women are restructuring their marriages; they want an open marriage, they want to have sex with guys. The sexual revolution and woman's revolution have been confused, they are two different things, but one option obviously is that women should be able to get their sex where they want it. Other women are getting out of the family-unit type of living, although they stay in this area. Two of my really good friends live with a third woman and a guy. And they're just friends. The town is usually not aware of the extent to which this is happening. These are not people you're going to find at your PTA meetings.

Q. Does liberation mean the end of marriage?

A. Not always. Marriages can be redesigned. One of my friends has brought her husband along with her into the movement. He is taking part in a men's rap. Other women simply say, It's not practical for us to get divorced, but from now on you live the way you want to live and I'll live the way I want to live, and I'm not going to tell you an awful lot about it. And, incidentally, I'm not talking about sex at all.

Q. Some people think you and others are extremists. Are you?

A. Some people think that when we have a lesbian rap, that's too far out. Others don't approve of our taking on Little League.

Q. Some are shocked when they hear you have nude sessions.

A. We had a nude rap. One of the ways of starting a consciousness-raising group is to have women talk about their feelings about their bodies. It's just fascinating. You can sit there with airline stewardesses and models and hear them say, My body has always been awful. My breasts are too little, my breasts are too big, my legs are too long or short. It's so crazy. I have never heard a woman say, I like my body. It's a matter of conditioning. Pictures of nude or semidressed women are all over the place, as the thing that's supposed to turn the world on. So a woman looks at this, and, no matter how gorgeous she is, she says, I don't fit.

And so one of the things we did—and it took us six months to do it, I mean it was really heavy to do—was to sit there and tell each other what we thought of each others' bodies. For most people it was a big shot in the arm, although a few were freaked out about the lack of privacy of it. It was a hard thing to do; somebody says, My thighs are too big, and everybody says, Gee, we think your thighs are beautiful.

And then there is self-help. Self-help is a cornerstone of the women's movement. Everyone in the movement accepts self-help.

Q. What is it?

A. Well, self-help is looking at your own cervix with a speculum and a mirror and a flashlight. Now, who in the world would want to see a cervix? I mean it sounds really freaky—until you consider that a lot of women's lives turn on the fact of motherhood and therefore gynecology, and that essentially we are known for our sexual purpose. And here is this fellow who is in charge of it, and you have never seen it. With a guy, you know, his prick and his balls hang out; you can see them and touch them.

So we look at the cervix. For one thing, you can tell almost immediately if you're pregnant. You can see the onset of fungus diseases which women get all the time. And in a way you are taking control of your own life. So it may seem like a dumb, crazy, far-out thing to do, but now it has become a very common thing in the women's movement, and in almost every conference there is a self-help workshop to teach women how to do it.

Q. What about your marriage?

A. We're separated. We're still in contact with each other, he comes out more or less every other week. We don't see the people we used to see—we see people who are involved in the movement. Our social life is a lot more diverse in terms of age.

Q. Are people afraid of you?

A. Men are afraid. The threat is genital. As Susan Brownmiller writes, the relationship almost always exists on a sexual level, a genital level. Men have traditionally possessed women. Now women are possessive of their own sexuality and are not defining themselves the way men would like to see them. And this is a revolutionary idea.

Q. Is the idea of rape central to relationships as they have existed?

A. Sure. It's always buried in our consciousness. If I'm driving along and see a boy hitching, I have to size him up. It's something a guy doesn't have to do. And if it's a question of my son hitching or my daughter hitching, well, I've got to have second thoughts about my daughter. It's just this whole feeling. Most of the guys she encounters may be safe, but it's very likely that my son will never have a problem like this and my daughter will. You see, that's the problem with rape, no matter how careful a woman is, it can happen, anyhow.

Q. And the act of rape extends metaphorically into all relationships?

A. Sure. Just turn on the television any hour of the day or night, or look at the ads for the movies.

Q. Do men need liberation?

A. Well, in a way, I think, men have become victims of their own system. Obviously, not every guy is running the system. It's hard to tell if anyone is running it, it's so fucked up. But a guy goes off and makes his forty thousand or fifty thousand and keeps a whole bunch of happy slaves at home, presumably with the boat and the tennis rackets—but nobody is really happy. Being kept is like being on welfare. You can pretend to like it. You can put on the mink coat—and try not to think of the animal exploitation and the rape of the land and the thing in Vietnam and how all of these things come out of this macho thing that men have about the way we should be dressed and where their territory should extend to.

Q. What next?

A. What I really think we're trying to do is tear down the whole world. Perhaps most women will never go this far. But they are drawn by the raw pull of it, and Exurbia is affected as they move.

17

Blowing Wild

An exurban pediatrician makes an interesting discovery about two of his patients, a boy and a girl, each eleven years old. They disclose to him that they have been having sexual intercourse with each other for two years. Though fully aware of the sexual precocity of many of the children in town, the pediatrician finds this story too much to believe. But investigation convinces him that it is true. The two children declare that they are in love with each other. The parents, it turns out, are aware of this; or, at least, aware that "something is going on." The mother and father of the girl are very upset. The boy's mother (she is divorced) says that she sees nothing wrong with it. It is an "honest" relationship, free of "hypocrisy." The pediatrician confesses that he is out of his depth on this one.

Two suburban mothers converse at a party. Each is on her third cocktail. One asks, "Is Andrea still at——?" The other replies, "Oh, no. She decided to take a year off." It transpires that Andrea has remained in the university town. She is "working." Andrea's mother asks her companion, "How about Alan? The last I heard he was on the West Coast." Alan's mother answers, "Yes, Alan decided to travel around, you know, to see something of the country. He had a good time and learned a lot. But he's home now, thank God." The two women sip their drinks. A quiet eavesdropper knows a little more of the story. Alan, in his travels, has become a disciple of an aging "fifteen-year-old" Indian guru. Now home, Alan never leaves the house. He sits in his room, staring out the window through matted hair. Andrea is working in the town where she attended college, but her work is of a semivolunteer nature. She is an inmate of a campus brothel.

150

An exurbanite boards the commuter train in Westchester, gets off at Grand Central Station, and begins to walk the five blocks to his office, where he works as executive vice-president of a packaged-food company. At a street corner he begins to thread his way through a half-dozen young people. They wear robes, their heads are shaved, they hop up and down, chanting what seems to him to be gibberish. One of the chanters bobs over in front of the commuter. He steps to the side to pass. The robed person says, in a singsong voice, "Hi, Dad. How's business?" It is his daughter, whom he has not seen for eighteen months. He begins to say something, but his daughter has now joined her fellows, and he is not sure which one she is. The vice-president stops off near his office, and for the first time since he can remember, has a drink before lunch.

"I think sex is beautiful," says a seventeen-year-old girl in Morris County, New Jersey. "Couples should be allowed to express themselves as freely as they want, in any way they want, but not with any guy that walks down the street." Another girl, fifteen, observes, "Sex is so much in the environment. Every movie you see has sex in it. They teach you about it in school. You walk down the street and you see the Planned Parenthood building. Today, sex is no secret. When my parents were my age, sex wasn't as open, and having it was something very daring and special. But now it doesn't seem that special, and so kids feel it's a normal thing to do."

A senior English class in an exurban high school receives the following assignment: "Write a composition of at least three paragraphs and about a page and a half long on *one* of the following topics: The Generation Gap Between Me and My Parents; The Generation Gap Between Me and (All, Some, or One of) My Teachers (or Teacher); Honor Thy Father and Thy Mother, *if* They Deserve That Honor; Feeling Guilty About Hating Your (Mother, Father, Parents)."

The head of the guidance department in an exurban school system reports that 85 percent of the high school students say that they smoke or have smoked pot, and 60 percent have tried harder drugs. In junior high school more than half have smoked marijuana and about 25 percent have experienced harder drugs. The percentages are lower for elementary school, but still significant. Nevertheless, the counselor goes on, the growing problem is not drugs but alcohol. High school alcoholics are common. Drinking in junior high school is not unusual. Teachers are becoming accustomed to seeing students drunk in class.

A nine-year-old black boy from the inner city returns home from two weeks in the suburbs as a fresh-air vacationer. He tells his mother of his most vivid memory. He was astonished at the bad language used by the kids in the town he visited.

A girl acts in plays put on at one of the most celebrated of exurban high schools. She goes on to undistinguished bit parts in two TV shows. Then she rockets to prominence as one of the country's leading stars of pornographic films. Her acrobatic versatility makes her a leading light in the world of skin flicks. The new star reminisces in a slick, sex-oriented magazine: "Let me start out by saying I was a cock teaser in high school. I think every chick who runs for homecoming queen in every high school in America is a prick tease." She goes on to describe her first sex experience in graphic terms: "We were both so hot to fuck that nothing would have stopped us." The first time was an anguished comedy of errors. After that, it was easier. "A few weeks later I found myself doing it again. No football player this time, no cars ... just a nice, good-looking, normal, average student. It was great. A great fuck."

Educators meet to discuss a ten-year decline in college board scores.

A survey of five thousand high school students at fifty schools in New England and the mid-Atlantic states discloses that 90 percent would not go to their parents for help with a drug or drinking problem.

The Illinois Dangerous Drug Commission says that 22 percent of the state's youngsters between fourteen and eighteen use both drugs and alcohol. "They use alcohol as a substitute for drugs or in combination with drugs, but in both cases for the same purpose, which is to get high."

Dr. Herbert Hendin studies Columbia/Barnard students and

reports *(The Age of Sensation)* on what he sees as causing the rising incidence of suicide, drug use, and sexual impotence among the young. These young people have been engulfed by rage and pain. They try to obliterate these feelings with drugs. They approach life with a cynical disregard for anything but immediate sensation. They are responding to messages that have been transmitted to them by their parents.

A study of men who smoke marijuana shows that the drug can interfere with the production of male sex hormones to such a degree as to result in impotence or infertility.

In an exurban town including about fifteen hundred teenagers, there are five identifiable suicides within one year. Seven other deaths, mostly traffic fatalities, are considered to be suicidal.

The board of finance of an affluent suburb is presented with a request for $200,000 for an additional maintenance appropriation for the school system. Questioning discloses that the money is needed to repair extensive damage in the school buildings. The damage is attributed to vandalism by the students.

An exurban student writes: "We have 'one of the best school systems in the nation,' but it is like a greenhouse. Most of the parents working out in the 'real world' are at home with members of any number of races, but apparently feel this is too strong stuff for their children. In addition, they think that integration, or low or middle income housing, means ghetto, crime, drugs, disciplinary problems, etc.

"The result is that their children see white clearly and regard all other shadings as threatening. The children who are groomed to be leaders, in a school system that equals that of the finest private schools, are filled with inhibitions out in the 'real world.' "

As the number of teenaged bicyclists in a town increased, so did the number of bike-auto accidents. However, the increase was far greater than traffic specialists estimated that it should be. Policemen were hearing many stories from bike riders who claimed that adult automobile drivers were deliberately passing so close as to brush the bikers off the road. At first skeptical, the police finally concluded that this was indeed the case in a great many instances.

What does one call a situation in which two groups of people disagree on almost everything, are often at odds with each other, and from time to time physically attack each other? It is certainly not the conventional image of family life. There are other, more apt, words.

In Exurbia there is a constant state of conflict between adults and their children. We are at war with our kids. We maintain that we have given them every advantage, and we decry their ingratitude. We are embarrassed by their seemingly deliberate failure to accomplish, their slovenliness, and their licentiousness. We are appalled at their self-destructive indulgence in liquor and drugs. We are hurt by their rejection.

The kids usually seem to be indifferent to us, often hostile. They appear to be willing to go to any extreme to shock us, worry us, or make us feel ashamed. And they are effective. We think about kids a lot, and our thoughts are almost never pleasant or tranquil. In *Liberal Parents, Radical Children,* Midge Decter addresses the younger generation, chiding them for their insensitivity to what has been given them. "You, as the exemplars of this new selflessness, and we as your parents—not to mention that entire society that was about to be so redeemed—should have been deeply gratified."

Instead, look at those kids!

What has happened? That's what we are all asking in Exurbia. We attribute the problem to various causes. Some of us castigate the schools for failing to instill discipline, some of us blame each other, and some of us blame ourselves.

There are certain phenomena of suburban life that may have more of a bearing on the situation with our kids than we have so far recognized.

One factor is the broad scope that exurban life gives us for "distancing" our offspring.

When a family lives in fairly close quarters, there is continuous mutual contact. When a father works close to his home, he is apt to be involved in this frequent interplay to a considerable extent. When a mother observes the traditional woman's role of homemaker, she is in constant touch with the kids. There is little chance for lacunae to develop.

But the family that moves to Exurbia achieves, not "togetherness," but *apartness.* Americans give lip service to the idea of togetherness, but they act as if togetherness is what you have to live with when you can't afford anything better. Togetherness, forced or otherwise, forces parents and children into certain traditional roles: the loving parent, the dutiful child.

In Exurbia there is no need for this kind of "togetherness." In fact, everything in Exurbia conduces to apartness, including the apparent preferences of all family members. The father has farther to go to work; he leaves earlier, gets home later. Moreover, he gives so much of himself to the job—not necessarily the productive part of the job, but rather the political and ceremonial adjuncts of it—that even when he is in the same room with the other members of the family (and this may happen only on rare occasions), he is still apart.

The mother has places to go and things to do. She is not your common housewife. She is too bright and too energetic for that. She does things. At one time, these might have involved mostly volunteer community efforts. Nowadays, she is more likely to have a paid job. But whatever, Mother is up and about. There is no reason for her to spend a lot of time with the kids.

The house is big. The children possess their own domain, even when they are quite young. The parents are in a position of general supervision, but it is more the rule than the exception that exurban youngsters enjoy privacy from an early age. The process of distancing begins in infancy.

Everybody is mobile in Exurbia. Mother and Father, of course, have wheels. As the kids grow older, they hitchhike; before you know it, they are driving.

So at any given time in a typical exurban family, there is the opportunity for distancing. No one need remain in the company of anyone else. It comes to be expected that each will "do his own thing." The number of listings of separate telephones for the "Chadwick Children" is a testament to the apartness that informs Exurbia.

We now know that, in the absence of restraints, children become people at an earlier age than had previously been suspected. Togetherness inhibits development as a distinct individual. The child, frequently in the company of parents and siblings, finds that life is easier if a role is played.

The apartness that is the norm in Exurbia removes these restraints. Children soon become people, individuals. The suburban father may always have assumed that his son would excel scholastically and athletically; go to a "good" college; get a good job; and altogether be a "credit" to his family and to the upbringing he has received.

But the son has become his own person without the process being apparent to his parents. The young man has been operating at a distance. He has developed his own set of values, and he has bought certain important concepts. One of these concepts is that his parents are less interested in him as a person than as a creditable reflection of themselves. Another is that the way in which he has been brought up is infused with hypocrisy.

These ideas accepted by the exurban youngster are apt to be hazy and ill-formed. Moreover, the follow-through is likely to be, in the eyes of parents, inconsistent. The youngster will take the fruits of affluence—the motorbike, the stereo, the car—as his due, and yet he will denounce the mode of life from which they spring. But the exurban teenage person will often go beyond that. He will say and do things that seem deliberately calculated to hurt his parents, and he knows how to hurt. He can zero in on the chinks in his parents' armor and penetrate to the most sensitive spots. He will be foul-mouthed, promiscuous, and indolent. He will drink and dope. He will fail and drop out. And while doing these things, he will constantly reiterate the message that everything he is doing is his parents' fault. "Where did we go wrong?" is the stock question. Trite or not, it is a question that parents are always asking themselves because they have an affinity for guilt.

Many exurbanites have never quite managed to overcome a guilty feeling about living the Good Life. They overlay it with rationalizations; they ignore it; they compensate by pugnacious defenses of their life-style. But many of them are still vulnerable in that spot. And their children manage to pierce them there.

The kids are reacting to their own stresses. They have great freedom and great resources, but there are great expectations riding on them. They resent the expectations, and they strike back. They have their own guilts to expiate. They are well aware that they are "advantaged." That they don't seem to feel any better for being advantaged does not help; it only makes it worse.

Don't these kids love their mothers and fathers? It is an interesting question, and it is not so susceptible to a simple answer as many—grown-ups and youngsters—would like it to be. People don't necessarily love other people simply because they are related to them. And they certainly don't love other people because they are dependent on them. The contrary is more likely to be true. It is not that kids in Exurbia are unaware of, or indifferent to, the tradition that children love their parents. The distancing common to many exurban families leads instead to a certain amount of dispassionate scrutiny. The tensions between what seem to kids to be the real truths of existence and the ways in which their mothers and fathers live their lives grow rather than diminish.

And so the kids do not, in many cases, love. Moreover, having gone their own ways and drawn on their own resources since they were quite young, many suburban kids do not feel obliged to even maintain the semblance of love and dutifulness. They may try sometimes, but they are not very good at it.

So we have a situation, particularly with the exurban family that has gotten older, of a number of people, old and young, who more or less live with each other but between whom the differences and the tensions are more apparent than the affinities. In such a situation there is not much love; love cannot be expected to burgeon under these circumstances.

Parents try to deal with the indifference and the alienation of their kids in various ways. Many exurban mothers and fathers go to what is sometimes an extreme to be "understanding," to be "with it." Mothers wear patched jeans; fathers let their hair grow. Mother and Father try to talk knowledgeably about pot, and perhaps they smoke it. This, of course, does not win even acceptance—let alone love— from the kids. It merely makes the older folks seem grotesque.

Other parents try to ignore the rebellion of their offspring. Still others try to be indulgent. But whatever the method chosen to cope and to present an acceptable public stance, there is usually a great deal of disappointment and hurt.

The kids are hurting, too. They frequently wish to be able to love, but feel that they are not given the basis for it. The tradition that children revere their parents is not enough. We are talking here, not of children, but of sophisticated young people. The distancing they have experienced, and the very advantages that their parents set such store by, have made the kids sophisticated. They are too sophisticated to go blindly along with what they consider to be arrant hypocrisy.

Hypocrisy is something that nobody has a good word for. Everybody is against it. No doubt these children of Exurbia have heard, time and time again, their parents deride the hypocrisy of acquaintances, politicians, eminent divines, and the like. No wonder the children react against it.

And yet hypocrisy is necessary. It is, in many ways, art. It is politics. It is social intercourse. It is beauty and romantic love. Hypocrisy is *civilization*. Let's face it.

The exurbanite family began to fragment when its members went beyond deriding and lamenting hypocrisy and decided to really try to do without it. Neither adults nor children have anything to replace it.

And so the kids of Exurbia grow up very quickly. Precocity is prized. Psychiatrists and physicians warn that the "superior" school systems of Exurbia are all geared to forcing growth that should not be forced. The "distanced" kids acquire antennae that bestow upon them perceptions far beyond the norms that used to exist. One example of this was seen in an elementary school in one of our more celebrated Exurbias. One fifth-grade teacher—an old-fashioned soul—was noted for her big event of the year, the "Story Book Parade." At this performance, attended by parents, grandparents, and friends, each child would in turn come onto the stage, in costume, and give a little impersonation of some favorite character of fact or fiction: Robin Hood, Dorothy of Oz, Abraham Lincoln, Florence Nightingale, and so forth.

There were no rehearsals; the teacher would be as surprised and delighted as the guests. Prizes were awarded for best costumes and most imaginative presentations. And then, at the height of "Story Book Parade" a few years ago, there came the turn of one particular girl. Shedding her coat, she pranced onto the stage. Her costume was an abbreviated, skintight garment and mesh stockings. She wore floppy ears on her head and a pom-pom on her rump. A basket hung by a strap from her neck. The little girl began to throw packages of gum to the assemblage, exclaiming sweetly that she was a Playboy bunny. The impact of the occasion was heightened by the fact that this was one of those fifth-grade girls who are preternaturally well-endowed. The reception was mixed. "Story Book Parade" was not renewed for the following season.

Exurbia's kids are at once heavily armored and highly vulnerable. They have been sheltered and exposed at the same time. They have grown in amazing strength, beauty, and variety, but their growth has been hothouse growth. They are not "street-smart," but they are culture-wise. They know the psychiatric jargon; many have already been under considerable psychiatric care. They know what to scorn and what to reject; but they have few things to love and cherish. They seek things to believe in; they wind up "believing" in sexual freedom or ecology or the stars or fifteen-year-old gurus. Some things they are sure of: They will never indulge in hypocrisy; they will not be conformists; and they will not be like their mothers and fathers.

These are the people who grow up in Exurbia.

18

Homo Suburbis:
Four Vignettes

Kittering

Kittering grew up in Raleigh, North Carolina. He went to college at Chapel Hill. When he was recruited by the Company, he worked first in Atlanta, then Houston, then back in Raleigh. So, though Kittering had traveled a lot—in fact, all over the world—he was a Southern boy, and he thought of himself that way.

There were always Negroes in Kittering's life. His earliest memories were of Winnie, who had worked for the Kitterings for thirty-five years, until she died. Kittering did not, of course, go to grade school with Negro kids, but he had known Winnie's kids and played with them.

It was after Kittering was out of college, working, that things began to change: Martin Luther King, the marches, the lawsuits, the "outsiders" who came down from the North. Kittering's attitudes toward the Negroes—it took him a long while to assimilate the term "blacks"—went through stages, but no stage in itself was complicated. He hated no one. He understood frustration and, as a general proposition, considered it wrong to keep people from voting, or to make them sit in the back of the bus. At the same time, he could not see why a man who owned a restaurant could not decide whom to serve and whom not to serve, and he could not see why people would want to go "where they were not wanted."

But he could not really get mad at the blacks. They, after all, had had a pretty raw deal. That was the way of the world, they were victims of history, but you could not deny that they had had it rough.

Were they his equal in all respects? Kittering did not ask himself questions like that; he did not ask himself any needless questions that might be tough to answer. He did not see all that many blacks, and he did not have occasion to come to concrete terms with abstract questions. Kittering was remote from it all. When his anger or contempt was aroused, it was directed at the agitators from the North or the Lester Maddoxes and Bull Connors of the South. To the "good old boys" with which the Company abounded, Kittering responded with a shrug of amused indulgence. A lot of them were shrewd businessmen; you could not write them off. Beyond that, Kittering had little truck with them.

When the first black moved into the executive floor at the Company, Kittering was probably the first to drop in for a chat. Kittering's principal feeling was curiosity. He neither liked nor disliked the idea of a black manager; it was inevitable. As the months went on, they talked together and worked together. There was no social intercourse; they never became friends. There was too much reserve on each side; and besides, while Kittering had to admit he admired a great deal about the new man, he could not really say he liked him. How much of this was personality and how much culture, Kittering did not worry about. He was no barrier-breaker.

When Kittering got the opportunity to move North, he and his wife talked about it a lot. For both, it would be uprooting. But the opportunity was there. Actually it was a little more involved than mere opportunity; if he turned down the move, nothing drastic would happen, but his future would never be quite the same with the Company. The kids were young enough to handle the change, and the Kitterings were, they felt, still flexible. Kittering accepted the move.

The Company took care of everything, including expert advice on the exurban town in which to live. The Kitterings bought a house, and, during the summer, moved North. Nothing was startlingly different, in fact, but a great many things were different in nuance. The change was most marked for Kittering's wife. The kids seemed able to accept everything quite happily, and Kittering himself had his work, which remained pretty much the same, North or South.

You did not get to know your neighbors very quickly, the Kitterings learned. There were, at first, two main avenues to the formation of friendships: people Kittering knew at work, and the parents of kids with whom the Kittering kids went to school.

In the city, where Kittering went every day, there were, of

course, black faces, although they were no more abundant in the executive suite than they had been in Raleigh. In the town, there were not many to be seen. Kittering's wife tried to get hold of a reliable cleaning woman, but she soon learned in practice what her first acquaintances had told her; good ones were hard to come by. A service sent a girl, who came from the neighboring city and had to be picked up at the railroad station. Mrs. Kittering found that she could not really talk to her, and after two weeks the girl did not come anymore. Then there was an older woman, but one day Mrs. Kittering came home and found her drunk. After that, although still hopeful, the Kitterings tried to make do with an expensive and not-too-thorough cleaning service.

It did not take long for the Kitterings to feel that they were settling down in Exurbia. Kittering felt strange in the commuting groove for a week or so; after that, his adaptation was so complete that he might have been doing it all his life. Penny Kittering showed a resilience that surprised even herself as she slipped into the short-car-trip rhythm of the archetypical exurban young-married. The Kitterings got around. They entertained and were asked out. People liked them. And—after it became clear that the Kitterings took no offense at all about it—there were questions, and some kidding, about the South. To many of the new friends, the marked Southern accents of the Kitterings came as a novelty.

It was at the Rosens' that the Kitterings were introduced to the Wrens. Bob Wren was an advertising account executive; Ann Wren a psychologist. The Wrens had been in town for about five years. They were black; not coffee-colored, but very black.

And it struck Kittering, as he stood talking to the new acquaintances, that everyone in the room was watching them, without seeming to. The introduction of the Kitterings to the Wrens was obviously an occasion of some social import; a Big Deal. Kittering knew that Penny had sensed the scrutiny, and she was a little annoyed; this was evident to Kittering as he noted the almost imperceptible extra effort that Penny was putting out to be especially gracious. The Wrens seemed impervious to the atmosphere, and Kittering wondered if they were aware of anything. He stopped wondering about Ann Wren as she directed at him one single, amused side glance from her exotic, faintly slanting eyes.

That night, back home, the Kitterings talked about it. They agreed that the Wrens were very nice and very intelligent people.

Kittering laughed about the uptight watchfulness of the hosts and guests as they observed the confrontation; Penny was a little less understanding, but ultimately forgiving.

They saw the Wrens several times after that within a short space of time; the constellation into which the Kitterings had settled was fairly fixed. And of course they must have the Wrens the next time they entertained, which they did. Kittering by now gave no visible evidence of taking any special note of the Wrens; Penny Kittering still talked about them, about Bob Wren's intelligence and quiet wit and how attractive Ann Wren was. Kittering found that, at parties, picnics, and the like, he was enjoying, more and more, the Wrens; or if truth be told, Ann Wren. They spent a lot of time talking with each other. Once Liz Rosen, nodding toward Kittering and Ann as they stood chatting in a corner, said something to Penny Kittering about "how *wonderful* it is that you and the Wrens have hit it off so well. You know, frankly...." And so on. That night Penny asked Kittering, as an aside, what it was that he and Ann found to *talk* about, and Kittering said, smiling, that they had so much in common.

It was three months or so later that Kittering and Ann Wren became lovers, physically. These things take some arranging. There were stories about overnight business trips, the rendezvous in the city ("Anywhere closer would not be exactly inconspicuous," Ann had said), dinner, the hotel, some gentle awkwardness, and then a most successfully negotiated night.

The meetings continued, continue now. At the beginning there was never any talk about anything except the occasional liaisons. Then one night Kittering said something, jokingly, about how he was, after all, a buttoned-up kind of guy and maybe they might think about some more permanent arrangement. Kittering has continued to talk about it. Ann Wren has never given any positive sign of agreeing, but her responses have changed from the initial joking brush-off, to earnest argument that the whole idea is insane, to pensive, and sometimes wistful, silence.

When Kittering meets Bob Wren now, he cannot help looking at him, wondering if he detects something in Wren's attitude; a deep, cold current of hostility, a sardonic contempt? But no, he cannot say that he sees anything there. Sometimes Kittering, who has never been given to daydreaming, thinks things like "If only Bob and Penny..." Every now and then he wonders if something might be going on, but he concludes it is his imagination. Penny has never said anything. But she does sometimes seem unusually crabby. She is more sharply critical of their friends than ever before, including the Wrens. The other night, as Kittering was in the bathroom, he heard Penny speaking about something that Ann Wren had said to her at the PTA meeting, and then Penny muttered some words that could have been "That black bitch!"

There are times when Kittering wonders where it will all come out. There are other times when he does not give a damn.

Morgan

Morgan was a New Yorker. When he moved to Connecticut, he remained a New Yorker. He watched the New York TV stations, he read the New York papers, he subscribed to *The New Yorker*, and, better yet, *New York*. The people the Morgans knew were all New Yorkers. They entertained themselves in New York, they kept up their ties to New York, they maintained a complete New York life-style.

When they thought or talked local politics, it was always New York politics. Hartford might as well be the capital of Montana. The Morgans barely knew the name of the town's first selectman; they thought the title itself was a quaint way of styling what in any decent place would be called a mayor. The doings of town bodies were a sealed book.

When the kids started going to school, Morgan's wife drifted into the PTA. Her colleagues practically dragged her to some meetings of the board of education. Then she began to attend sessions of the town council when educational matters were on the agenda.

None of this interested Morgan. Occasionally he was asked—by his wife and others—if he might not want to attend this or that meeting. He laughed it off.

Then one evening the Morgans went to dinner at the Fergusons'. After dinner, Ferguson announced, everybody was attending the council meeting. Morgan was annoyed; while this had been planned, he somehow hadn't gotten the word. He had been looking forward to a repeat of the usual after-dinner cordial and conversation about business and national trends; a conversation at which, if town matters came up, they were treated with derision.

Ferguson pointed out that the council would be debating a public-works proposal that would make an enormous difference in everybody's tax bill. Now Morgan, like everybody else, thought that taxes were exceptionally high; and in a vague way he accepted the proposition that people who lived in the town ought to at least know what was going on in the town, if only for self-protection. But his threshold of concern had never gotten low enough for him to act on that acceptance.

Under protest, Morgan went to the meeting. He could not believe what he saw: forty men and women uttering strident idiocies, a moderator who would have been fired from any self-respecting corporation for running such a shambles of a meeting, and pompous windbags gabbling on and on about the "need for change" who were rebutted endlessly by equally pompous windbags lamenting any alteration in the "character of the community" and denouncing the tax load. Morgan could not get out fast enough.

However, he absorbed a sufficient amount from his first exposure to town government to put the experience to good use. Morgan was a pretty good amateur impressionist and lampoonist, and for some months after that he held forth at parties with his version of a representative town meeting, which some people, at least at first, found hilarious. Finally Morgan's wife pointed out that he was beginning to repeat himself. Morgan dropped the act, but stayed away from anything to do with town affairs.

Then the thing about the boat moorings came up. Morgan owned a boat. He didn't get out on it as often as he would have liked. One reason was that his mooring was well outside the harbor, necessitating a laborious trip in a dinghy and considerable wear and tear on the craft. There was a waiting list for preferred moorings; Morgan was on it and understood that he was working his way toward the top. He understood, too, that there were plans to lengthen the breakwater and thus establish many more moorings, at which time he would be in good shape.

Now Morgan heard that there had been a change. The breakwater was not to be extended after all. Indeed, nothing was to be done to improve the boating scene; apparently the town fathers were mumbling about how things were tight and the money was needed elsewhere.

Morgan was furious. He readily permitted himself to be enlisted on an ad hoc committee to Safeguard the Rights of the Boating Community. He went to strategy meetings, he contributed money for advertisements, he buttonholed his friends.

And he began to attend meetings of the town bodies involved in the action: the boards of recreation and finance and the council. Moreover, Morgan was frequently to be seen on his feet, exhorting these functionaries to do their duty.

While Morgan's somewhat caustic style was not welcome to many of those who found themselves on the receiving end of his strictures, his abilities at organization and persuasion—honed in a multitude of conference room skirmishes—impressed other people. Morgan was urged to run for the council. Since the boating question was still hanging, he accepted, made an energetic campaign, and won.

Morgan's interest in town affairs grew. His attendance record at meetings was excellent. He took his committee assignments seriously, and it was now commonplace to see him in the audience at sessions of other bodies, even when the agenda contained nothing that might have been thought remotely interesting to the old Morgan.

Once the plan for ensuring new moorings was established, Morgan's style changed. When he first took office he was deeply involved in pushing through one project. Once that goal had been achieved, Morgan turned his talents in the direction of keeping anyone else from pushing through any other favored project. Night after night, people with a special interest would appear: the school people, the tennis people, the apartment people, the commercial-development people. On all of them Morgan trained his guns. He did his homework. He was gifted at dramatizing the greediness of those who would use tax money to further their own interests. He was fiery in excoriating the crassness of those who would heedlessly make wholesale changes that would destroy the town's character. Morgan could make a taxpayer ache with potential pain over a proposal to spend money; he had picked up a surprising amount of knowledge about the history of the town, and could weave a tapestry to depict a "heritage" that must never be touched in any way, lest its sacred fabric dissolve away.

Morgan's constituents kept reelecting him. True, as time went on, more and more of them were offended by his opposition to projects they supported; but since Morgan was also opposed to many more projects that they abhorred, the consensus was that he was a good man to have in there.

You can still see Morgan at almost any meeting, and you can count on him to get to his feet to assume his role as watchdog of the treasury and Horatius at the Bridge fighting off the forces of change. No one listens to Morgan anymore, but he is accepted as one of the staples of town government.

Recently a man named Campbell was persuaded, after years of adamant resistance, to attend a council meeting. Campbell could not believe what he witnessed. He could not get out of there fast enough. But Campbell absorbed enough to provide himself with ample material to deliver an entertaining version of a town meeting for the edification of others. Campbell's one-man act is still holding them spellbound at parties. The centerpiece of his performance is an imitation of Morgan that never fails to leave everyone laughing to the point of utter helplessness.

Frame

There were times, when Frame stood on the platform with the other commuters, that he wondered what the hell he was doing there. The men he traveled with were always on their way to London, or coming back from vacation on la Playa del Oro. Frame did not travel to places like London in his job; occasionally he went to Springfield, Massachusetts, or Bethlehem, Pennsylvania, or some such place, but that was all. And as far as vacations were concerned, the Frames simply had not been able to afford one. Or at least that's what Frame's wife kept saying, to Frame's annoyance and humiliation.

But you had to play the part. Frame had drifted into a relationship with a group of riding companions, and he felt obliged to hold up his end. These were Big Men, obviously; they all had more important jobs than Frame, that seemed evident to him. And they all seemed to have immeasurably more money. They had worries, but their worries—at least those they gave voice to—were of an entirely different order from his. They talked about boats and the shape of the fairways and the lousy meals on airlines. Frame wondered when he might be able to get a suit made for himself. The ones he bought off the rack were by no means up to the current fashion, and Frame was painfully aware that they did not fit him nearly so well as the suits that all his friends wore.

Of course it had been a mistake to buy the place in the expensive suburbs, but at the time Frame had been in the grip of a euphoric spate of optimism about where he was going on the job, and the move had seemed a natural one. They had moved. The job that Frame had aspired to had gone to another man who was five inches taller, had a deep voice, and wore shoes that, though never polished, looked as if they had cost $150. A similar opening had gone to another commanding personality, and now Frame had the sneaking suspicion that he was never going anyplace.

Some days he wanted to shift his location on the train, to get away from the constant reminders that the others had Done Things, while he was nobody; but that would have been a conspicuous retreat. Frame imagined what they would say about him.

So he stuck it out. From time to time he would try to assume the role of a man who had Done Things, but he never felt that he carried it off very well. He suspected that they were secretly laughing at him.

One of the staple topics of conversation was the terrible service on the commuter line. Every now and then, when the train was particularly hot or cold or particularly late, someone would say that they ought to do something, that they should refuse to pay money for treatment like this. But there was a tacit agreement that nobody had the guts to do it.

Then came the morning that the train went into its familiar whining crawl and stopped, to sit immobile for an hour. Distracted trainmen disappeared. At last the apparatus returned to a semblance of life and began to creep along the track, though very slowly. The trainman, at last, appeared to take the tickets.

The others greeted the trainman—red-faced and grim—with the kind of insulting banter that he had been hearing as he passed through four previous cars. But they surrendered their tickets. The trainman looked at Frame. He said, "I refuse. The service you have provided—or failed to provide—this morning does not merit payment."

Frame's companions smiled broadly. The trainman, his face a little redder, asked again for the ticket. Again Frame refused.

Frame's companions smiled more broadly, their eyebrows rising slightly. The trainman asked, and asked again. Frame continued to refuse. Now it had gotten quiet in that section of the car. Frame and the trainman had an audience. The trainman, beyond patience, reached threateningly toward Frame. He leaned back in his corner seat, folded his arms, stared straight ahead. The nearby commuters cheered. The trainman fumed. Frame felt an inner glow.

The trainman went on down the aisle, taking other tickets. The group around Frame congratulated him. He said, "I thought it was about time somebody *did* something, instead of just talking about it. Maybe if we all do this, we'll get somewhere." He was beginning to see himself in the forefront of a surging wave of rebelling commuters, not only here but perhaps even in other places, maybe all over the country.

At this point, the conductor arrived. As he approached, one of the others said to Frame, "Well, fun's fun, but now you better come across. This guy looks like he means business." There was no question of money being passed; Frame had bought a thirty-day ticket at the beginning of the month, and everyone, including the crew, knew it. It was simply a matter of producing it.

But this Frame would not do. He sat, adamant, as the conductor at first kidded, then pleaded, then threatened. There was, by this time, a change in the atmosphere. The other commuters were studiously immersed in their newspapers, darting an occasional uneasy glance at the rebel.

The conductor went away. Frame felt that now the skirmish was over, the victory had been won. He started to talk with animation about the things that could be accomplished through commuter pressure, but no one seemed to want to talk about it.

When the train reached the terminus, Frame reached up and got his briefcase from the rack. As he turned, there was the conductor with a policeman. The policeman said, "Sir, I guess I can understand how you would get a little mad sometimes, but this man is only doing his job. You made your point. Now if you will just take out your ticket, everything will be okay."

Frame was alarmed. He hadn't thought it would come to this. He glanced around; a few commuters still paused in the aisle, watching curiously. Frame refused again. The policeman sighed, "You know, if you don't, I am going to have to arrest you for theft of services. We don't want to have to go through anything like that, do we?" Frame said, "Theft of services? This road has been robbing *me* and everyone else of services for years!"

That was a good one, he felt, and he looked around to see how everyone had taken it. But nobody was left.

At this point, Frame thought about packing it in, showing the ticket, and going to work. But something would not let him do that. He refused, and continued to refuse.

Frame was arrested and booked. He spent what seemed like hours in a precinct station. Finally he got home. There was a brief story about it in one of the city dailies, and a somewhat longer story in Frame's hometown weekly. He determined that he would not plead guilty, though assured that, if he did, that would be the end of it. He wanted a lawyer. The Commuter's Association, a vocal but somewhat exiguous group, offered moral support but said there was no money in the treasury for a lawyer. To approach such an organization as the American Civil Liberties Union was alien to Frame's gut feelings. He hired a lawyer, despite his wife's emphatic declarations, supported by ample proof, that they could not afford it.

Frame is fighting the case. He sees it as a crusade. He spends his nights, sometimes all night, poring over research material he has amassed as ammunition in his fight against the railroad. Frame's bosses are starting to look askance at him. His wife has—unknown to Frame—sought psychiatric help from a community agency.

But, worst of all, the triumph is beginning to turn to ashes for Frame. The exhilaration of the fight is fading. He rides the train; he shows his ticket; he sits with the same people. But they tend not to talk about the episode, and sometimes Frame catches them looking at him oddly. Frame is beginning to realize that they do not regard him as a man of guts and principle.

They think he's crazy.

Renfrew

To Renfrew, Saturday and Sunday at his home in Exurbia were like R&R to an infantryman—a brief respite from the constant danger and tension of front-line combat. When Renfrew first moved to the suburbs, he was a recreational eclectic. He did everything. He golfed, he played tennis, he jogged, he boated, he partied. This was not just fun. It was a necessary battery-recharging period to get him ready for Monday morning.

Renfrew's wife accepted this for quite a while. She and the kids were conditioned to minister to Daddy's bruised psyche, shore up his will to fight another week, and stay out of his way when he needed quiet. And Renfrew needed a lot of quiet. The package-goods empire within which he was carving a career was an arena in which no quarter was given.

From Monday through Friday the family did not see much of Renfrew. He was usually late; at home he retired into his den to work; and he traveled a lot. In the house, on the wing, or at the office, Renfrew was working.

But he always kept the weekends free; not for the family, but for himself. Not that he never talked with anyone. Renfrew liked to relax on occasion—to the extent that he could ever relax—and tell his wife about the events of the week. He told her about the high-pressure meetings, the Byzantine intrigues, the earth-jarring confrontations and the marketplace maneuvers that constituted his life. And Ruth Renfrew, like Desdemona, loved him for the dangers he had passed, and gave him for his pains a world of sighs.

Renfrew found that throwing himself into every conceivable leisure activity was not restful. He might enjoy doing a number of different things on weekends, but enjoyment was not the primary objective. The idea was to keep him in fighting trim. And so gradually he became more selective, paring his weekend interests down to a few—and finally to the one that he found gave him the biggest payoff in replenishment.

The choice that Renfrew arrived at was surprising to those who knew him. It might have been thought that he would, like so many of his friends, become an obsessive golfer. Or he might have concentrated on boating; he had many of the traits that make for a superb handler of small boats.

Renfrew did not go in these directions. He became an assiduous gardener and lawnkeeper. From the time that the Renfrews had moved into the house, he had taken considerable interest in the flowers, shrubs, and trees surrounding him; and, characteristically, he was not willing to leave all the decisions up to some yardman or lawn service. He had sought advice, weighted and sifted it, experimented with seeds, weedkillers, conditioners, fertilizers, and soils. He studied local flora. He had acquired and become skillful with the best equipment. In short, Renfrew approached the problem of making things grow as he approached any problem. He was damned good at it, and, furthermore, he liked it.

There came a time when Ruth Renfrew's Desdemona-like willingness to do nothing more than provide the warrior with surcease from battle began to wane. The children were more able to manage on their own. All her friends were doing interesting things. She decided that it was time for her to get involved in some new activities.

It was not easy at first for Ruth Renfrew. She felt a little guilty about doing volunteer work. She had been thoroughly infused with the woman-belongs-in-the-home attitude, and to get out of the house on business of her own required a certain amount of rationalization and determination. Ruth Renfrew wound up putting it to herself this way: They owed a certain debt to the community. A man with Renfrew's ability would be a great asset, in any part-time role he was willing to assume, but her husband was so busy that he could not do it. Therefore, inadequate though she might be as a replacement, she should try to do something at least to make a contribution. Besides, the development of another interest would make her a more interesting and vital partner. And, of course, there was the fact that, for all intents and purposes, Renfrew was not around during the week.

So Ruth Renfrew began to do volunteer work. In a small way, at first. She didn't take on anything requiring a lot of time, or any great planning or decision-making ability. She fetched and carried; she sorted mail and stuffed envelopes; she made phone calls; she made herself into a pleasant and reliable footsoldier of volunteerism.

But things did not remain this way. The local veterans of community service knew a good thing when they saw one. Ruth Renfrew was more than just pleasant and reliable; she was capable. Gradually—so gradually that she hardly noticed—Ruth took on more responsibility. She was still unwilling to accept a post with a title and a fixed area of operation—but she could, and did, involve herself to a growing degree in ad hoc committees and one-shot projects. Now she was often out to meetings at night. This presented no problem for Renfrew. Absorbed in his own thing, he would nod abstractedly when Ruth said she would be going to a session at the community center; and that was that.

Emboldened by her new awareness of previously unsuspected

abilities, and responsive to the recognition and appreciation she was getting, Ruth finally agreed to take on a volunteer job with a title; although, she was anxious to point out, she could not work at it anything like full-time.

Soon, however, Ruth's involvement was so close to full-time as not to make any difference. Her weekends were still her own, and the weekends were the only time when she was really required to be available as sounding board, playmate, and pepper-upper. Even on weekends, Renfrew was so caught up in his companionship with growing things that Ruth was needed less and less.

Renfrew was working harder—impossible though that might have seemed—during the week, and, in compensation, gardening more extensively on weekends. He was working harder because the economy was sagging and it took tremendous effort to keep volume where it should be. Was there any other reason why Renfrew felt under pressure? Nothing that he admitted to himself; but, after all, a man had always to be on his guard. There might—just might—be somebody down there in the ranks who could be the one to challenge Renfrew successfully. Not that he believed any such thing could happen; he had fought off challenges through the years, and he was at the top of the heap, or near it.

The merger came as a shock. Renfrew, with all of his vaunted sensitivity to trends, had simply not anticipated it. Things went on, though, for several months; and then one day, incredibly, the board chairman told Renfrew that he was out. There would, of course, be a severance arrangement—not as much as they would have liked, "You know how things are today"—but Renfrew was through. He was fired.

Of course Renfrew would move into another spot right away. His reputation was universal; there would be any number of companies bidding for him, including those who had floated offers to him through headhunters, and those competitors whose market shares had diminished when Renfrew had gone head-to-head with them.

But somehow the anticipated offers did not materialize. There were tantalizing lunchtime conversations. There was talk about heading up new subsidiaries. But nothing concrete. Oh, there was a tentative offer here and there, but they were nickel-and-dime outfits, and Renfrew turned them down cold. The big job, though, did not come through. Times were tough, Renfrew knew that. A lot of people were afraid of hiring him because he was a threat; he knew

174 The End of Exurbia

that, too. To a lesser degree he was aware that he made some people in the industry uneasy. They thought of him as an intense, ruthless, driving son of a bitch. And that approach seemed to be going out of style.

Renfrew waited, confident that he would land on top. And he waited, and waited. Incredibly, money began to loom as a problem. The Renfrews lived big, and they did not have all that much in reserve. Inflation eroded the severance check with remarkable speed.

Then one day Ruth Renfrew said, hesitantly, that she had moved into a somewhat different phase in her work. She was doing more or less the same things that she had done as a volunteer—but now she was getting paid for it. She was diffident in broaching the news, but firm in her resolve to stick with the job, which she had already taken, and which, to Renfrew's surprise, paid pretty well. Not in his class, but pretty well.

Renfrew greeted this information with mixed emotions, which seemed too complicated to sort out. The best and safest approach appeared to be that of a pat on the head. Renfrew told Ruth that this was great, and why shouldn't she be paid for what she was doing? Beyond that, he gave every impression of not taking it too seriously.

Three months went past. The contacts were drying up. Renfrew had second thoughts about a couple of the "nickel-and-dime" outfits, but they were no longer open. He got in touch with several acquaintances in the industry and indicated, casually, that he might be available to take on certain assignments, even though they were not quite at the level he was used to, just to help out and to keep his hand in while a very important proposition was being finalized. Their responses varied in degrees of evasion, but they boiled down to the idea that they would not insult Renfrew by offering him work for which he was overqualified, and they were sure that he would soon be back in full harness in a job worthy of his talents.

Even with what Ruth could bring in, the money was running out fast. Renfrew was, for the first time in his life, really worried about it. He thought about consulting, but he knew that the last—and often the first—resort of myriad out-of-work executives was to set up in business as consultants, getting cards and stationery printed and renting a small office in which nothing much happened. Even if he could pick up a buck here and there, he could not bring himself to do it. No, it would have to be something that would not make him look bad.

It was a passing remark made by Ruth Renfrew—dismissed at first, then considered, then acted on—that gave Renfrew a direction. What else was he good at, besides the package-goods business? Well, he was good at making things grow. After a lot of thought, he came to a decision. He would make his expertise in this area available, at a fee.

It was amazing how quickly it grew. Renfrew managed to take on a couple of jobs for acquaintances. The results he got were remarkable, well worth the money. He expanded, bought equipment, advertised, hired some people (including two other on-the-beach managers with green thumbs). Times were tough, but it turned out that there was money to be made in landscape planning and estate maintenance—if you were good at it. And Renfrew was good. No formal training, of course; but he knew dirt and the things that grew in it, and he was a planner.

The parallel new careers of the Renfrews burgeoned. Ruth was now involved in the world of budgets, conferences, decisions, correspondence—and internecine intrigue. Renfrew's new work had none of that, but he loved it. He would listen to Ruth as she retold the day's events, how this individual could not be trusted to follow through on a project, how that person was after her job, how she was planning to discomfit the competition in some altruistic but nonetheless cutthroat area. Sometimes Renfrew would offer some sharp comments and judgments; often he just sat and smiled. The roles were reversed, but why not? Let Ruth find out what the rat race was really like. All that was behind him.

Then came the call from the headhunter. A new, aggressive company; a new line of products; a big opportunity. It was Renfrew's chance to return to the fray. Of course he said he was no longer interested, but, just for the hell of it, he was willing to have lunch.

In the end Renfrew took the job, selling the landscape business out to his second-in-command. Soon he was back at the old game. But something has gone out of it for Renfrew. He's not as bold as he used to be. He hesitates; he shops for opinions; he hedges. He works as hard as he used to, but he can't seem to relax as he once did. Somehow, working around the place has lost its appeal. Ruth has her own job, her own concerns, and her own tensions to dispel during the leisure hours. The kids are grown, and Renfrew never really did get to know them. He tries to put everything he has into the work, but he suspects that "everything" now is not what it once was, and he nurses a growing awareness that the chief executive of his company is not entirely happy with the bottom-line results. And there are young tigers in that jungle, pacing and waiting for him to slip.

The other day Renfrew was at the road, and one of the trucks that he formerly owned went past. The driver waved happily. And Renfrew felt, suddenly, so tired that he had to go back to the house and lie down for a while, a thing he had never done before.

19

Why the World Can't Afford Exurbia Anymore

At the height of the 1974 fuel and food-price crisis, two exurbanites chatted over cocktails. One remarked that he had heard about a shortage of fertilizer that was driving up the price of food. Interestingly enough, one reason given for the shortage and expensiveness of fertilizer was that suburban weekend gardeners were using so much of it there was not enough left over for the farmers.

The other exurbanite, an enthusiastic gardener, nodded and smiled, as if he had just heard something that made him feel very good. "Yes," he said, "it's true, and yet I can tell you from personal experience that that is a lot of bunk."

The problem cannot be dismissed quite that breezily. The Good Life in Exurbia is getting more and more expensive. An increasing number of suburbanites are asking themselves, Can I afford it? Maybe that's not the big question. Maybe it's, Can the rest of the country afford Exurbia?

Take energy, for example.

In the United States we consume about 350 gallons of automobile gasoline per capita every year. But in Westport we are consuming a lot more than our share. A study conducted in 1975 showed that gas stations in Westport sold 500 gallons for every man, woman, and chil ' residing in the town. The survey covered only service stations in the town; it is reasonable to assume that Westporters buy a lot more gas outside the community than nonresidents buy within.

So, in Westport, we are using up gas at a rate that exceeds average national usage by something more than 45 percent. We are also using up home-heating fuel at more than the national average. When fuel prices zoom, we find it harder to live in Exurbia. It is understandable that, concerned with our own problems, we tend to overlook what it is costing others—outside the suburbs—to maintain us in our spacious areas and our simple, "rural" way of life.

There is probably no way to calculate the full cost of the metropolitan regions and the nation at large for keeping exurbanites in a state of simple, but comfortable, bucolic seclusion. But there are some ways to begin to reach an estimate. The Suburban Action Institute conducted "A Study of Exclusion" for the Commonwealth of Pennsylvania, funded in part by a grant from the U.S. Department of Housing and Urban Development. The report focused on a number of areas of "diseconomy" that result from suburban practices of restriction.

Reduced Building of Houses

The construction industry, and particularly its residential component, has come to be the "sick man" of the American economy. Periodically there are optimistic flashes from Washington that seem to indicate a pickup in house-building, but the actual figures continue to be sluggish. You can't put up houses if zoning regulations do not permit them, or if the land they occupy is too expensive. The exclusivity of suburbia has contributed heavily to the subdued state of residential construction. The Home Builders League of New Jersey tried to come up with figures that would estimate the gross impact of *not* building houses. They estimated that the annual regional loss from nonconstruction is approximately $150,000 for each single-family unit and $100,000 for each multifamily unit not constructed.

When home-building activity is diminished, there is a considerable ripple effect on other economic activity, on job-creating spending, and on tax revenues. With houses in short supply, the cost of buying or renting a house goes up, fueling inflation. When a region becomes sufficiently short of housing, its labor supply is diminished. Industries do not move in. Industries already in the region think about moving out.

New houses cost money. Houses that are *not* built cost money, too.

Low Turnover of Housing

Housing experts use the term "filtering" to describe the process by which better housing becomes available to lower-income families at prices they can afford. The basis for the concept is that every new house puts into motion a sequence of moves. Studies show that a housing opening in the suburbs will be filled by a move from the urban fringe; the chain of moves extends back into the central city. The sequence also extends back from higher- to lower-income families. So, filtering implies a direct connection between new suburban construction and lower-income housing, and between house-building in the suburbs and improvement of housing conditions in the city. The building of 1,000 new homes will, on the average, allow 3,545 families to move. This number will include more than 300 poor families and more than 1,000 of moderate income. The building of moderately priced homes will permit more poor families to move than will the building of expensive houses.

Suburban exclusion cuts down on filtering. Fewer poor families move out of the central city. The inner city festers and deteriorates. More families continue to need housing subsidies and other public assistance. The costs, tangible and intangible, of reduced filtering are pretty high.

This does not mean that there is no action in the Exurban housing market. Houses are bought and sold. New faces appear in the affluent suburbs. A lot of this happens because corporations like to transfer executives from one location to another. They are transferring them at the rate of 700,000 per year. Most of these mobile managers leave one Exurbia for another. *Business Week* (October 28, 1972) cited a survey showing that sixty-eight per cent of American managers in the twenty-five to forty age bracket move at least once every three years, twenty-three per cent move every two years, and eighteen per cent move annually. Long-haul transfer is a way of life at places like GE, ITT, Standard Oil of New Jersey. At IBM it became popular to remark that the initials stood for "I've Been Moved." A senior executive of an oil company says bluntly: "Moving is the life's blood of our business—it's as simple as that. . . . If a guy wants to get ahead, he expects mobility. Growth means movement."

Do managers like to move around at such a rate? For a long time top management did not worry about this very much. Then, in the mid-sixties, the question started getting asked. The answers were troublesome. Members of the academic community disapproved. The anthropologist Lionel Tiger observed that "an important consequence of the corporate commitment to moving managers around is that their wives and children are deprived of the fundamental human requirement of social continuity and personal stability; that the managers are debarred from becoming effective members of the communities in which they find themselves; and that by forcing people to adapt to the company's scheme, rather than adapting the company to the people who work in it, American business is disenchanting the sons and daughters of its own executives, and in some degree impairing the effectiveness of the executives themselves." Harry Levinson of the Harvard School of Business questioned whether "just rotating a man around provides the kind of experience he should have today."

By 1970 industry was confronting a novel form of insubordination. Executives were refusing to accept transfers. Then came the recession. Vocal resistance to transfers subsided. The moving vans began to roll again, and they have been rolling ever since.

But that doesn't mean that executives will continue to transfer at the current rate. Resentment—by wives, children, and the executives themselves—will increase. Corporations will compare the costs—tangible and intangible—of moving a manager against the supposed benefits. When the practice diminishes the exurban housing market will diminish further.

Reduction of Employment Opportunities

Everyone deplores the high rate of unemployment. Not everyone realizes what unemployment costs, but there is general acknowledgment that the figure is high.

We are constantly being reminded that, in a period of high unemployment, there are still many jobs that go begging. Some use this information as a comforting "off-the-hook" factor, saying, "The jobs are available, why don't they take them?" Others, more realistic, know that it is no use talking to an unemployed individual about a job a hundred miles from his home if that individual is unable to move.

Exclusion cuts down sharply on the mobility of the worker. When he cannot find housing near the work site, the job might as well not exist. The out-of-work person pays a price. The employer pays a price in a diminished labor pool and consequently higher payroll costs. And the public at large pays a price for the continuing rate of unemployment.

Suburban exclusionary practices reduce job opportunities in another way. To qualify for most jobs, the individual must be educated and trained. Opportunities to obtain specialized training do not abound in the inner city. Furthermore, the forced homogeneity of urban ghettos narrows expectations and impels young people to drift into the least-skilled, lowest-paying modes of employment.

The problem of unemployed or underemployed city workers is monumental. In *Underemployment in the Urban Ghetto*, Bennett Harrison cites figures showing subemployment rates ranging from 24.2 percent in Boston's Roxbury district and 34.2 percent in North Philadelphia to a staggering 47.4 percent in the slums of San Antonio (which has recently joined the ranks of America's ten largest cities). Within these areas, public money goes down the ratholes of crime, inadequate housing, and public welfare.

Ignoble as the exurbanite's indifference may be, it is at least done under the illusion that what happens there has little to do with him. He is wrong. What happens there has a lot to do with him, and with everyone outside the ghetto, if only in terms of the money it is costing.

For one thing, lack of housing for labor in suburban areas inflates the prices that the exurbanite is paying. When workers are in short supply, payroll costs go up and the costs are passed on to the consumer. A study of Long Island labor markets found that "the need to attract blue collar workers from greater distances to secure a full work force at the suburban plant makes it necessary to offer wages that are higher than in the city." Furthermore, despite these higher wage levels, "employers continue to be plagued by job vacancies and high labor turnover."

In the suburbs of Chicago, researchers found that when workers had to commute from the city to work in the suburbs, employers were compelled to pay a premium ranging from 2 percent for janitors to 13.5 percent for accountants. And a survey conducted in Bucks County, Pennsylvania, showed that when workers must travel long distances to work in the suburbs, absenteeism and erratic participation surge upward, adding to recruiting and staffing costs.

Commuting is an expensive proposition. Exurbanites who ride public transportation moan about the mounting cost and the miserable service. Those who drive must cope with rising gasoline prices, the irritations of traffic, and the burden of keeping up at least two cars.

Commuters complain about these things, but for most they are not matters that produce overwhelming anxiety. More often than not, the exurbanite's griping about his commuting trouble and expense is a form of boasting. He has *chosen* to live far away from his job; he is one of the privileged few who are in a position to undergo the vicissitudes of commuting. Seen from this viewpoint, commuting is like the rigorous discipline to which members of a prideful elite corps are subjected. (When you hear Marines griping about the obstacle course, they are most likely expressing their pride.)

But what about the "wrong-way" commuter, whose trouble and expense are far less voluntary? The low-paid worker from the city who has to get to suburbia to keep his job is also enduring the difficulties of commuting, usually in a form that proportionately is far more burdensome and far less tolerable than the load carried by his affluent counterpart.

"Right-way" commuters don't think about this. After all, the railroad tracks and the highways run in both directions. But the mass-transportation service for the "wrong-way" rider is tough; schedules accommodate those going in the other direction.

Reverse commuting carries a hidden social cost. A study by the National Committee Against Discrimination in Housing found that "present systems and facilities preclude reverse commuting for all but a few central city residents. Public transportation is almost useless for most trips to work that originate in a central city neighborhood and end at a suburban establishment."

The onus of reverse commuting falls heaviest on those least able to afford it. For example, among those who hold lower-paying jobs in Bucks County, 80 percent of the black and 61 percent of the Puerto Rican workers must commute from Philadelphia, as against 19 percent of white workers. More than 13 percent of the reverse commuters in this area earn less than $4,000 a year.

In Detroit, according to Robert Smock (*The Inner-City Worker*), 30 percent of the white and 34 percent of the black workers in the city have to travel to jobs in the suburbs.

Indeed, in some places, reverse commuting has grown to such an extent that the term "reverse" is hardly applicable. A recent survey of job patterns in Westchester County, New York, projected that soon there will be more workers traveling from New York City to jobs in the suburbs than there will be people commuting in the other direction. However, the average income of those working in the suburbs is less than half that of those who make the traditional commute into the city.

Reduced Economic Activity

Exclusivity cuts down housing availability. Lack of housing can push a region in the direction of economic stagnation.

In the New York metropolitan region, the Regional Plan Association estimates that, by 1985, "white collar and service jobs will exceed available manpower by 300,000 positions, while the blue collar labor force will exceed the blue collar jobs by about 90,000." In New Jersey, the Middlesex-Somerset-Mercer Regional Study Council looks at the difficulties that employers are running into in attracting workers, and predicts that the situation will grow worse. If prevailing patterns of employment hold up, more than 60 percent of the tricounty region will be in the under-$10,000 range, but under existing zoning regulations, there will be no housing that they can afford.

In 1972, the League of Women Voters of Bergen County, New Jersey, reported: "The International Business Machines Corporation purchased land for administrative offices and a computer facility in Franklin Lakes [a town of 7,500, about ten miles north of Paterson]. After experiencing great difficulty in relocating the first 100 of the 1,200 anticipated employees, the division's Director of Relocation asked for help in locating housing for company employees, citing the lack of new housing and the shortage of housing selling under $30,000, and the particular difficulty in finding homes for non-white employees of the division." At this time, all available land in Franklin Lakes was zoned for one-acre lots; the average price of a home was $50,000.

The president of the Quaker Oats Company declared a few years ago that the company would not locate facilities in places that did not offer open housing. "We expect the communities we locate new facilities in to offer equal opportunities comparable to those we offer in our own employment. Thus, prior to our decision to locate a major food plant in Danville, Illinois . . . we advised the city fathers that passage of an open housing ordinance would impress us as an indication of the city's intent for social progress. The ordinance passed, and two days later we approved location of a new plant in Danville."

This last quotation suggests some particularly fascinating possibilities. In many respects it is the giant corporations who are the agents of social change. They do not play this role because of an overwhelming sense of altruism; it is a function of realistic response to necessity and economic common sense. Corporations, to grow, must build new facilities; not just factories, but desirable, "clean" installations like computer centers, administrative offices, and laboratories. Many suburban communities lust after such "clean" installations as enrichment for their sickly tax bases. Executives who live in these suburban communities would welcome some relaxation of the tax burden; they would also, if possible, like to work nearer to where they live. And they want their companies to continue to prosper. But, at the same time, the zoning laws that maintain the "character of the community" in which these exurbanites live preclude any such change.

Public Service

Suburban communities are becoming increasingly strapped for the money needed to keep up the high-level amenities to which residents have become accustomed. Their citizens are less and less willing/able to pay for these services.

Low-density housing is a growing problem in providing services. For example, a first-rate hospital cannot exist in an area containing too few people to make such a facility logical. A shortage of workers for public services drives up the cost. If it is impossible for firemen, policemen, teachers, sanitation workers, clerks, maintenance men, and so forth to live in a community, it will obviously cost more for the community to obtain people—particularly capable people—to do this work.

The provision of utilities is getting to be extremely costly in Exurbia. The sparser the residential density, the more it costs to provide services. A study of Bucks County projected costs of sewer and water services for various lot sizes. Here is what was found: "Sewage costs per lot on a 20,000 square foot lot rose 54 per cent over costs for a 9,800 square foot lot; on a 40,000 square foot lot, they rose 151 per cent; and on an 80,000 square foot lot, 288 per cent. The per lot costs of providing a piped water supply for a 20,000 square foot lot were 60 per cent higher than for a 9,800 square foot lot; for a 40,000 square foot lot, 161 per cent higher; and for an 80,000 square foot lot, 302 per cent higher."

The high costs of low density can stretch the resources of suburban communities beyond their resources. Stephen Sussna, writing in *Land Economics*, points out that the Illinois Department of Community Affairs has already reported several communities that are unable to provide sanitary sewers or badly needed road repairs because of the financial burden dictated by their low-density development.

Reduced Opportunity for Savings

Poor people may not get much from those who are more fortunately situated, but they certainly receive ample quantities of what John F. Kennedy once referred to as the "ultimate luxury"— free advice. Often this advice takes the form of Benjamin Franklin–style injunctions to be thrifty.

There is no denying that if poor people save money they will not be poor anymore. This will be a boon to everyone in the country, notably the poor themselves. The trick is, how do they do it?

Traditionally, home ownership has been the major vehicle of asset accumulation for low- and moderate-income families. Equity in single-family homes accounts for almost one-half the wealth of lower-income groups and more than one-third the wealth of families in the $10,000–15,000 range. Ownership of a home not only gives people a means of accumulating equity in an orderly fashion; it provides an incentive, and it inculcates the habit of thrift that conduces to greater wealth.

But exclusionary residential patterns are making this desired end a practical impossibility. People do not become householders if they cannot buy houses. And they cannot buy houses they can't afford.

When the suburbs of a region restrict available housing to those who are already affluent, this area for enhancement of wealth and improvement of the economy is closed off, with costs that are borne by many people, including those who have already made it to Exurbia.

School Costs

When a community restricts itself to a relatively small number of people who are able to afford expensive homes, and when the community keeps out everyone else by forbidding any relaxation of zoning regulations, school costs go up. The community will either have to watch its school decline in quality, or it will have to bear an inordinate tax burden to maintain "quality education," or it will have to agree to some form of regionalized busing to somehow equalize the cost of schooling.

It might be mentioned, also, that even when a community is willing to be highly taxed to keep up a small but expensive school system, the maintenance of that system consumes resources that are in short supply in the region and the country at large.

Land Costs

The exurbanite is happy when the assessed value of his house and land go up (although he is unhappy when confronted with the tax bill). The rising price tag on what he owns makes him a man of even greater affluence; or it does, at least, until he tries to sell the place.

However, there is the future to think of, and a very near future at that. When exclusionary practices impose large-lot development, housing availability becomes scarce throughout the region. This causes the price of land for other uses to rise (and it can, eventually, actually cause the value of the large lot to fall).

In the short run, affluent suburbanites may be paying less than their "fair market share," at the expense of lower-income people who must compete for houses that are made scarce by the closing off of expansion in the suburbs. In the long run, this can lead to real land shortages. Right now, we do not often include land among those precious resources about which we worry, but continued exurban exclusivity can change this situation for the worse.

Transportation Costs

Low density increases transportation costs. It places near-exclusive emphasis on the automobile. Families must travel considerable distances to work, play, and shop. A second car becomes a practical "must." The development of mass transit is restricted in the region because the suburbanite who is compelled to drive will not support it.

And then, of course, there is the pollution that goes hand in hand with excessive reliance on passenger automobiles. The cost of transportation in low-density suburbs is borne primarily by suburbanites; pollution affects everyone in the region.

Lack of Regional Development

Some of the severest costs of exclusivity can be measured in terms of what does not happen. When multifamily homes are banned—and when large lots must be used for building—only the wealthiest families can afford to live in the community. Common use of resources is cut to a minimum. Water pipes, utility lines, and sewer systems are strung out for many extra miles; if people were housed in higher density patterns, the same installations could serve many more families. Long stretches of road must be built and maintained for the thousands of cars needed to move suburbanites around; the sparsity of habitation precludes mass transit, which would move more people with greater economy. Land is underutilized. Economies in the expenditure of heating oil are not implemented.

There are diseconomies in Exurbia that are less measurable, but no less significant. The sequestered community loses touch with the rest of the world. Its children grow and learn in an artificial atmosphere. At the same time, the inevitable decrease in the tax base of the inner city reduces the opportunity for children who grow up in these areas to receive first-rate education.

Exclusivity goes hand in hand with racial segregation. Proponents of the status quo maintain that any segregation is caused by financial, not racial, factors. The effect, nevertheless, is racial separation. A growing intermingling of Americans of all classes, creeds, and colors does not happen as long as the barriers remain.

Another thing that does not happen is the kind of balancing of population that eliminates sharp changes in circumstances and needs. For example, as Exurbia and its children grow older, modern school buildings must be closed because they are no longer needed. A more balanced population would eliminate this problem. When population groups are isolated and homogeneous, swings in the magnitude of differing needs tend to be extreme, and the means used to cope with them are thoroughly uneconomical.

And then there is the glaring lack of a regional mustering of energy, ingenuity, and cooperation to solve current problems and to prepare the way for a healthy future. This may be the greatest diseconomy of all.

The situation would not be so bad if only one or two communities in a metropolitan region practiced exclusionary zoning. But in many areas this policy is not the exception but the norm. Not long ago, a study conducted for the state of New Jersey of eight representative counties disclosed that 82 percent of the usable land is zoned for plots of more than one-half acre, and 60 percent for one acre or more, while only 8 percent is presently available for multifamily housing.

Exurbia is expensive, and not just for the exurbanite. Everyone who lives in a region is paying part of the cost of exurbanization. And in terms of social costs and high usage of scarce resources, the entire population is paying for the continuation of exclusive enclaves.

As the costs increase—and they will—and as the perception of them spreads, the already tenuous grasp that the exurbanites have on their position will become even weaker. When a movement for change combines social fervor, class antagonism, and economic common sense, it is hard to withstand.

20

Where Will the Flowers Bloom Tomorrow?

The "flower children" of the 1960s were largely the sons and daughters of Exurbia. They were the kids who dropped acid and dropped out. They fled their comfortable environs for the purportedly innocent squalor of Haight-Ashbury and the supposedly idyllic togetherness of the communes. They made pot commonplace. They burned the campuses and fought the Guardsmen. They made evasion of military service an honorable cause.

The movement never really caught on with the children of the lower middle class and the poor. The rebelling youngsters came into the cities from the suburbs. They were not joined by the city youngsters, who tended to look upon the flower children as rich snobs who had dropped in on a slumming trip.

Since so many of the young rebels a few years ago grew up in Exurbia, it may be useful to examine the role and influence of the Exurban Dream in what happened to its kids—and, more importantly, in what will happen to them in the years to come.

The leading philosophical voice of the extreme exponents of the youth revolution was Herbert Marcuse (emphatically not a youth). Among Marcuse's contributions was his assurance to the young that it was right and proper for them to refer to their fathers as "mother-fuckers," inasmuch as these individuals had committed (in some way) the archetypical incestuous crime. However, Marcuse's inspiring exhortations were essentially negative. He urged the destruction of the establishment, reasoning that only in the ensuing chaos could the millennial new order grow. In the end, nobody was talking like Marcuse anymore, including Marcuse himself, who turned peevishly on his acolytes, calling them ignorant and ill-mannered agitators.

It remained for another academician to sum up the youth experience of that tumultuous decade in its most positive and grandiose terms. In *The Greening of America*, Charles Reich—a law professor at Yale—gave shape to campus disorders, dropping out, dope, dirt, and rebellion in the form of a proclamation that America was on the threshold of a new revolution that would reclaim society from its encasement in "metal and plastic and sterile stone" and make life worth living again.

The Greening of America was bought and debated—probably more than it was actually read. The author had chosen a title that hinted, however vaguely, of peace, solace, and pantheistic optimism. He had, moreover, done what all aspiring authors try to do: He had successfully encapsulated his concept under a catchy handle— Consciousness III. What was happening to young people was Consciousness III, and for a while no cocktail party in the exurban archipelago was official unless that term threaded its way through the drone of conversation.

Consciousness III is, as Reich sees it, the successor to Consciousness II, which emphasized laws, the state, technology, manufactured goods—*things*—and gave rise to the corporate state. (Consciousness II leads to conformity and regimentation—for example, under its aegis, "School is intensely concerned with training students to stop thinking and start obeying.") Consciousness III breaks out of this rigid mold; it says, "I'm glad I'm me." It starts with self. "In contrast to Consciousness II, which accepts society, the public interest, and institutions as the primary reality, III declares that the individual self is the only true reality." (In this respect, Consciousness III has a certain ring of Ayn Rand's philosophy of selfishness, celebrated in *Atlas Shrugged*. Somehow the new concept, though it "returns to the earlier America: 'Myself I sing,'" is assumed to give human beings unprecedented sensitivity and regard for each other.) Consciousness III is *liberation*.

Reich says: "Consciousness III rejects the whole concept of excellence and comparative merit that is so central to Consciousness II. III refuses to evaluate people by general standards, it refuses to classify people, or analyze them. Each person has his own individuality, not to be compared to that of anybody else. Someone may be a brilliant thinker, but he is not 'better' at thinking than anyone else, he simply possesses his own excellence. A person who thinks very poorly is still excellent in his own way." One might conclude from this that the adherents of the new philosophy would be consummately tolerant of others, including their parents; the evidence does not seem to support such a conclusion.

Nevertheless, another important aspect of the new culture, as described in Reich's book, is the idea of "community among people." It rests on two concepts: "respect for the uniqueness of each individual and the idea expressed by the word 'together.' "

This is Consciousness III: the rejection of the supremacy of the established order, the apotheosis of self, the extirpation of merit, and the concept of community. It is Consciousness III, in Reich's formulation, that will revolutionize society. "We are only beginning to realize the incredible vastness of the changes that are coming." The central fact of the movement is its "assertion of the power to *choose* a way of life." No more "machine slavery," relegating people to the roles of automatons in a mechanical world.

Reich recognizes that Consciousness III is, at this writing, still a youth movement. But he does not see it as temporary. The observation of St. Paul to the Corinthians, "When I was a child, I spake as a child. . . . When I became a man, I put away childish things," does not pertain to Consciousness III. It will flourish; it will *Green America.*

There was, at the time, little disagreement with Reich's comment: "The new generation insists upon being open to all experience." In retrospect it might not appear that *all* experience was actually included—just new ones, experiences that departed from a way of life that had been familiar from childhood. Reich observes and remarks the tendency of young people today to prolong the period of youth, and to keep all options open. He does not concur with the feelings of some that commitment to Consciousness III resulted in the opposite effect, that of closing out options, significantly those options relating to working at jobs in industry. This is because young people "refuse to play a role while at work that forces them into a different personality than is actually theirs." They "will not be a 'nigger' while on the job."

Consciousness III does not call for instant dismantling of the system. Its essence lies in participation without commitment. "If a person is working within an institution but does not share the institution's goals, and does not desire to rise in the hierarchy, if his interest is not in the affairs of the institution itself but in his own work, he unexpectedly has a great deal of freedom." This process of "de-institutionalization" will be followed by that of "de-alienation: making the work meaningful to and satisfying to the worker himself."

The new consciousness, though now a youth movement, will spread, says Reich hopefully. "The values we describe must be accepted democratically by a whole people, as our Bill of Rights was once accepted." What is important is the concept. The corporate state sampled all values and ignored all laws; a "true human community" is based on respect for each individual's uniqueness and privacy. It will burgeon, and it will lead to the Greening of America.

Charles Reich lavished prodigies of creativity and applied logic on the concept of Consciousness III. Where is it today?

A headline in the business section of *The New York Times*, January 4, 1976, reads: A "REALISTIC GENERATION" OF YOUTH TURNS TO BUSINESS. The story reported what many sources have been saying: Young people are showing a renewed and lively interest in "going into business." The MBA degree has acquired new luster; applications for admission to the business schools at Columbia and NYU have risen by 25 percent, mirroring developments in other universities throughout the country. Dean Boris Yavutz of Columbia's Graduate School of Business says, "Young people have begun to realize that not all jobs in business involve money-grubbing, money-crunching work."

A candidate for an MBA agrees. "In undergraduate school I felt our economic structure was a contradiction to human life. What I conceived of as business values could not coexist with my studies of humanities. I was ignorant of economics. I still want to change things, but the best way to do that is from the inside out. It's always a temptation to let your values be compromised. . . . But in business, if you can keep your values and vision intact until you reach the top, you can affect other people's lives enormously."

Another student puts it more bluntly. "The 60's thing has ended. Changing the community is more difficult than students thought. Now they want some negotiable skills to give them more clout. Young people want jobs, and students are interested in anything that looks safe." The recognition of the paramount importance of getting a job, rather than reforming the system, is widespread. "In this economy I can't pick and choose. It's all in the hands of the employer."

What happened to Consciousness III? Optimistic proponents

might comfort themselves with the notion that it is as viable as ever, that these kids are as keenly attuned as before to the music of the spheres, but that they are merely shelving the rhetoric. They will, in this view, join the ranks of the establishment as quiet toilers in the cause, but they will constitute a swelling Fifth Column that will, one day, accomplish the Greening of America in a bloodless revolution.

Others, more cynical, say that the young are simply learning the lesson that all learn from life. It was all very well to demonstrate and riot and drop out for a while, but, in the crunch of a tight economy, they are now realizing that one needs money to live comfortably. Kids want to live comfortably, and they are now doing what is necessary—joining the establishment—to get money. No doubt there is a lot to be said for this view. An episode in the athletic world may serve as an analogy. Early in 1976, the British heavyweight Joe Bugner announced his retirement from boxing. Bugner explained that he had once had boundless love for the sport, but all of his love had dissipated in his bout with Muhammad Ali. We might conclude that there is nothing more likely to dispel one's love for the "sport" of boxing than fifteen rounds with Muhammad Ali. In the same vein, we might speculate that there is nothing more likely to reverse one's bias against material things than an enforced spell of poverty.

There is another way to look at the present movement of young people back into the mainstream of industry. This view takes into account the fact that the youthful rebels of the 1960s were, to a considerable extent, children who had grown up within Exurbia.

The simple view of the youthful rebellion against the system is that it was essentially negative in character, a rejection of what had been experienced rather than a positive affirmation of a new way of life. The ingenious arguments of Reich and others do not render this opinion untrue.

What were the kids of the suburbs rebelling against? It is convenient to answer, "The system," with the system comprising the corporate state, the multinational company, the pervasiveness of advertising, the idea of planned obsolescence, the grip of conformity, the dog-eat-dog nature of the corporate jungle, and all of the other excrescences commonly attributed to the capitalist system. But here we must enter a caveat; it is reasonable to say that these young people were rebelling against a system, yes, but a system as they saw it. It was the perception of the establishment and its effects that did so much to turn kids off.

And in what did this perception consist? The exurban child knows that he is growing up in a protected environment. He watches television; he hears about the cities. He is aware that his community is exclusive, and that there are angry voices raised against this exclusivity. When the suburban student goes to school with a poor kid, it is—lamentably—often true that they will not become bosom friends. But the idea of exclusion becomes very real to the suburban child, and it has a compelling effect.

The youngster in the affluent enclave takes for granted the amenities of suburban living; after all, what does he have to compare it with? But the knowledge of a whole other world out there excites his curiosity, his sympathy, and ultimately his resentment of the idea of exclusion.

The suburban youngster knows that the particulars of his life are based on money and success. He may not be able to discourse about these matters in learned terms, but he realizes that the house and the nice grounds are bound up, usually, with what his father does.

And what does his father do?

He goes away in the morning with a briefcase to do something of which the utility—let alone the benefit to society—is not clear. He comes home at night—if he comes home—with the same briefcase. He worries about his job. Maybe he drinks too much. Around the house he is often tired. When he talks about his work, he does not talk about things made or deeds done, but about trips planned and made, lunches eaten, conversations conversed, and backs stabbed.

This is the closest that the suburban child comes to firsthand knowledge of what work in the corporate society is all about. It is not surprising that he does not find it an enchanting prospect.

In school the kid from Exurbia feels pressure. He is targeted for college—for a "good" school, his parents hope. His progress often seems to be measured in terms of preparation for college boards rather than objective learning or accommodation to real life.

The suburban youngster does not really have a chance to form disinterested judgments on the favored atmosphere in which he grows, any more than a fish can make objective judgments about the water he has always swum in. But, unlike the fish, the child may well come to feel that there is something wrong with the whole scene. The stresses of life in his enclave are communicated to him; they are impressed on his system. Reich is correct in that today's young people want to keep their options open. They are aware that there must be alternatives to the lives their parents are living, and they want to be able to explore them.

But this, as we are finding out, does not mean that the youngster will automatically reject the possibility of working in the corporate society—of which exurban living is the mark of accomplishment. On the contrary, he wants this option, and he is tending to choose it.

To live one's own life, to enjoy the things one wants to enjoy, to savor a variety of experiences—these seem to be things that young people want. You do not get to do those things if you are a revolutionary. The revolutionary system-changer may give himself over to the toil and hardship of dedicated antisystem activity so that those who come after him will enjoy a free and happier life, but he soon finds that his dedication closes off most avenues of conventional happiness for himself. By and large, the sons and daughters of Exurbia are not all that dedicated. They want more freedom, and they want to be able to fulfill themselves in a greater variety of ways. If the choice lies between rigid dedication to a cause and the finding of a good life within the system, the latter will inevitably be the path most heavily traveled.

And, to a considerable extent, this is the choice. For one thing, there is the matter of material goods. Suburban children—who enjoy them—have come to demean them. The youngster from the inner city is not nearly so quick to proclaim his contempt for *things.* Clothes, records, tapes, stereos, cars—these are things, the products of the corporate society. And the rising generation, though many older people deplore its economic ignorance, certainly senses that these things are available because they are products made to be sold in the marketplace for a profit. If nobody works, then there are no products.

Our children also come to the realization that it is not just the kind of suburban existence that their parents live that takes money. In this society, most choices are related in some way or other to money. The flowers of the new existence grow out of the dunghill of commerce.

Reich declares that "the great and urgent need of these times is transcendence. To survive, to regain power over our own lives, we must transcend the machine." This does not mean destroying the machine, or shunning its products. To the extent that the machine represents work, transcendence is intimately bound up with work. The attainment of the freedom to soar into the empyrean depends on a lot of effort. Some of the highest cultures in civilized history were built on slavery.

Today's kids have more sense about all this than we give them credit for. They understand that the machine, and things, and systems can offer amenities leading to greater enjoyment of life. They understand also, that one need not be enslaved by these entities. They do not expect to live their self-fulfilled lives on the basis of what other people produce. They are willing to be numbered among the producers.

It is not really surprising that the flower children of yesterday are the MBA candidates of today. Their willingness to obtain the requirements for entry into the commercial world is not—as some exurban parents would like to think—a stamp of approval for the whole package. It simply represents a recognition of reality. By making himself able to get and hold a job that pays well, the youngster is keeping his options open. He is staking his claim to a piece of territory in the real world. How fully he mines it, and what he does with the proceeds, is up to him. He has not opted out of society; he wants to be able to make a choice. And he knows that dropping out and spending two years doing nothing but contemplating the indecipherable utterances of a mini-guru closes off his options.

But this does not mean that the junior exurbanite is willing to sell his soul to the job in the way that he feels his father did. When Charles Reich talks about de-institutionalizing work through remaining aloof from the conventional goals, he is accurately describing the attitude that these young people will bring to the job. They want to work for money. They want to do their work well. And then they want to be let alone. They will not sell to the employer the "whole man" (or woman). They are utterly unwilling to eat, sleep, and breathe the job. And they are not always intent on rising to the position of chairman of the board.

The overlords of industry—including, of course, the exurban sires of these new, "cool," recruits to the world of work—will do well to take the new spirit into their calculations. The employer who continues to insist on hiring only those who are willing to exalt the job above all else will be closing himself off from a vast reservoir of talent. Employers who accommodate themselves to the attitude of the young will have to make some changes in their thinking. At present, for example, the emphasis in management is not so much on the way a man does his present job as on the qualities of "drive," "ambition," and so forth that he shows in pushing toward the job next highest on the ladder. When a man shows some diminution of that upward thrust, he's marked as through, no matter how well he may be doing what he does now.

Kids from the suburbs have seen what the up-or-out concept has done to their fathers (and mothers, and themselves). Many of them know what it is like to be part of the baggage of a corporate nomad, moving from exurb to exurb at the behest of a giant employer. They don't want to live their lives that way. When business changes its thinking to allow for this attitude, it may well discover that enterprise is run better than before. The new worker who gets satisfaction from what he does, but who will not engage in corporate jungle-fighting to get a bigger job, is apt to be a more valuable asset than the constant upward striver.

Reich's second step is "de-alienation." This involves making work meaningful and satisfying to the worker himself. Here Reich is echoing the thoughts of a long line of observers of the work scene, including Abraham Maslow. Maslow said in 1954 that there was a hierarchy of human needs, with physiological needs—food, shelter, and so forth—at the lowest level. The hierarchy rises through the levels of Safety, Social Needs (love, affection, the need to belong), Esteem, and Self-actualization. His contention was that the job must afford the worker a chance to satisfy not just the lowest and most basic needs but the higher ones as well. Fifty years ago Elton Mayo of Harvard was saying similar things.

So the idea that the job must offer satisfaction beyond the paycheck is not a new one. It has, however, been honored more in the breach than the observance. We hear, now and then, of attempts at what is now called "job enrichment," but there are always considerations that take precedence over giving work more of a self-fulfilling quality.

Now there is a whole generation of young people who have seen the results of well-paid work that does not offer the worker much else in the way of satisfaction. They will have none of it. As they move into industry, their influence is likely to give new impetus to the concept of jobs that satisfy, not just pay. They will respect work as necessary. Since it is necessary, they will try to shape it in a way that offers them maximum fulfillment. They will acknowledge that one must work to get money because money buys the means of living a good life, but they will be less inclined than their parents to commit themselves to a constant upward spiral of achievement that ultimately takes precedence over all other considerations. They will not divest themselves of the need for status, but their ideas of what constitutes status, and their ways of displaying it, will be different.

These young people seem to be adopting a form of Kierkegaard's idea that man must live dually, in time and in eternity. They will try to find satisfactions within the system while making contributions to the system. At the same time, their souls are their own. Moreover, they will make changes in the system as they see it, if only to eliminate its most destructive features.

So, more and more, the young people who grew up in Exurbia will turn their backs on revolution and work in the corporate society. Where will they live? With regard to many, the answer is plain. They will live in what is now Exurbia.

First, it is a pleasant place to live. The new generation likes quiet, grass, trees. Its members have, if anything, a greater regard for nature than their parents, and a deep desire and need to enjoy its bounty and preserve its character.

The need for status has not been flushed out of human genes in Lysenko-like fashion by the upheaval that has taken place in one generation. Status remains desirable, and so does the desire to make a good home and environment for one's own children. These youngsters may not like many aspects of what their elders have done with Exurbia, but this does not mean that they reject it as a prize not worth winning.

Then—and this is perhaps the most powerful reason—these children grew up in Exurbia. There is something in most of us that calls us to the place—or the kind of place—we lived in as children.

True, Exurbia's children have been leaving Exurbia. But what choice have they had? Their options have been narrow. One has been to continue to live with their parents well into young adulthood. A lot of suburban youngsters are doing this. It is far from an ideal situation. The strains upon the household grow, often past the point of tolerance. Exurban parents must maintain the attitude of loving their children and wanting them around, but the facade begins to crack. The parents have their own problems. To mention just one factor, Harry Levinson, the interpreter of executive stress, has commented on the tendency of the aging executive to hate the young. This hatred is all too often turned upon the most obvious and available representatives of youth, his own sons and daughters who continue to eat his bread and live under his roof. The fall-out from such a situation is frequently palpable in the psychiatrist's office or the police court.

Where else can the kids go and still remain in the environs in which they grew? They cannot afford $50,000 and up to buy a house. There are no apartments for them to move into. Like as not, regulations prohibit their parents from putting additions on the house that would provide separate living quarters, even if this were a desirable course. Some youngsters share houses with friends. Others move into rooms in the community, whether or not such accommodations are sanctioned by law.

These are not permanent solutions to the question of how young people who have grown up in the suburbs can live in the same—or similar—communities as adults. The answer will come as Exurbia becomes Semiurbia. The barriers will be breached. The apartments and the smaller houses on smaller lots will come in. New and different kinds of people will move in, younger people, poorer people, people with diverse backgrounds. Prominent among the new inhabitants of the previously exclusive and homogeneous exurbs will be the sons and daughters of the Exurban Dream. They will come with a dream, but with a difference.

These young people will not necessarily keep the torch of youthful conscience burning bright as they grow into middle age. Many of them will, alas, become as self-concerned as their elders were, and will wish to blot out the concerns of the outside world to a comparable degree. But a lot of them will still wish to make a greater contribution to the society at large than their parents did, and even those who don't will be unable to close off the realities of life. It will be impossible; life will be next door.

When the young people of the former exurbs are working in the system and living in its bedroom environs, there is apt to be far more recognition of regional responsibility than one sees now in Exurbia. This is not to say that today's mature exurbanite is incapable of changing and acclimating himself to a more heterogeneous community. He can; he will have to. But his children will make an even greater contribution.

It is, to a considerable degree, these offspring of Exurbia who will make the new semiurbs work. They will accept the proposition that one does not have to own title to nature and keep undesirables away from it to enjoy it. They will develop a pride of community that will be a positive, rather than a negative, pride. And the community with which they are concerned will be a broader entity than today's Exurbia.

We are not talking here of the Apocalypse; we are talking of change, growth, and adjustment. What is going to happen in the suburbs will not be the Greening of America, in the sense that that term is usually understood. Rather it is the *browning* of America—a cultivation of a richer and more variegated soil out of which a better society can grow.

21

The Coming of Semiurbia

Exurbia is finished.

It can no longer exist as an entity conveniently close to, but utterly aloof from, the city. The isolated exurban community of today will become part of the larger regional community of tomorrow. The process is already in motion.

Exurbia will become *Semiurbia.*

How will exurbanites cope?

The strategies are limited. Some will look for a substitute Exurbia, a community that comes as close as possible to providing the exclusivity, status, and amenities of the old setup.

Others will "stonewall" it. They will dig in and try to ignore what is happening around them, fighting to the last to preserve every shred of what they had.

Still others will take the "evolutionary" strategy. They will accept the fact of Semiurbia—and try to make it work.

For the group seeking a substitute, the condominium approach will become an attractive alternative.

A condominium is a multiple-dwelling complex in which the resident enjoys full ownership of the unit in which he lives, and joint ownership of the common ground. A condominium may be a high-rise building or a garden or "town house" arrangement. You buy your condominium—they can range from $15,000 to upwards of $200,000—and then you pay regular charges for maintenance.

Actually the idea of condominiums as places to live is very old. There were condominiums in ancient Rome. (The word is from the Latin, meaning joint domain.) Rome had a housing crisis like the cities of today, and condominiums were an answer for those who could afford them. The custom continued through the Middle Ages but fell into disuse when walled cities became passé. Condominiums were revived in Europe in the twentieth century, spread to Great Britain and Latin America, and then, in mid-century, hit the American real-estate scene with a bang. The (then) Territory of Puerto Rico was the first to legalize the condominium in the United States. The new rage spread rapidly. In 1961, Congress amended the National Housing Act to extend government mortgage insurance to this kind of housing. By 1968, every state had passed laws making it easier to build or buy condominiums.

The thrust behind the movement is not difficult to discern. We are becoming a nation of multiple-dwellers. Impelled by the realities of money, the increasing shortage of space, and the mounting difficulties of keeping up a home, Americans are turning to the condominium as a way of life. Another factor in the popularity of the concept is that the country is getting older. Older people do not wish to cope with the sometimes dubious joys of owning a home. The condominium seems to offer equity and various living amenities without overcrowding or the necessity to mow the lawn. Furthermore, the nature of the condominium leads to homogeneity; the prospective purchaser can at least think that he will be with the sort of people he will enjoy, and share with them the kind of surroundings he likes.

In 1960, three-quarters of Americans lived in single-family houses. By 1970, the number living in multiunit dwellings had risen to one-third. Ruth Rejnis (*Everything Tenants Need to Know to Get Their Money's Worth*) remarked on the fact that in 1973 there were 797,000 new apartment starts, as against 325,000 in 1966. The condominium is an inevitable development because it seems to promise the best of both the apartment and single-family house worlds.

A condominium can be far more than a place to live. It is a way of life. For example, at On Top of the World, a three-thousand-member establishment near Tampa, Florida, residents may choose among such activities as swimming in the pool, shuffleboard, the theater, riding the private transportation system, daily recreation schedules, and adult education courses from parapsychology to creative writing.

Your dyed-in-the-wool exurbanite turns up his nose at condominiums. Sometimes, in despair (feigned or real) over taxes, expenses, and house troubles, he may contemplate the possibilities of moving into such a milieu. But there are problems. Selling the house may mean taking a bad tax beating, and there may not be anybody to buy it. Moreover, the exurbanite may feel that his house and mortgage are among the best things he has going for him. Inflation is a daily irritant, but he has a real stake in inflation if he's been a householder for the right length of time. His property has zoomed in value, at least book value, and his relatively low-interest mortgage is probably unmatchable.

But beyond the practicalities, the confirmed exurbanite wants to own his own house and piece of ground, and he will continue to fight to maintain the "character of the town," meaning to keep out those who are different in background, occupation, ethnicity, size of income, and general outlook on life.

The fact is that the exurbanite is living, in effect, in one great big condominium. He owns his own "unit," a house on one or two acres. He has a common stake in the rest of the community. He uses his influence, in conjunction with like-minded neighbors, to see that the community furnishes him with wide-ranging recreational opportunities: golf courses, tennis courts, open-air drama and music, a mooring for his boat. His "community-condominium" offers expensive education for his children. And, above all, he can keep control over the kinds of people who will be his neighbors in the community.

He enjoys the simulacrum of rusticity. The shops and business establishments are obliged to conform to aesthetic standards that impose a facsimile of old-fashionedness. He can drive through town and look at a lot of open spaces, woods, beaches, or lawns. And he reaps the benefit of this pleasant uniformity without having to pay to control it. He knows that the man who happens to own six acres in a part of town five miles away cannot offend his sensibilities by putting up apartments on the land, or indeed by building more than three houses on it.

So, in a very real sense, the exurbanite is enjoying the benefits of condominium living without enduring the disadvantages. He does this by exercising what he has come to think of as his inalienable right, the right to zone out what he does not desire.

One course for Exurbia is to create the illusion of rural simplicity through lavish applications of money. This involves what we might call the "Hurley's" approach.

For years there was an incongruity in midtown Manhattan. In the early 1930s, the great Rockefeller Center complex had been built in the upper Forties and low Fifties, between Fifth and Sixth avenues.

But, at Forty-ninth and Sixth, one old four-story building huddled defiantly among its towering modern neighbors. In 1930, the partners who owned this structure successfully fought off the massive powers behind the huge development, so the sixty-five-story RCA Building had to be erected around it.

In the ground floor of this old building there was a bar that had been there ever since the building went up in 1870. This establishment—called Hurley's—had long been a hangout for newspapermen. When Rockefeller Center soared up around it, Hurley's became a favorite haunt of the radio and television people and high-powered communicators who worked near it.

But the lease by which Hurley's clung to life was a finite thing. Rockefeller Center owned the ground underneath it and the building around it. In 1975, the lease ran out. Rockefeller Center refused to renew it. The building was leased to a new tenant, David Wolf.

What would Mr. Wolf do with the place? Demolish it? Of course not; that would be doing violence to the decades of cherished tradition that invested Hurley's. Well, then, would Mr. Wolf let the place stay the way it was? Wrong again! What is the sense of leasing a fine old establishment and leaving it just the way it was?

The new tenant started to completely gut the four-story structure in order to effect a complete interior and exterior renovation at a cost of $600,000. The purpose of all this was to create "a real old-fashioned nineteenth-century tavern of wood and copper, with everything but the sawdust." Among other features, old-fashioned gas lamps were to be installed around the exterior of the building.

Some few traditionalists will whine, but the new-old Hurley's is destined to be a great success. Most people prefer fake-old to real-old. It works better; the modern amenities embedded in the atmosphere are far more to the taste of most of us than the truly old-fashioned. This is the Disneyworld approach. Perhaps we will see a Disneyworld approach to supercondominium living.

Here's how the Disneyworld approach can work.

Zoning will be broken. The apartments will come in. The Westporter, going downtown on a Saturday morning to buy the newest miracle fertilizer in his "old-fashioned" hardware store, will find congeries of black kids lounging in the tiny park next to the library. They will talk loudly; they will engage in horseplay and shove each other around; they will laugh a lot. Now, in all this they will act no differently from the white kids who hang around there now, but they will *look* different. The commuter, skilled by long practice at whipping his GT into a just-vacated parking space, will find himself beaten out by a nondescript blue-collar type whose 1969 Plymouth has fenders that barely cling to the rusted body. The commuter's wife, beginning her excursion through the supermarket in tennis clothes, will encounter people who are strange to her eye. These people will come in all shapes and sizes and colors; they will not conform to the trim, tanned look that has been the norm. They will buy the cheaper cuts and argue with the butcher about them. The commuter's son will get into a fight at school; the opponent, a black kid, will bring to the encounter a street-wise efficiency that lies outside the exurban experience.

This is certainly a "change in the character of the community." The exurbanite will not want to live there anymore; it will have been ruined for him. But where can he go?

He can try to move farther out, to some community that is as yet "unspoiled." This will give him more aggravation and a much longer commute. Furthermore his new community will not remain "unspoiled" for long. The citification of the towns radiating outward from the city will be as inexorable a process as the development of forests, where the aspens grow first, are replaced by spruce and fir, and finally give way to the oaks, maples, and beeches.

Flight is not the answer. The exurbanite will have to find a secure enclave in which to enjoy the atmosphere that he was looking for in a plush suburb. In this enclave he will want to be sure that he will be with people like himself, yet at the same time he will wish to be given a sense of living in the real world.

Drawing on the lessons of Disneyland and the metamorphosis of Hurley's bar into "a real old-fashioned nineteenth-century tavern," we can begin to see the outlines of this new haven for the harried achiever.

It will be a condominium, although it will not call itself that. It will be expensive and exclusive. It will be planned and artificial, but the best artifice that money can buy will be devoted to giving the place an unplanned, natural look and feel. And, indeed, it will cater to the exurbanite's real needs (which he does not always express) better than the current exurban archipelago has ever done.

Let us consider, then, such an enclave. It will be open by the end of the century. Call it WestportWorld.

WestportWorld is a multiple-dwelling complex that is camouflaged as a single-family community. Its land-use density is much higher than that which existed in the Westport of old, but the casual onlooker will not be able to discern this right away. There will be some single-family houses, some "town houses" (two- and three-story attached houses), and some low-rise apartments. The dwellings are clustered, yet screened by trees and bushes. There is open space and recreational space. And there are institutional, service, and commercial areas.

Everything conforms to an aesthetic approach that goes to great lengths to give WestportWorld a feeling of unstudied simplicity, age, and rusticity—although, of course, everything within the complex is brand new.

The rough layout of WestportWorld is in concentric circles. (Dante would have no trouble recognizing the plan.) At the center, on the highest ground, are the single-family houses. There is plenty of space around these clustered dwellings. There are trees, wooded areas, streams, even small waterfalls. The terrain is uneven, graded to resemble the rocky ridges that dominate the area in which old Westport stood.

The houses at the center of WestportWorld are the most expensive, perhaps $300,000 and up. Here is where the greatest achievers live—the high-powered lawyers, surgeons, and psychiatrists; the presidents and chairmen of the board; the "celebrities."

Grouped around the center are the town houses. These attached units boast practically all of the luxuries of those in the very center; there is just a bit less space, although one would be hard put to figure it out. Here are the exurbanites who have not quite reached the top—the executive vice-presidents.

Radiating farther out from the center are the garden apartments—not so posh as those more toward the middle, but still extremely desirable. And then, in satellites clustered around the main residential complex, there are certain other dwelling areas. Here, in one satellite grouping, is where the elderly live, in single-story apartment houses, among gently graded lawns that make it easy to get around. In another satellite we find the "young people's housing." This is where the grown and growing children of the exurbanite family can live, short- or long-term, usually in one-room apartments.

Strategically placed, we will find the stores, the lake, the golf course, the tennis courts, the country club, the restaurants, the nightclubs, the clinic, the professional offices, the community center, and the schools.

Oh, yes; WestportWorld has schools, private schools. Here the children of Exurbia can learn the way their parents want them to learn. The school system is not an "alternative" system—that is to say, it does not offer a choice between "traditional" and "progressive" education. The exurbanite who comes to WestportWorld is sick of the whole business about educational ideologies. He wants schools that do not give him headaches, that teach the kids what their parents learned, that put a damper on rebellion, that exert enough (but not too much) discipline, and that turn out students who can get into prestigious universities.

WestportWorld is not a formal political unit. However, within its confines the resident can find a wide variety of quasi-political and community-action forums with which he may get involved if he wishes. He, or she, can attend meetings until the eyes glaze over, mount campaigns, engage in polemics, do good works, and become happily immersed in intrigue.

One of the seductive aspects of life in WestportWorld is the designation of specific parts of the community for older people and for young people. The exurbanite can find a place for his aged mother—whom he of course loves dearly, and to whom he feels a great duty—without the inconvenience of having her living in his own abode. When his kids are old enough, he can feel that they have the option of living nearby without being underfoot all the time. The kids may not avail themselves of that option, but it is there. The existence of the specialized satellite complexes eases the resident's burden of guilt and makes his life happier and less complicated. He does not even have to admit to himself that he has been driven to distraction by his old parents, and was growing to hate his son. He finds an unadvertised blessing (but one that has by no means been overlooked by the canny planners of WestportWorld) in the limitation on his immediate space, which gives him the rationale for placing troublesome dear ones at a certain distance.

There is social life within WestportWorld, plenty of it, all anybody could want. Those who wish to swing sexually, or try to, have ample opportunity to do so. There are always cocktails, dinners, theater.

Naturally, there are the problems that beset the old Westporters. Some people lose out; they can't afford WestportWorld anymore;

they have to leave. Other people can't afford it, but stay anyway. There is an unabated level of strain and tension, a continuing quota of crackups. Those who get into emotional trouble are ministered to by on-site analysts, psychiatrists, and counselors. This is a thriving industry in WestportWorld; its practitioners live in the center, up on the hill.

Of course, WestportWorld is resented. There are many on the outside who revile its denizens, who accuse them of callousness, who deplore them as social ciphers. But the WestportWorlders don't care. They have what they always wanted out of Exurbia, and they have it even better than they ever had it in the real Exurbia. And best of all, nobody can come and take it away from them. It's no longer the situation of years ago in old Westport, when malcontents whined about the townspeople monopolizing the beauties of nature and preventing people from making use of their own property as they saw fit and ignoring the "needs of the region." WestportWorld is private property. Its wonders and beauties are artificial; no one can say that those who enjoy them have preempted the pleasures that God is said to have placed on earth for the enjoyment of all. WestportWorld costs plenty, but then the really good things in life do cost plenty. You have to work to make it to WestportWorld. You have to succeed. But when you get to WestportWorld, you know you have arrived. And you don't have to worry about *them.*

It goes without saying that WestportWorld is fenced, guarded, and patrolled by a private elite force.

WestportWorld is the affluent commune that will beckon the exurbanite when urbanization at last drives him out of his happy home. Of course, not every inhabitant of the endangered suburbs will go the WestportWorld route. Some will be unable to afford it. Others will not want it. There will be those who, seeing that the city is coming to them, will figure that they may as well go to the city. There will be a great many who will stay where they have been living, in spite of "creeping urbanization," unfrightened by the apartments and the influx of "them," undismayed by more people on the sidewalks, more cars in the lot, and more bodies per square mile. They will stay, but they will no longer be exurbanites.

And for many, that will be a relief. They will meet different kinds of people than they ever met before. There will be a lot more variety in the life of the former exurbanite who accommodates himself to the coming of the hordes. He will discover that many of the Goths and

Huns who enter the gates of civilization bring with them their own brand of civilization and their own varieties of sensibility.

When the zoning barrier breaks, those who have lived behind it will face some interesting choices. In the process of making these choices they will learn about themselves. They will find out what they really consider to be important. As long as Exurbia holds out, it is quite possible for the individual to say he lives there because he loves nature and is a vigorous partisan of green things and fresh air— when all the while what really keeps him there is status and exclusivity. When the individual has to make a choice, he must, to some degree, think about himself and his ideas of what life ought to be. Having made a decision for, say, WestportWorld, the exurbanite is apt to be a happier and a more serene man. He knows what he wants, and he has acted on it. He need no longer be a closet snob, passing as a lover of the bucolic. He has come out affirmatively for the values he cherishes. Having done so, he will find life less· complicated, and, sometimes, less guilt-ridden.

22

Strategies for Semiurbia

Most exurbanites will stay in the old neighborhood, some because they elect this course, some because they have no choice. These people have two options: "stonewalling" or accepting the evolutionary process.

The stonewalling strategy entails fighting to the bitter end, without accommodation to change. And the end is apt to be quite bitter. The pressures from outside will mount. Within the boundaries of the stone walls, there will be disharmony and division.

The breaches in the stone walls will come suddenly. Exclusivity will break down in ways over which the old exurbanites have little control. The apartments will come in, located in what many will consider the worst possible places.

The newcomers—many of them poor and black—will be viewed with fear and revulsion. They will respond in kind.

There will be ugly scenes in the affluent suburbs. Up until now, Exurbia has not been extremist. There has been no reason for extremism. But ugly things will happen. Suddenly there will be street crime—not in the degree that was feared, but enough. The first rape will be an earthquake.

Safety and "law and order" will become big issues. The stonewalling suburbanite who was once willing to devote a lot of tax money toward the ideal of "quality education" will now be all out for one objective—police protection.

Blight and sprawl will proliferate because there is no plan and no spirit of accommodation to keep them from doing so. The old exurbanite, hard-pressed to afford what has turned sour, will at last have to consider the alternative he rejected sometime back—moving away. But where can he move?

The evolutionary strategy is designed to prevent the worst effects of what is going to happen anyway. It assumes that change is inevitable. It acknowledges that the fight for exclusivity is a lost cause. Based on these assumptions, it calls for planning that will facilitate healthy change.

Realistic planning will accept the proposition that the community has a responsibility to the region at large. There will be arrangements for cheaper housing of higher density. At the same time, the principles of open space and common ground will be incorporated—not to preserve an illusion of rurality, but to create new and pleasant communities for a broader range of people.

Along with cheaper housing, the community will undertake responsibility for providing services that meet the needs of its old and new residents. There will be day care and family counseling to a greater degree than heretofore. The role of the school as problem-solver as well as educator will be institutionalized.

People of diverse backgrounds and incomes will meet with each other to try to moderate conflict, plan for growth, and build a workable new community. This is not to say that the evolution strategy will usher in the millennium. There will be conflict, and unhappiness, and great difficulty. But there will also be, at least, the opportunity for people who have been separated by a wide gulf to see each other, get to know each other, and look for areas of mutual interest. To the extent that people make the semiurbs work, they will build influence and power that can be devoted to obtaining things that will be badly needed—revitalized intra- and interurban transportation, for example.

The evolution strategy or the stonewall strategy? Exurbia, in its various manifestations, is making the choice now.

The viable successor to Exurbia will be built on a number of concepts. Here are a few of the principal ones.

Mandatory Planning

Most communities have something that amounts to a town plan. However, in this context, planning means the devices that can be used to maintain the status quo and prolong the illusion of rurality. The "plan" is relied on to keep out apartments and distasteful businesses and people who do not conform to the exurban pattern in outlook and income.

But before long there will be a new concept of planning applied to the suburbs. Exurbia will not like it, but it will have to accept it. Acceptance will be mandatory if the community is to receive state and federal aid for sewers, roads, transportation, and the other areas in which the suburbs must rely on the larger political entity.

The community plan for the suburb of the future will have to meet certain criteria. It will have to provide "adequate" housing opportunity for low- and middle-income people. Now, for a time, lawyers will feast upon disputes over the interpretation of "adequate" and other terms that will be embodied in legislation and court decisions, but the thrust will be clear. The Exurbia that is composed exclusively of big, expensive houses on large lots will move into a phase of drastic modification. Zoning will change to permit smaller and cheaper houses, apartments, and town houses. Open land will no longer be an amenity that can be taken for granted. The beauty, livability, and character of the community will have to be provided for, and this will mean planning.

We will see a growing tendency toward "ecological zoning," under which building plans will be scrutinized with regard to their effect on the balance of nature in the area.

So, as the age of Semiurbia moves from dawn into midmorning, residents of the once-exclusive enclaves will be obliged to involve themselves in "high-density" planning. The "high" in high-density is, of course, relative; we are not talking about densities approaching those in the inner city. Nevertheless, people will be living a lot closer to each other than before; and as this becomes a reality, the suburbs will become deeply involved in planning. It will be a matter of legal necessity and survival.

The former exurb will now be part of a region. It will not have the autonomy it once had in taxation, housing, or education.

Common Land

The early settlers had the option of acquiring unlimited private land. Nevertheless, they built their villages around the central principle of *common* land. The householder lived on his own property and farmed his own patch of ground. But, with all the other inhabitants, he had access to ample common land.

This was the custom because it made sense. It was economical to pasture the animals on one large plot, owned by all and available to all. The householder took under his own purview only enough ground to meet his needs.

Today, in the suburbs—many of them occupying the same sites occupied hundreds of years ago by the settlers who instituted the commons—the idea of common land has gone out of fashion. The householder is impelled to acquire for his private use a large piece of territory. He does not farm it or use it for pasturage. His possession of a big lot is, ostensibly, for the purpose of leisure and recreation. The capacity to sit and let his eye roam over green grass and trees is supposed to enable him to relax.

There is, of course, another purpose. The possession of a large plot of ground proclaims the householder's success to the world. This is, emphatically, conspicuous consumption. The exurbanite who sits in the middle of his two acres is saying to himself and to others, "This is mine. It is the fruit of my labors and the symbol of my achievement. I do not need this ground to raise crops or feed animals. I have it because I can afford to have it. Some may say it goes to waste. If that is the case, then so be it. The property is mine. I can afford to let it go to waste."

The costs of this conspicuous consumption are mounting. The exurban householder himself is encountering difficulty in continuing to afford his symbol of success. Inflation has eroded his financial position. His kids have grown and moved away. They won't live with him anymore, and they cannot afford to live near him.

There is still, of course, the matter of equity. Real estate is the single largest possession of the exurbanite. The land he lives on is where his money lies. But when he thinks about converting his investment into cash, he has problems. Who can afford **to** buy the place? If it were broken up into smaller lots and developed, the conversion into cash would be possible. But zoning laws forbid it.

Furthermore, there is the larger aspect of what it costs to maintain the private ownership of excess property. A large share of the expense is borne, in various ways, by people who do not enjoy the amenities of Exurbia.

The costs of low-density land use, in themselves, constitute a powerful factor contributing to change. When they are considered in conjunction with the other pressures—emotional and factual, external and internal—it would seem that the time has come to contemplate the practicality of the large-lot orientation of today's exurbs.

Common land once made economic sense. Today it makes recreational sense. Planners of the semiurban communities that will replace the exclusive suburbs will reinstitute the concept of the common. Houses of varying size will stand on smaller plots, clustered around open space and sited so as to give all householders in the cluster access to land that is not built on.

The open space will be private property, held in common by all householders in the complex.

The Rebirth of Mass Transportation

Exurbia is keyed to the automobile. Reliance on cars is expensive, wasteful, and ecology-destroying.

As suburbs turn into semiurbs, the automobile will begin to lose its favored position. Some of those who are admitted to the previously exclusive enclaves will renounce buses and trains and go all-out for the family car. Others, however, will not be willing to give up their dependence on the cheaper modes of travel. The car will lose its cachet.

The semiurb will mount its own intracommunity systems. The "Minny Bus" will become an accepted means of getting around, instead of a hotly debated novelty. Public transportation within the community will become more desirable as more businesses move into suburban areas.

As the confirmed exurbanite gives up exclusive reliance on his car, he will experience some withdrawal symptoms. But as the economies become clear to him, his pain will diminish. He will contemplate the possibility of owning one car instead of two, and of having a means for his kids to get around town independent of auto transportation. The resurgence of practical intracommunity public transportation will come to be considered one of the more pleasant aspects of the end of Exurbia.

Since the need to excel—and the desire to manifest excellence in material ways—will not disappear, the competitive instincts of at least some exurbanites will turn toward the building of really superior public-transportation systems instead of the purchasing of more expensive cars. Many will find that an innovative and sprightly set of local buses can be a bragging point and a conversation piece. The creators of Westport's pioneering Minny Bus system realized this; it is not for nothing that the buses that carry previously auto-borne commuters to the train station are not made by Ford or General Motors, but rather by Mercedes-Benz.

Equal Education

The suburban educational system is a failure. Spending top dollar for schooling has not been justified by results. Now all this is changed. School budgets are voted down. Teachers, once applauded, are viewed with mistrust and antagonism. The teachers react by becoming more militant unionists. Amity is replaced by alienation. As the college board test scores decline, the clamor for a "return to basics" mounts.

And the school buildings are empty. The suburban population ages. The kids grow up and leave school. There are fewer small children to take their places. Families with young children cannot afford to move into the town. School board members and administrators confront the thankless task of trying to explain to furious parents why they are closing down superbly equipped school buildings. The exurbanite does not want to pay more for exclusive education, but he does not want the economizing knife to cut too deeply, either.

These are some of the antieducation pressures existing inside the walls. Outside, the levelers are at work. They agitate in the legislature and they sue in the courts to change the local property-tax basis for funding education. Their goal is to equalize educational spending. They claim that, under the Constitution, every child is entitled to the same number of dollars to be spent on his schooling.

In the new semiurbs, there will not necessarily be a rigid equalization of educational funding, but certainly a far more uniform picture than the one that now exists. Spending for schools will not depend largely upon local taxes. Allocations will be made on a regional or statewide basis.

The diseconomy and illogic of closing suburban schools while urban students overcrowd older buildings will be recognized by adoption of a broader regional approach to the location of school facilities. Where good school buildings exist, kids will be sent to fill them. The tightly drawn boundaries around suburban school systems will lose their meaning.

Initially this will be done through busing. Busing, of course, has become a four-letter word. It is bad enough for many suburbanties to consider the busing of city (black) children into their neighborhood schools. "Reverse busing"—the transportation of exurban children into city schools—is unthinkable.

When busing has been ordered to achieve racial balance—as, notably, in Boston—a typical complaint of opponents has been that the practice requires sending children to "dangerous, crime-ridden ghetto schools," and means that children are "taken out of a safe, clean place and sent to a place of danger." This view—analogous to the attitude that condoned extensive busing to maintain segregation but condemns less-extensive busing to promote integration—will be widely trumpeted. But the fervor of the argument will decline. Reasonable people in the suburbs—impelled by circumstances toward a broader view—will begin to think about the proposition that *no* child should attend a school that is dirty, crime-ridden, and dangerous. The proposition that busing enhances achievement in school will shrink in importance. This has turned out to be a dubious claim at best.

Moreover, the transportation of children to fill unused classroom space will be undertaken not for the purpose of integrating the schools—although this will be one of its more egregious effects—but to fulfill the commonsense concept that it is idiotic to have some schools bulging at the seams while other, superior school buildings accommodate dwindling enrollments, to the point that an increasing number are closed.

The busing will not be "reverse" busing. Suburban kids will not be transported to the inner city. The schools there cannot accommodate them. It is the city kids who will be taken to the available suburban classrooms.

At first, exurban opponents of all this will proclaim the idea that city children and parents deplore this kind of busing as much as they do. They will be proved wrong. People who live in the inner city, on the whole, will demonstrate that they want as much "quality" education as they can get, and that a trip on a bus is a small price to pay for it. It will become apparent to the suburbanite that, given the circumstances pertaining in the dwellings and streets—let alone the schools themselves—of the inner city, the city kids are a lot safer and better off riding a bus than walking to their "neighborhood" schools.

In time, the busing question will be obviated. As exclusivity breaks down, the suburbs will open up to younger and poorer families who will send their children to the schools no longer being occupied by the sons and daughters of old-line exurbanite families.

There will be a leveling of educational expectations and practice. As spending evens out and student bodies become more hetero-geneous, experimentation will decline. City parents have, as a rule, been more inclined to insist on the time-honored educational verities than have suburbanites. Pressure from broader-based groups of parents will lead toward a return to the "basics." There will be far less of a tendency to gear certain systems almost exclusively to the student who is expected to go on to college, as is now the case in Exurbia. Many parents will lament this. Whether or not it will truly represent a handicap to the bright, achievement-oriented student is another matter. Ultimately, college admission policies will adapt themselves to the new realities of "leveled" education. The absence of clear-cut "superstar" school systems may make life somewhat harder for admissions officials, but then that's life.

The Social Whirl

The established social order in Exurbia is geared to married couples who fall within a certain age range. The exurban dinner or cocktail party will be attended, as a rule, by pairs of husbands and wives whose ages are roughly within ten years of those of the host and hostess. Some of these people are neighbors, but on the whole the relationship is not based on geographical nearness. There is little sense of neighborhood in the affluent suburbs, at least in the sense that people get together regularly with those who live closest to them.

This social configuration ignores one of the growing realities of Exurbia. Marriages are breaking up at an accelerating rate. The suburban community is thus increasingly peopled by "singles." Many of them are women who are approaching, or have arrived at, middle age. They have stayed in town because the house was the most tangible and convenient asset that could be realized in the divorce settlement. In other cases the couples are still technically married but separated and edging toward divorce. Time was that the man deemed a divorce to be a blight on his corporate career, and so attempted to maintain the facade as long as possible. The wife clung to the form of marriage because she could not see anything else to do, and because there might be hope, however vain, that the thing would be patched up.

Divorce—that is to say, *one* divorce—is no longer much of a stigma for the ambitious executive. Moreover, his wife is apt to see options she did not see before, and so be more willing to precipitate the final break. And staying together "for the sake of the kids" is losing its pull as a rationale for feigned togetherness, particularly when the kids are pretty much on their own, anyway.

So a whole other social network has arisen in the suburbs. Singles—voluntary or otherwise—comprise a significant element of the population. Organizations like Parents Without Partners thrive. The separated, divorced, or widowed adult can, in most Exurbias, participate in some social activity every night of the week.

The two social networks—married and single—hum along lines that do not intersect. The presence of a single is not a regular occurrence at a party of marrieds. The newly freed woman may be invited a few times—as a matter of duty and conscience—but after a period she finds that she is out of her former circle. Singles in Exurbia refer over and over again to this phenomenon as one of the unanticipated pains of being on one's own. It hurts, and it often leads to dark mutterings by the divorced woman that her former friends won't invite her because they are afraid of having their husbands stolen.

This may be a reason in some cases, but the more prevailing cause is a simple sense of what is fitting. Birds will shun a member of the species that fails—even in some subtle way—to conform to the general pattern. The pattern in the traditional social Exurbia is one of married couples—no matter how much strain may be involved in maintaining the form. A single is awkward, and what is awkward is best ignored.

So the suburbanite who is trying to make a social go of it alone finds entries to the traditional circuit closed off. The options that remain are limited. Some singles just stay home and brood. Others try to make the job—if a job can be gotten—a surrogate for social life.

For a great many the choice lies between the unofficial or the official singles network. The nexuses of the unofficial network are to be found in cocktail lounges. Word gets around the singles community about the bars you go to to meet new friends, depending on age and taste. The frustrations in this milieu are many, and the casualty rate is high.

The official network consists of Parents Without Partners, and the like. Here the action is safer and occasionally fruitful in terms of making new friends or more-than-just friends. But a lot of the singles who go this route are ultimately frustrated by what they consider to be exclusion from the mainstream of social intercourse.

Singles in Exurbia tend to drink a lot because drinking is a necessary adjunct to the available means of meeting people. Some drink too much. Others, abandoning previous inhibitions about sex, go far and deep in the other direction. Every exurb has its quota of women who try to make every trip to the filling station the beginning of a "meaningful relationship."

As Exurbia gives way to Semiurbia, this situation will change—for several reasons. The community will offer residence to younger people who are not hung up on marriage, monogamy, or a family-oriented household. Dwellings will be closer together; one will see more of his neighbors. The suburban party of the future is apt to be a more heterogeneous gathering. You may invite some couples. You will probably also invite some singles, without any particular regard for pairing off men and women. And you will invite the people from the new little house down at the corner, the inhabitants of which consist of three women, two men, and three children, none married and none of the adults living in any fixed relationship with any of the others.

In the broader community, relationships will not depend on similarity of status and financial position to the extent that they have in the past. The predominance of legal marriage as the basic social unit will diminish. With this relaxation the gravitational pull of the marriage vow—already weakened by years of distancing—is apt to weaken further. Monogamous marriage is not likely to make a comeback in Semiurbia, but there just might be a higher incidence of real friendship and true love.

Parenthood

The bearing and rearing of children is not likely to make a big comeback in Exurbia. The young residents of the suburbs will tend to have two children at most.

Children require space. Space is expensive. Big families will not fit into the higher-density patterns of the semiurbs. So, logistics and economics militate against having babies. Moreover, the young people of tomorrow's suburbs have a view of life that does not give primacy to starting a family. There are other things to do, and taking care of kids keeps you from doing them. To a considerable extent these young people will give up children to achieve their version of the Good Life. They are in no way committed to the proposition that procreation is the main purpose of sex.

Women will want to keep their options open and avoid becoming tied down too early. So, the idea that life in the suburbs is a desirable goal principally because it is a good place for kids to grow up will be far less prevalent, even as a pious fiction.

Children who are born and grow up in Semiurbia will be mothered, to a large degree, by remote control. The proliferation of day-care centers will be put to full use by these young mothers, before the kids reach school age and after they are in school. The concept of day care will be extended upward through the eighth grade, and outward to contain elements of development and conditioning far beyond mere baby-sitting.

But this, of course, does not mean that parents will not love their children or that they will ignore them. On the contrary, youngsters who have reached maturity in today's Exurbia are demonstrating that their ideas of parenthood are different from those of their own mothers and fathers. These young parents are tougher; they are less permissive. They have seen what happens when parents are always trying to be "with it" and are desperately afraid of appearing unsophisticated or unmodern or not "understanding." The children of Exurbia have exploited their parents' weakness and ambiguity and inability to convey a definite sense of values. However, there is no way that these children of arrogance, now grown, are going to get into the same situation with their own offspring. Young parents who grew up in Exurbia are not afraid to say No. They are strict. They seem, instinctively, to be reverting to a concept of parenthood that their own parents rejected.

Kids of the Suburban Kibbutz

In Exurbia, there has been increasing modification of the concept of *Motherhood* in the accepted sense that Mother's first duty is to extend a mantle of protectiveness over the children.

The suburban father has traditionally been an absentee parent. He commutes away in the morning and comes home at night with a briefcase and a head full of corporate woes. He is too tired to get involved with the kids. The weekends are not much different. They are devoted to providing R&R for Daddy so that he can return to the battle on Monday morning in some semblance of shape. The children are conditioned to stay out of his way or acquiesce in his wishes. Since the distancing factor in Exurbia makes this fairly easy for them to do, getting along without Daddy becomes a way of juvenile life. Even when there is some kind of joint family activity, it is far from certain to provide for togetherness. The favored weekend resorts are those advertising a full range of programs for the small fry, freeing the adults for their own brand of fun. A skiing trip, for example, does not offer the youngsters much of a crack at Dad's company, except in the strained confines of the automobile trip. We ski alone.

So it has been up to Mother to handle the parental role. She has chauffeured the kids around, gone to the PTA meetings, presided over the Brownies and Cub packs, sat at the Little League games. When the school does not seem to measure up to its responsibilities, it is Mother who is on the phone to voice a complaint. When things go wrong, she is expected to do the bulk of the worrying and take the rap.

By and large, the children of Exurbia—whether they live in "broken homes" or not—gain an early experience of a single parent, usually a female one.

Now Mother is beginning to ask pointed questions about her role. She may not join the local chapter of NOW or walk a liberation picket line or even evince much support for her more militant sisters, but she sees that others are finding alternatives to the role of total motherhood. Women are going to work. Sometimes it is an economic necessity, sometimes a matter of choice, often a combination of these. It is no longer socially unacceptable to do things that preclude the function of spending every possible minute with the children.

What happens to the kids?

Day care is becoming an important concept in Exurbia, and it will grow in importance. Day care is what is done with the little kids when Mother is not around to take care of them. More and more suburban communities are feeling the pressure to provide adequate day-care facilities. This pressure will intensify. There will be a wider selection of day-care opportunities, public and private.

As suburban communities have been evaluated to a significant extent on the basis of their school systems, they will increasingly be judged on the kinds of day care that they can provide. One hotly debated question will be: How far does day care extend? Some will wish to confine it to organized baby-sitting. There will be others advancing the concept of "early childhood development," maintaining that more and better things can be done for the kids than just getting them together to play until Mother comes to pick them up.

A lot of Exurbia's children have had to grow up pretty much on their own as it is. The spread of day-care centers will be simply a recognition and a formalization of that fact. Many will lament what seems to be an inhumane denial of the parental role. However, it remains to be seen if extended removal from what may well be a strained home atmosphere will really be bad for these kids. Eager platoons of sociologists will be lusting to study these progeny of the suburban kibbutzim.

23

The Closing of the Affluent Frontier

In 1893, Frederick Jackson Turner published his famous essay on *The Significance of the Frontier.* Turner said that the existence of the frontier had been the most important influence in shaping the country. "The peculiarity of American institutions is the fact that they have been compelled to adapt themselves to the changes of an expanding people—to changes involved in crossing a continent, in winning a wilderness, and in developing at each area of this progress out of the primitive economic and political conditions of the frontier into the complexity of city life."

The frontier shaped individual attitudes and approaches to life no less than it did institutions. The frontiersman had to do much on his own: clear the land, build the house, cultivate the crops. But his situation also imposed on him the necessity for cooperation with his neighbors: He worked with others at the barn-raisings, the husking bees, the building of churches and schools. Moreover, the frontiersman developed a dependency on government for his land and his protection. He needed government and "big business" to build the railroads that would take his produce to market.

Out of the confluence of these frontier-based realities grew, according to Turner, the unique character of the American nation. The closing of the frontier would have a profound effect on the country and its people.

The commuter to the suburbs fails emphatically to cut a figure like that of the idealized frontiersman. Oh, the exurbanite may be a towering presence at a client meeting, and you can't deny that he makes good money, but on the whole he is the subject of derision, scorn, and often hatred—albeit these feelings are often mixed with envy. The efforts of writers to romanticize the briefcase-bearing corporate leader are usually funny, although they do not have that intention. More often the exurbanite is an antihero. He is shown as an individual whose false values and single-minded drive to success have ruined his life and the lives of those around him.

Nevertheless, the exurbanite is a frontiersman, though perhaps an ignoble one. Exurbia has constituted a kind of frontier in American society. It has no long, sweeping boundary; the exurban archipelago dots the American terrain. The enclaves of the archipelago are surrounded by those who are trying to get into these desirable places. Formerly, the effort to enter was confined to the career route—"making it." When you had worked hard and successfully enough to qualify, you were ready to make the big jump on the game board of life and move to an affluent suburb. Never mind about the actualities of life there; forget about whether or not it was really what you wanted; don't be sidetracked by considerations of what life in Exurbia really meant to you and the wife and the kids—when you moved into the big house on two acres in University Park, you had *made it*.

Now, Exurbia is surrounded by vast crowds who have the effrontery to claim a right to enter without "making it." They want the rules changed. And they are going to get them changed.

When Exurbia is successfully stormed, a frontier will close. This event may not bring with it the dramatic profundities of the closing of the Western frontier as seen by Turner, but it is not without significance.

Exurbanites constitute an elite. There are all kinds of elites—of blood, of money, of intellect, of savagery. The exurban elite is a hybrid. You have to be tough; you need money; and you usually need brains of some sort.

The exurban elite is *insulated*. It dwells on the affluent frontier of society. Its members need not be troubled by many of the more unpleasant manifestations of the world; at least not at first hand. The marketing executive who commutes to the big city from Paradise Park gets paid $100,000 a year to know what the common man will buy. This executive does not ever get to meet the common man; he does not have to. He pays large sums to research specialists to tell him all he needs to know.

The exurban elite runs the country. It decides what will be seen on television; it sets the patterns for business; it makes the laws. All of this momentous activity takes place in a hermetically sealed environment. The exurbanite, whisking from his house to his executive suite and back again, need never have any more than the most fleeting contact with anyone who is good for less than $50,000 a year.

The insulation of our elite has considerable consequences. The college-enrolled sons of Exurbia did not have to go to Vietnam if they did not want to go. The children of Exurbia are not bused into slum schools. The men and women of Exurbia never see rats. They are not obliged to go to clinics staffed by indifferent doctors and nurses. On the streets of their town, it is quite unusual to see drunks sleeping in doorways. The exurbanite may be burgled, but he is not likely to be mugged.

So the exurbanite deals with the affairs of the world, but he does not soil his hands with them. Reality comes to him in beautiful and antiseptic wrappings. Packaging is very important, as all marketing men know. The exurbanite and the community in which he lives are triumphs of packaging.

The frontier was a great magnet for, and consumer of, human energy. Turner saw the great optimistic tides of humanity rolling westward, expending prodigious efforts to settle a wilderness. When the land frontier closed, that energy no longer had a clear-cut direction, but the energy—at least in potential—was undiminished. Some of it went into productive channels. Some was wasted.

There is boundless energy and ability in Exurbia. People get there because they are good at what they do. They are masterful organizers, skillful communicators, potent persuaders, able decision-makers, cogent planners, effective executors, competent solvers of problems, capable resolvers of conflict, perceptive thinkers. They are dynamos of disciplined energy.

The cities need help. They need the kind of energetic effectiveness that abounds in the suburbs. But the cities do not receive the benefit of this energy. As long as the lines of demarcation between city and exurb remain sharp, the exurbanite will continue to think of "us" and "them." He will use his skill and expend his energy to maintain his advantageous position and to keep "them" out.

When that battle is lost, is it too much to hope that at least some exurbanites will join "them"? When it is no longer fruitful to use great talent to try to maintain exclusivity, will people use that same talent to make not just an affluent town but the heterogeneous area around that town a better place for everybody to live in?

To some extent—perhaps to a considerable extent—that is the

way it will go. The elitist will wish to remain a member of the elite; it is in his nature to do so. But what is the nature of elitism? He may try to cling to the vestiges of his erstwhile exclusivity, but realism will tell him that this is a losing game. And it is at that point that he will become a productive member of the larger community.

We may then see the burgeoning of a new concept of elitism, an elitism of service and contribution rather than acquisition and exclusivity. In some respects the motives may still be largely selfish. An exurbanite finds that he now lives in a community with a steadily growing population of lower-income people, including blacks and Spanish-speaking individuals. He may not like it, but it is a fact. He looks at the high-rise apartments going up and reviews his fears that they will turn out to be garbage-littered warrens of crime and corruption. But, he tells himself, maybe that is not inevitable. And, he adds, he will be damned if he will let his town turn into a citified nest of slums.

So he turns his ability and energy to doing something to prevent his fears from becoming fact. He will meet unprecedented problems, suspicion, rebuffs, frustration. But he brings to the confrontation a background of accomplishment and a self-confidence born of being able to get things done. He sets out to work with "these people" to get things done. In the beginning his only motive may be a selfish wish to avoid embarrassment. As he proceeds, he may find other rewards.

We exurbanites have looked pretty bad—selfish, frivolous, insensitive to human need and suffering, materialistic, faintly ludicrous, and irrelevant. We did not set out to be that way. We have thought of life as something to be attacked. We have attacked it, and we have, within the limits of our basic strategy, done well. Now we are finding that our strategy was faulty, that the premises on which we have always operated were phony from the start.

But we are proud, and, I am afraid, stubborn. When one devotes his whole being to achieving something, he is going to go through prodigies of rationalization to make that achievement seem worthwhile.

We told ourselves that we were moving to the affluent suburbs primarily for the sake of the kids—the open space, the air, the good schools, the positive environment in which to grow. The schools have disappointed us; and so, if truth be told, have our kids. They have grown, all right, but into strangers. They look at us distantly, mockingly, scornfully. They do not understand us; they mistrust us; they do not confide in us; and they reject what we stand for. We tell them that we have done it for them, and it seems to make them angry.

We assumed that life in Exurbia would be very pleasant. We had worked hard for the Good Life; we deserved it. And there's no denying it, it *is* pleasant. It is damned nice to live in a big house, to have money for recreation and casual expenditures, to enjoy the beautiful surroundings and facilities, to spend time with people who talk our language and whose company makes us feel good.

But everything is relative. The reality has not quite measured up to the expectation. This basic truth of existence is, naturally, not confined to Exurbia. But our expectations were higher than those of other people. We felt that we had to struggle harder and accomplish more to get where we are. So, when it doesn't pan out the way we might have liked, the shock can be severe.

We do not give up illusions without a fight. Having made the commitment to the Good Life in the suburbs, we are going to continue to try to resolve the dissonances. One of the prominent ingredients of our dissonance is guilt. We feel vaguely guilty about a lot of things. Have we let down our families? Have we wasted our gifts? Have we turned our backs on others who need our help? But we don't talk about those feelings. We don't permit them to surface. We aggressively keep them down by asserting loudly that what we have is good, we are entitled to it, and we are going to keep it.

Most of us are not divorced from reality; we are just slow to acknowledge it when it is unpleasant. Now we are coming to the point when we will have to acknowledge certain truths. The catalyst for the reevaluation will be the growing realization that all this is about to change. When we see for certain that our idyllic enclaves are being pierced, we will be confronted with a new set of dissonances. It will be easier for us to conclude that the grapes were not that sweet.

This will not usher in the millennium. We will still be hard-driving, accomplishment-oriented people who have advantages and who are impelled to use those advantages for personal benefit. We cannot change our basic nature. But our behavior can be modified.

Of course we will still be operating on behalf of our self-interest. But self-interest casts a broad net. When our image of ourselves and what we want to be is infused with a degree of commitment to a region and to people who are not like us, we will get involved. Still selfishness? Of course. But we are not talking here so much of motivation as of effects. Whatever the reasons impelling us to take on a greater sense of community responsibility, we will approach the task of carrying out those responsibilities with energy and skill. We will be mistrusted and rejected, but that is nothing new to us. Our self-confidence and drive will give us—at least some of us—an adequate protective armor. Involved in a wider community, we will work to make it a better community. We will not necessarily do this out of altruism; we are not altruists, and we are skeptical of those who so style themselves. We will do it because we still want the places we live to be pleasant, desirable, and a fitting culmination to a lifetime of difficult and often ruthless effort.

And we are apt to find rewards in this new approach to the idea of community. Eventually our kids will, perhaps, see something more in us than they have been seeing. This will not happen overnight, or to a marked degree; it may not even seem to happen at all. The distancing of our offspring is not a phenomenon peculiar to Exurbia; we have come to see what Oscar Wilde meant when he said: "Children begin by loving their parents; as they grow older they judge them; sometimes they forgive them." But *we* may feel that we are doing more to earn their respect and love—particularly those of us who do not fall into the same old trap of saying, and even believing, that "we have done it all for them."

In many ways our pursuit of happiness has been paradoxical and self-defeating. We have chosen to be members of an elite based on acquisition and pleasure, rather than on contribution, community, and commitment. Having made the choice, we measure our rewards in terms of comfort and delightful experience. But we are restless people. Experiences lose their power to delight when we undergo them again and again. Yet we have locked ourselves into a narrow corner in which the range of possible experiences is limited, and the possibility of new ones diminishes, no matter how much time and money we expend. We party and we play; we work like hell in tasks of prestige and power; we travel to different places. But after a while it all seems to be a matter of seeing the same people and doing the same things. Since this is what we have chosen, what we have worked for, and valued above all else, we tend to deceive ourselves that it remains always fresh and enjoyable. But it is not. It gets monotonous. We are pushed toward doing some really important things, but within our narrow compass there are not so many different things to do.

Now we will be faced with a change. We will be embedded within a larger community; our isolation will be gone. Many of us may still try to hang onto exclusivity, and may do a pretty good job of it. But a lot of others will concede that things are different, and that the real world has impinged on our existence.

We may, many of us, rediscover the satisfaction of accomplishment that is not reflected in a paycheck. We have always been proud of our ability, but we have come to measure that ability less by internal standards than by external recognition, and we have bought the proposition that the paramount—and often only—real recognition of accomplishment is money. When we are compelled to do things for a wider community—compelled, let us remind ourselves, not so much by altruism as by pride and the determination to make our journey's end continue to be worth the trip—we will newly savor the pleasure of accomplishment for its intrinsic value, a capacity that we have not entirely lost but have only enameled over.

Our outlook on life will change, and not for the worse. We will see at first hand that people whom we consider dumb can be smart, that there are things in life to be enjoyed that have nothing to do with two-acre zoning, that closer contact with the earth does not necessarily make us dirty, but nurtures us.

When the last barriers are broken, we will have a chance to experience new things and to achieve accomplishments in new areas. Life will be simpler. Maintenance of the Good Life as we have envisioned it has become an immensely complicated proposition. It is not just the money; it is the increasingly cumbersome intricacy of having fun. When certain options are closed off, we will relish more fully those that remain open.

Bibliography

Babcock, Richard F. *The Zoning Game*. Madison: University of Wisconsin Press, 1969.

Coleman, James S. *Equality of Educational Opportunity*. U.S. Government Printing Office, 1966.

Crandell, Richard F. *This Is Westchester*. New York: Sterling Publishing Co., 1954.

Decter, Midge. *Liberal Parents, Radical Children*. New York: Coward, McCann & Geoghegan, 1975.

Department of Community Affairs, Commonwealth of Pennsylvania. *A Study of Exclusion*. 1973.

Donaldson, Scott. *The Suburban Myth*. New York: Columbia University Press, 1969.

Downs, Anthony. *Opening Up the Suburbs*. New Haven: Yale University Press, 1973.

Franklin, H. *The Courts and Urban Growth Policy*. Paper delivered at 1971 National Planning Conference, American Society of Planning Officials.

Goldstein, Lee. *Communes, Law and Commonsense*. Boston: New Community Projects, 1974.

Gottmann, Jean. *Megalopolis*. New York: Twentieth Century Fund, 1961.

Holt, John C. *How Children Fail*. New York: Pitman, 1964.

Holt, John C. *What Did I Do Monday?* New York: Dutton, 1970.

Keats, John. *The Crack in the Picture Window*. Boston: Houghton Mifflin, 1957.

Kerner, Otto (Chairman). *Report of the National Advisory Commission on Civil Disorders*. New York: Bantam, 1968.

Kozol, Jonathan. *The Night Is Dark and I Am Far from Home*. Boston: Houghton Mifflin, 1975.

Le Shan, Eda J. *The Conspiracy Against Childhood*. New York: Atheneum, 1967.

Loth, David G. *Crime in the Suburbs*. New York: William Morrow, 1967.

Masotti, Louis H., and Hadden, Jeffrey K. *Suburbia in Transition*. New York: New Viewpoints, 1974.

Mendelker, Daniel R. *The Zoning Dilemma*. Indianapolis: Bobbs-Merrill, 1971.

Mumford, Lewis. *The City in History*. New York: Harcourt, Brace & World, 1961.

National Commission on Urban Problems. *Building the American City.* U.S. Government Printing Office, 1968.

President's Commission on Urban Problems. *A Decent Home.* U.S. Government Printing Office, 1969.

Reich, Charles A. *The Greening of America.* New York: Random House, 1970.

Reische, Diane, ed. *Women and Society.* New York: H. W. Wilson, 1972.

Rist, Ray C. *The Urban School: A Factory for Failure.* Cambridge: MIT Press, 1973.

Seeley, John R. *Crestwood Heights.* New York: Basic Books, 1956.

Silberman, Charles E. *Crisis in the Classroom.* New York: Random House, 1970.

Spectorsky, A. C. *The Exurbanites.* Philadelphia: Lippincott, 1955.

Suburban Action Institute. *A Study of Growth and Segregation.* New York, 1975.

Toll, Seymour I. *Zoned American.* New York: Grossman, 1969.

Wattenberg, Ben J. *The Real America.* New York: Doubleday, 1974.

Wood, Robert C. *Suburbia, Its People and Their Politics.* Boston: Houghton Mifflin, 1959.

Index

233